What Henry James Knew

Cynthia Ozick is a member of the American Academy of Arts and Letters and has won various prizes and awards for her novels, short stories, poems and essays. Her books include *The Pagan Rabbi and Other Stories*, *Bloodshed and Three Novellas*, *Trust* (a novel), *The Messiah of Stockholm* (a novel), *The Shawl* (a novella and story), *Art & Ardour* (essays) and *Metaphor & Memory* (essays). Her work has been translated into most major languages.

BY CYNTHIA OZICK

Trust
The Pagan Rabbi and Other Stories
Bloodshed and Three Novellas
Levitation: Five Fictions
Art & Ardor: Essays
The Cannibal Galaxy
The Messiah of Stockholm
Metaphor & Memory: Essays
The Shawl
What Henry James Knew
and other Essays on Writers

Cynthia Ozick

WHAT HENRY JAMES KNEW

and Other Essays on Writers

Published by Vintage 1994

2 4 6 8 10 9 7 5 3 1

Some of these essays first appeared in *The New Yorker*, *Commentary*, *Midstream*, *The New Republic*, *The New York Times Book Review*, *The New York Times Magazine* and *Dark Soliloquy: The Selected Poems of Gertrud Kolmar*, published by The Seabury Press.

First published in Great Britain by Jonathan Cape Ltd, 1993

Vintage
Random House, 20 Vauxhall Bridge Road, London SW1V 2SA

Random House Australia (Pty) Limited
20 Alfred Street, Milsons Point, Sydney
New South Wales 2061, Australia

Random House New Zealand Limited
18 Poland Road, Glenfield,
Auckland 10, New Zealand

Random House South Africa (Pty) Limited
PO Box 337, Bergvlei, South Africa

Random House UK Limited Reg. No. 954009

A CIP catalogue record for this book
is available from the British Library

ISBN 0 09 942531 9

Printed and bound in Great Britain by
Cox & Wyman, Reading, Berkshire

Contents

Introduction

WHAT DID HENRY James know? H. G. Wells once accused him of knowing practically nothing. In the Jamesian novel, Wells charged, "you will find no people with defined political opinions, no people with religious opinions, none with clear partisanships or with lusts or whims, none definitely up to any specific impersonal thing." Wells concluded: "It is leviathan retrieving pebbles."

James was desperately wounded. He was at the close of his great span of illumination—it was less than a year before his death—and he was being set aside as useless, "a church lit but without a congregation." Replying to Wells, he defended himself on the question of the utility of art. Literature, he asserted, is "for use": "I regard it as relevant in a degree that leaves everything behind." There followed the famously characteristic Jamesian credo, by now long familiar to us. "It is art," he wrote, "that *makes* life, makes interest, makes importance . . . I know of no substitute whatever for the force and beauty of its process." And though he was speaking explicitly of the novel's purpose as "the extension of life, which is the novel's great gift," there is evidence enough that he would not have excluded the literary essay, of which he was equal master, from art's force and beauty. Thus, what Henry James knew.

To which Wells retorted: "I had rather be a journalist, that is the essence of it."

In the quarrel between Wells and James, James's view has been overtaken by times and habits far less elevated in their literary motives (and motifs) than his own, and by radical changes in the aims of education and in the impulses that drive the common culture. What James knew was the nobility of art—if, for him, the novel and the literary essay were not splendors just short of divine, then they were, anyhow, divining rods, with the capacity to quiver over the springs of discovered life. What Wells knew was something else—the future; us; what we are now. He welcomed the germinating hour of technology's fecundity, and flourished in it. James, we recall, switched from pen and ink to the typewriter, not because he was attracted to machines—he was not—but because he suffered from writer's cramp. He never learned to type himself; instead, he dictated to a typist—a technological regression, in a way, to the preliterate oral; or else an ascendance to the dominant priestly single voice. Wells, by contrast, was magnetized by the machine-world. Imagine him our contemporary: his study is mobbed by computer, printer, modem, e-mail, voice-mail, photocopier, fax, cable—the congeries and confluence of gadgets and conveniences that feed what the most up-to-date colleges advertise as "communications skills."

The truth of our little age is this: nowadays no one gives a damn about what Henry James knew. I dare to say our "little" age not to denigrate (or not only to denigrate), but because we squat now over the remnant embers of the last diminishing decade of the dying twentieth century, possibly the rottenest of all centuries, and good riddance to it (despite modernism at the start and moonwalking near the middle). The victories over mass murder and mass delusion, West and East, are hardly permanent. "Never again" is a pointless slogan: old atrocities are models (they give permission) for new ones. The worst reproduces itself; the best is singular. Tyrants, it seems, can be spewed out by the dozens, and their atrocities by the thousands, as by a copy machine; but Kafka, tyranny's symbolist, is like a fingerprint, or like handwriting, not duplicatable. This is what Henry James knew: that civilization is not bred out of machines, whether the machines are tanks or missiles, or whether they are laser copiers. Civilization, like art its handmaid (read: hand-made), is custom-built.

Let this not be mistaken for any sort of languorous pre-Raphaelite detachment from science or technology, or, heaven forfend, as a complaint against progress and its reliefs. Gratitude for anaesthesia and angioplasty and air travel, and for faxes and computers and frozen food and the flush toilet and all the rest! Gratitude, in truth, for Mr. Gradgrind and the Facts, and for those who devise the Facts—especially when those facts ease the purely utilitarian side of life. What distinguishes the data of medicine and science is precisely that they *can* be duplicated: an experiment that cannot be repeated will be discarded as an unreliable fluke, or, worse, as a likely forgery. In the realm of science, what is collective has authority. It is the same with journalism: if two reporters witness an incident, and the two accounts differ, one must be wrong, or must at least promote distrust. A unique view, uncorroborated, is without value. Wells, in discrediting James, was in pursuit of public and collective discriminations, as opposed to the purely idiosyncratic; he was after consensus-witnessing, both in science and society, and a more recognizable record, perhaps, even of lust and whim. Defined political and religious opinions, clear partisanships, persons definitely up to some specific impersonal thing.

Defined, definite, specific—how, what, when, where: the journalist's catalogue and catechism. Naming generates categories and headings, and categories and headings offer shortcuts—like looking something up in the encyclopedia, where knowledge, abbreviated, has already been codified and collected. James's way, longer and slower, is for knowledge to be detected, inferred, individually, laboriously, scrupulously, mazily—knowledge that might not be found in any encyclopedia.

"I had rather be a journalist, that is the essence of it"—hark, the cry of the common culture. Inference and detection (accretion heading toward revelation) be damned. What this has meant, for literature, is the eclipse of the essay in favor of the "article"—that shabby, team-driven, ugly, truncated, undeveloped, speedy, breezy, cheap, impatient thing. A while ago, coming once again on Robert Louis Stevenson's "Virginibus Puerisque"—an essay not short, wholly odd, no other like it, custom-made, soliciting the brightness of full attention in order to release its mocking charms—I tried to think of a single periodical today that might be willing to grant print to this sort of construction. Not even "judicious cutting," as editors like to say, would save Stevenson now. Of course there may be an instantly appropriate objection to so mildewed an observation. Stevenson is decidedly uncontemporary—the tone is all wrong, and surely we are entitled to our own sounds? Yes, the nineteenth century deserves to be read—but remember, while reading, that it is dead.

All right. But what of the "clear partisanship" of a book review encountered only this morning, in a leading journal dedicated to reviews? "Five books, however rich and absorbing, are a hefty number for the reader to digest," the reviewer declares, commenting on Leon Edel's multi-volume biography of Henry James: "a little amateur sleuthing some years ago suggested to me that the number of people who bought Mr. Edel's quintet bore little relation to the number who succeeded in battling their way through them." (Amateur sleuthing may be professional gall. "Succeeded in battling," good God! Is there a paragraph in Edel's devoted work, acclaimed as magisterial by two generations, that does not seduce and illuminate?) Edel, however, is not under review; he is only a point of contrast. The book in actual question, a fresh biography of James—in one volume—is, among other merits, praised for being admirably "short." It is "attention span" that is victor, even for people who claim to be serious readers.

And writers may give themselves out as a not dissimilar sample. Now and then you will hear a writer (even one who does not define herself as a journalist) speak of her task as "communication," as if the meticulous making of a sentence, or the feverish uncovering of an idea, or the sting of a visionary jolt delivered by what used to be called the Muse, were no more artful than a ten-minute telephone conversation. Literature may "communicate" (a redundancy, even a tautology), but its enduring force, well past the routine of facile sending and receiving, is in the consummation, as James tells us, of life, interest, importance. Leviathan rises to kick away the pebble of journalism.

Yet the pebble, it seems, is mightier than leviathan. The ten-minute article is *here*, and it has, by and large, displaced the essay. The essay is gradual and patient. The article is quick, restless, and brief. The essay reflects on its predecessors, and spirals organically out of a context, like a green twig from a living branch. The article rushes on, amnesiac, despising the meditative, reveling in gossip and polemics, a courtier of the moment. Essays, like articles, can distort and lie, but because essays are under the eye of history, it is a little harder to swindle the reader. Articles swindle almost by nature, because superficiality is a swindle. Pessimists suppose that none of this is any longer reversible. That the literary essay survives in this or that academic periodical, or in a handful of tiny quarterlies, is scarcely to the point. It has left the common culture.

Some doubt whether there *is* a common culture now at all, whether it is right to imagine that "the West" retains any resonance of worthy meaning; or even that it should. To claim commonality is, paradoxically, to be written off as elitist. Politically, through exploration, exploitation, and contempt, the West has spread elitism and exclusion; but it has also spread an idea of democratic inclusiveness so powerful—all of humanity is made in the image of the One Creator—that it serves to knock the politics of contempt off its feet all over the world. The round earth, like an hourglass, is turned upside down these days, spilling variegated populations-in-motion into static homogeneous populations, south into north, east into west; the village mentality, with its comfortable reliance on the familiar, is eroded by the polychrome and polyglot. America, vessel of migrations, began it. Grumbling, Europe catches up. While the kaleidoscope rattles and spins, and tribe assaults tribe, no one can predict how all this will shake itself out; but the village mentality is certainly dead. The jet plane cooked its goose.

Between the last paragraph and this one, I took a quick trip to Paris. This is not the sort of thing a hermitlike scribbler usually does; generally it is a little daunting for me to walk the three short blocks to Main Street. But the rareness of such a plummeting from one society into another, perhaps because one's attention becomes preternaturally heightened, somehow illumines the notion of commonality. I crossed an ocean in an airplane and found, on the opposite shore, almost exactly what I left behind: the same congeries of concerns. The same writers were being talked about, the same world news (starvation, feuding, bombing) was being deplored; only the language was different. So there really *is* a "West"—something we mostly forget as we live our mostly Main Street lives. Suppose, then, the language were not different but the same?

And if "commonality" requires more persuasive evidence than a transoceanic flight, there is, after all, the question (the answer, rather) of English—setting aside Shaw's quip about America and Britain being separated by a common language. The mother-tongue, as the sweet phrase has it, is a poet's first and most lasting home, his ineradicable patriotism.* In my teens I read Katherine Mansfield: what did a New York-born Jewish girl whose family had fled the boot of the Russian Czar have in common with a woman born in New Zealand forty years earlier? And what did this

* I know a European writer of genius, in love with his language, whose bad luck it was to have been born just in time to suffer two consecutive tyrannies. It is a wonder that this writer lived past childhood. At the age of five, under Hitler, he was torn from his home and shipped to a concentration camp. Having survived that, he was spiritually and intellectually crushed by the extremes of Communist rule, including a mindless and vicious censorship. Currently, after the fall of the dictator, and having emigrated to America, he is being vilified in the press of his native land for having exposed one of its national heroes as a programmatic antisemite. After so much brutalization by the country of his birth, it would be difficult to expect him to identify himself as a patriot. But that is what he is. He is a patriot of his mother-tongue, and daily feels the estrangement of exile. *Pro patria dulce mori!*

woman of the farthest reaches of the South Pacific have in common with an island off the continent of Europe? How rapidly the riddle is undone: Keats and Shelley and Coleridge and Wordsworth, to begin with. The great tree-trunk of English literature . . . no, that grand image ought to give way to something homelier. Call it the drawstring of English letters, which packs us all into the same sack, at the bottom of which—as we tumble around all mixed up down there, North Americans, Australians, Nigerians, South Africans, Jamaicans, numbers of Indians, and on and on—lies a hillock of gold.

The gold is the idea (old-fashioned, even archaic, perhaps extinct) of belles-lettres. Some will name it false gold, since English, as language and as literature, came to the Caribbean, and to New York, and to all those other places, as the spoor of empire. (Spooky thought: if not for the Czar of All the Russias, and if not for mad King George III, and if not for their anachronistic confluence, I would not now be, as I am, on my knees before the English poets. Also: no native cadences of Hawthorne, Melville, Emerson, Thoreau, Dickinson, Faulkner, Mark Twain, Cather!) The Shropshire Lad for a while bestrode the world, and was welcome nowhere. But Milton and Mill and Swift and George Eliot and E. M. Forster came along as stowaways—"Areopagitica," and "The Vindication of the Rights of Women," and "A Modest Proposal," and *Daniel Deronda* and *A Passage to India*. These hardly stand for the arrogance of parochialism—and it is just this engagement with belles-lettres that allows parochialism to open its arms, so that the inevitable accompaniment of belles-lettres is a sense of indebtedness. "It takes a great deal of history to produce a little literature," James noted: everything that informs belles-lettres is in that remark, and also everything that militates against the dismissal of either the term or the concept.

If I began these reflections in curmudgeonly resentment of the virtual annihilation of what Henry James knew—of the demise of the literary essay—it is only to press for its rescue and reclamation. Poetry and the novel will continue to go their own way, and we can be reasonably confident that they will take care of themselves. But the literary essay needs and merits defense: defense and more—celebrants, revivification through performance. One way or another, the literary essay is connected to the self-conscious progression of a culture, whereas the essay's flashy successor—the article, or "piece"—is in every instance a pusher of Now, a shaker-off of whatever requires study or patience, or what used to be called, without prejudice, ambition. The essayist's ambition is no more and no less than that awareness of indebtedness I spoke of a moment ago—indebtedness to history, scholarship, literature, the acutest nuances of language.

Is this what is meant by "elitism"? Perhaps. I think of it as work, if work is construed (as it ought to be) as "the passion of exactitude and sublimity." The latter phrase I borrow from a young essayist in London—my daughter's age exactly—who, because of a driven Parnassian ardor and because he is still in his twenties, has, I trust, the future of belles-lettres secreted in his fountain pen. In the newest literary generation, the one most assailed by the journalist's credo of Now, it is a thing worth marveling at: this determination to subdue, with exactitude and sublimity, the passionless trivia of our time.

T. S. Eliot at 101

"The Man Who Suffers and the Mind Which Creates"

THOMAS STEARNS ELIOT, poet and preëminent modernist, was born one hundred and one years ago. His centennial in 1988 was suitably marked by commemorative reporting, literary celebrations in New York and London, and the publication of a couple of lavishly reviewed volumes: a new biography and a collection of the poet's youthful letters. Probably not much more could have been done to distinguish the occasion; still, there was something subdued and bloodless, even superannuated, about these memorial stirrings. They had the quality of a slightly tedious reunion of aging alumni, mostly spiritless by now, spurred to animation by old exultation recollected in tranquility. The only really fresh excitement took place in London, where representatives of the usually docile community of British Jews, including at least one prominent publisher, condemned Eliot for antisemitism and protested the public fuss. Elsewhere, the moment passed modestly, hardly noticed at all by the bookish young —who, whether absorbed by recondite theorizing in the academy, or scampering after newfangled writing careers, have long had their wagons hitched to other stars.

In the early seventies it was still possible to uncover, here and there, a tenacious English department offering a vestigial graduate seminar given over to the study of Eliot. But by the close of the eighties, only "The Love Song of J. Alfred Prufrock" appears to have survived the indifference of the schools—two or three pages in the anthologies, a fleeting assignment for high school seniors and college freshmen. "Prufrock," and "Prufrock" alone, is what the latest generations know—barely know: not "The Hollow Men," not "La Figlia che Piange," not "Ash Wednesday," not even "The Waste Land." Never "Four Quartets." And the mammoth prophetic presence of T. S. Eliot himself—that immortal sovereign rock—the latest generations do not know at all.

To anyone who was an undergraduate in the forties and fifties (and possibly even into the first years of the sixties), all that is inconceivable—as if a part of the horizon had crumbled away. When, four decades ago, in a literary period that resembled eternity, T. S. Eliot won the Nobel Prize for literature, he seemed pure zenith, a colossus, nothing less than a permanent luminary fixed in the firmament like the sun and the moon—or like the New Criticism itself, the vanished movement Eliot once magisterially dominated. It was a time that, for the literary young, mixed authority with innovation: authority *was* innovation, an idea that reads now, in the wake of the anti-establishment sixties, like the simplest contradiction. But modernism then was an absolute ruler—it had no effective intellectual competition and had routed all its predecessors; and it was modernism that famously carried the "new."

The new—as embodied in Eliot—was difficult, preoccupied by parody and pastiche, exactingly allusive and complex, saturated in manifold ironies and inflections, composed of "layers," and pointedly inaccessible to anybody expecting run-of-the-mill coherence. The doors to Eliot's poetry were not easily opened. His lines and themes were not readily understood. But the young who flung themselves through those portals were lured by unfamiliar enchantments and bound by pleasurable ribbons of ennui. "April is the cruel-lest month," Eliot's voice, with its sepulchral cadences, came spiralling out of 78 r.p.m. phonographs, "breeding / Lilacs out of the dead land, mixing / Memory and desire . . ." That toney British accent—flat, precise, steady, unemotive, surprisingly high-pitched, bleakly passive—coiled through awed English departments and worshipful dormitories, rooms where the walls had pin-up Picassos, and Pound and Eliot and *Ulysses* and Proust shouldered one another higgledy-piggledy in the rapt late-adolescent breast. The voice was, like the poet himself, nearly sacerdotal, impersonal, winding and winding across the country's campuses like a spool of blank robotic woe. "Shantih shantih shantih," "not with a bang but a whimper," "an old man in a dry month," "I shall wear the bottoms of my trousers rolled"—these were the devout chants of the literarily passionate in the forties and fifties, who in their own first verses piously copied Eliot's tone: its restraint, gravity, mystery; its invasive remoteness and immobilized disjointed despair.

There was rapture in that despair. Wordsworth's nostalgic cry over the start of the French Revolution—"Bliss was it in that dawn to be alive, / But to be young was very heaven!"—belongs no doubt to every new generation; youth's heaven lies in its quitting, or sometimes spiting, the past, with or without a historical crisis. And though Eliot's impress—the bliss he evoked—had little to do with political rupture, it was revolutionary enough in its own way. The young who gave homage to Eliot were engaged in a self-contradictory double maneuver: they were willingly authoritarian even as they jubilantly rebelled. On the one hand, taking on the puzzlements of modernism, they were out to tear down the Wordsworthian tradition itself, and on the other they were ready to fall on their knees to a god. A god, moreover, who despised free-thinking, democracy, and secularism: the very conditions of anti-authoritarianism.

How T. S. Eliot became that god—or, to put it less extravagantly, how he became a commanding literary figure who had no successful rivals and whose formulations were in fact revered—is almost as mysterious a proposition as how, in the flash of half a lifetime, an immutable majesty was dismantled, an immutable glory dissipated. It is almost impossible nowadays to imagine such authority accruing to a poet. No writer today—Nobel winner or no—holds it or can hold it. The four present American Nobel laureates in literature—Czeslaw Milosz, Saul Bellow, Isaac Bashevis Singer, and Joseph Brodsky (three of whom, though citizens of long standing, do not write primarily in English)—are much honored, but they are not looked to for manifestos or pronouncements, and their comments are not studied as if by a haruspex. They are as far from being cultural dictators as they are from filling football stadiums.

Eliot *did* once fill a football stadium. On April 30, 1956, fourteen thousand people came to hear him lecture on "The Frontiers of Criticism" at the University of Minnesota, in Minneapolis. By then he was solidly confirmed as "the Pope of Russell Square," as his London admirer Mary Trevelyan began to call him in 1949. It was a far-reaching papacy, effective even among students in the American Midwest; but if the young flocked to genuflect before the papal throne, it was not they who had enthroned Eliot, nor their teachers. In the Age of Criticism (as the donnish "little" magazines of the time dubbed the forties and fifties), Eliot was ceded power, and accorded veneration, by critics who were themselves minor luminaries. "He has a very penetrating influence, perhaps not unlike an east wind," wrote William Empson, one of whose titles, *Seven Types of Ambiguity*, became an academic catchphrase alongside Eliot's famous "objective correlative." R. P. Blackmur said of "Prufrock" that its "obscurity is like that of the womb"; Eliot's critical essays, he claimed, bear a "vital relation" to Aristotle's *Poetics*. Hugh Kenner's comparison is with still another monument: "Eliot's work, as he once noted of Shakespeare, is in important respects one continuous poem," and for Kenner the shape of Eliot's own monument turns out to be "the Arch which stands when the last marcher has left, and endures when the last centurion or sergeant-major is dust." F. R. Leavis, declaring Eliot "among the greatest poets of the English language," remarked that "to have gone seriously into the poetry is to have had a quickening insight into the nature of thought and language." And in Eliot's hands, F. O. Matthiessen explained, the use of the symbol can "create the illusion that it is giving expression to the very mystery of life."

These evocations of wind, womb, thought and language, the dust of the ages, the very mystery of life, not to mention the ghosts of Aristotle and Shakespeare: not since Dr. Johnson has a man of letters writing in English been received with so much adulation, or seemed so formidable—almost a marvel of nature itself—within his own society.

Nevertheless there was an occasional dissenter. As early as 1929, Edmund Wilson was complaining that he couldn't stomach Eliot's celebrated conversion to "classicism, royalism, and Anglo-Catholicism." While granting that Eliot's essays "will be read by everybody interested in literature," that Eliot "has now become the most important literary critic in the English-speaking world," and finally that "one can find no figure of comparable authority," it was exactly the force of this influence that made Wilson "fear that we must give up hope." For Wilson, the argument of Eliot's followers "that, because our society at the present time is badly off without religion, we should make an heroic effort to swallow medieval theology, seems . . . utterly futile as well as fundamentally dishonest." Twenty-five years later, when the American intellectual center had completed its shift from freelance literary work like Wilson's—and Eliot's—to the near-uniformity of university English departments, almost no one in those departments would dare to think such unfastidious thoughts about Eliot out loud. A glaze of orthodoxy (not too different from the preoccupation with deconstructive theory currently orthodox in English departments) settled over academe. Given the normal eagerness of succeeding literary generations to examine new sets of entrails, it was inevitable that so unbroken a dedication would in time falter and decline. But until that happened, decades on, Eliot studies were an unopposable ocean; an unstoppable torrent; a lava of libraries.

It may be embarrassing for us now to look back at that nearly universal obeisance to an autocratic, inhibited, depressed, rather narrow-minded and considerably bigoted fake Englishman—especially if we are old enough (as I surely am) to have been part of the wave of adoration. In his person, if not in his poetry, Eliot was, after all, false coinage. Born in St. Louis, he became indistinguishable (though not to shrewd native English eyes), in his dress, his manners, his loyalties, from a proper British Tory. Scion of undoctrinaire rationalist New England Unitarianism (his grandfather had moved from Boston to Missouri to found Washington University), he was possessed by guilty notions of sinfulness and martyrdom and by the monkish disciplines of asceticism, which he pursued in the unlikely embrace of the established English church. No doubt Eliot's extreme self-alterations should not be dismissed as ordinary humbug, particularly not on the religious side; there is a difference between impersonation and conversion. Still, self-alteration so unalloyed suggests a hatred of the original design. And certainly Eliot condemned the optimism of democratic American meliorism; certainly he despised Unitarianism, centered less on personal salvation than on the social good; certainly he had contempt for Jews as marginal if not inimical to his notions of Christian community. But most of all, he came to loathe himself, a hollow man in a twilight kingdom.

In my undergraduate years, between seventeen and twenty-one, and long after as well, I had no inkling of any of this. The overt flaws—the handful of insults in the poetry—I swallowed down without protest. No one I knew protested—at any rate, no professor ever did. If Eliot included lines like "The rats are underneath the piles. / The jew [sic] is underneath the lot," if he had his Bleistein, "Chicago Semite Viennese," stare "from the protozoic slime" while elsewhere "The jew squats on the windowsill, the owner" and "Rachel *née* Rabinovitch / Tears at the grapes with murderous paws"—well, that, sadly, was the way of the world and to be expected, even in the most resplendent poet of the age. The sting of those phrases—the shock that sickened—passed, and the reader's heart pressed on to be stirred by other lines.

What was Eliot to me? He was not the crack about "Money in furs," or "Spawned in some estaminet in Antwerp." No, Eliot was "The Lady is withdrawn / In a white gown, to contemplation, in a white gown" and "Then spoke the thunder / DA / *Datta:* what have we given?" and "Afternoon grey and smoky, evening yellow and rose"; he was incantation, mournfulness, elegance; he was liquescence, he was staccato, he was quickstep and oar, the hushed moan and the sudden clap. He was lyric shudder and roseburst. He was, in brief, poetry incarnate; and poetry was what one lived for.

And he was something else beside. He was, to say it quickly, absolute art: high art, when art was at its most serious and elitist. The knowledge of that particular splendor—priestly, sacral, a golden cape for the initiate—has by now ebbed out of the world, and many do not regret it. Literary high art turned its back on egalitarianism and prized what is nowadays scorned as "the canon": that body of anciently esteemed texts, most of them difficult and aristocratic in origin, which has been designated Western culture. Modernism—and Eliot—teased the canon, bruised it, and even sought to astonish it by mocking and fragmenting it, and also by introducing Eastern infusions, such as Eliot's phrases from the Upanishads in "The Waste Land" and Pound's Chinese imitations. But all these shatterings, dislocations, and idiosyncratic juxtapositions of the old literary legacies were never intended to abolish the honor in which they were held, and only confirmed their centrality. Undoing the canon is the work of a later time—of our own, in fact, when universal assent to a central cultural standard is almost everywhere decried. For the moderns, and for Eliot especially, the denial of permanently agreed-on masterworks—what Matthew Arnold, in a currency now obsolete beyond imagining, called "touchstones"—would have been unthinkable. What one learned from Eliot, whose poetry skittered toward disintegration, was the power of consolidation: the understanding that literature could genuinely *reign*.

One learned also that a poem could actually be penetrated to its marrow—which was not quite the same as comprehending its meaning. In shunting aside or giving up certain goals of ordinary reading, the New Criticism installed Eliot as both teacher and subject. For instance, following Eliot, the New Criticism would not allow a poem to be read in the light of either biography or psychology. The poem was to be regarded as a thing-in-itself; nothing environmental or causal, including its own maker, was permitted to illuminate or explain it. In that sense it was as impersonal as a jar or any other shapely artifact that must be judged purely by its externals. This objective approach to a poem, deriving from Eliot's celebrated "objective correlative" formulation, did not dismiss emotion; rather, it kept it at a distance, and precluded any speculation about the poet's own life, or any other likely influence on the poem. "The progress of an artist is a continual self-sacrifice, a continual extinction of personality," Eliot wrote in his landmark essay, "Tradition and the Individual Talent." "Emotion . . . has its life in the poem and not in the history of the poet." And, most memorably: "The more perfect the artist, the more completely separate in him will be the man who suffers and the mind which creates." This was a theory designed to prevent old-fashioned attempts to read private events into the lines on the page. Artistic inevitability, Eliot instructed, "lies in this complete adequacy of the external to the emotion" and suggested a series of externals that might supply the "exact equivalence" of any particular emotion: "a set of objects, a situation, a chain of events." Such correlatives—or "objective equivalences"—provided, he insisted, the "only way of expressing emotion in the form of art." The New Criticism took him at his word, and declined to admit any other way. Not that the aesthetic scheme behind Eliot's formulation was altogether new. Henry James, too, had demanded—"Dramatize, dramatize!"—that the work of art resist construing itself in public. When Eliot, in offering his objective correlative, stopped to speak of the "*données* of the problem"—*donnée* was one of James's pet Gallicisms—he was tipping off his source. No literary figure among James's contemporaries had paid any attention to this modernist dictum, often not even James himself. Emerging in far more abstruse language from Eliot, it became a papal bull. He was thirty-five at the time.

The method used in digging out the objective correlative had a Gallic name of its own: *explication de texte*. The sloughing off of what the New Criticism considered to be extraneous had the effect of freeing the poem utterly—freeing it for the otherwise undistracted mind of the reader, who was released from "psychology" and similar blind alleys in order to master the poem's components. The New Criticism held the view that a poem could indeed be mastered: this was an act of trust, as it were, between poem and reader. The poem could be relied on to yield itself up to the reader—if the reader, on the other side of the bargain, would agree to a minutely close "*explication*," phrase by phrase: a process far more meticulous than "interpretation" or the search for any identifiable meaning or definitive commentary. The search was rather for architecture and texture—or call it resonance and intricacy, the responsive webwork between the words. *Explication de texte*, as practiced by the New Critics and their graduate-student disciples, was something like watching an ant maneuver a bit of leaf. One notes first the fine veins in the leaf, then the light speckled along the veins, then the tiny glimmers charging off the ant's various surfaces, the movements of the ant's legs and other body parts, the lifting and balancing of the leaf, all the while scrupulously aware that ant and leaf, though separate structures, become—when linked in this way—a freshly imagined structure.

A generation or more was initiated into this concentrated scrutiny of a poem's structure and movement. High art in literature—which had earlier been approached through the impressionistic "appreciations" that commonly passed for critical reading before the New Criticism took hold—was seen to be indivisible from *explication de texte*. And though the reverence for high art that characterized the Eliot era is now antiquated—or dead—the close reading that was the hallmark of the New Critics has survived, and remains the *sine qua non* of all schools of literary theory. Currently it is even being applied to popular culture; hamburger advertisements and television sitcoms can be serious objects of up-to-date critical examination. Eliot was hugely attracted to popular culture as an innovative ingredient of pastiche—"Sweeney Agonistes," an unfinished verse drama, is saturated in it. But for Eliot and the New Critics, popular culture or "low taste" contributed to a literary technique; it would scarcely have served as a literary subject, or "text," in its own right. Elitism ruled. Art was expected to be strenuous, hard-earned, knotty. Eliot explicitly said so, and the New Critics faithfully concurred. "It is not a permanent necessity that poets should be interested in philosophy," Eliot wrote (though he himself had been a graduate student in philosophy at Harvard and Oxford, and had completed a thesis on F. H. Bradley, the British idealist). "We can only say that it appears likely that poets in our civilization, as it exists at present, must be *difficult*. Our civilization comprehends great variety and complexity, and this variety and complexity, playing upon a refined sensibility, must produce various and complex results. The poet must become more and more comprehensive, more allusive, more indirect, in order to force, to dislocate if necessary, language into his meaning."

He had another requirement as well, and that was a receptiveness to history. Complexity could be present only when historical consciousness prevailed. He favored history over novelty, and tradition over invention. While praising William Blake for "a remarkable and original sense of language and the music of language, and a gift of hallucinated vision," Eliot faulted him for his departures from the historical mainstream. "What his genius required, and what it sadly lacked, was a framework of accepted and traditional ideas which would have prevented him from indulging in a philosophy of his own." And he concluded, "The concentration resulting from a framework of mythology and theology and philosophy is one of the reasons why Dante is a classic, and Blake only a poet of genius." Genius was not enough for Eliot. A poet, he said in "Tradition and the Individual Talent" needs to be "directed by the past." The historical sense "compels a man to write not merely with his own generation in his bones, but with the feeling that the whole of the literature of Europe from Homer and within it the whole of the literature of his own country has a simultaneous existence and composes a simultaneous order."

A grand view; a view of grandeur; high art defined: so high that even the sublime Blake fails to meet its measure. It is all immensely elevated and noble—and, given the way many literary academics and critics think now, rare and alien. Aristocratic ideas of this kind, which some might call Eurocentric and obscurantist, no longer engage most literary intellectuals; nor did they, sixty years ago, engage Edmund Wilson. But they were dominant for decades, and in the reign of Eliot they were law. Like other postulates, they brought good news and bad news; and we know that my good news may well be your bad news. Probably the only legacy of the Eliot era that everyone can affirm as enduringly valuable is the passionate, yet also disinterested, dissection of the text, a nuanced skill that no critical reader, taking whatever ideological stand, can do without. This exception aside, the rest is all disagreement. As I see it, what appeared important to me at twenty-one is still important; in some respects I admit to being arrested in the Age of Eliot, a permanent member of it, unregenerate. The etiolation of high art seems to me to be a major loss. I continue to suppose that some texts are worthier than other texts. The same with the diminishment of history and tradition: not to incorporate into an educable mind the origins and unifying principles of one's own civilization strikes me as a kind of cultural autolobotomy. Nor am I ready to relinquish Eliot's stunning declaration that the reason we know so much more than the dead writers knew is that "they are that which we know." As for that powerful central body of touchstone works, the discredited "canon," and Eliot's strong role in shaping it for his own and the following generation, it remains clear to me—as Susan Sontag remarked at the 1986 International PEN Convention—that literary genius is not an equal opportunity employer; I would not wish to drop Homer or Jane Austen or Kafka to make room for an Aleutian Islander of lesser gifts, however unrepresented her group may be on the college reading list.

In today's lexicon these are no doubt "conservative" notions, for which Eliot's influence can be at least partly blamed or—depending on your viewpoint—credited. In Eliot himself they have a darker side—the bad news. And the bad news is very bad. The gravity of high art led Eliot to envision a controlling and exclusionary society that could, presumably, supply the conditions to produce that art. These doctrinal tendencies, expressed in 1939 in a little book called *The Idea of A Christian Society*, took Eliot—on the eve of Nazi Germany's ascendancy over Europe—to the very lip of shutting out, through "radical changes," anyone he might consider ineligible for his "Community of Christians." Lamenting "the intolerable position of those who try to lead a Christian life in a non-Christian world," he was indifferent to the position of those who would try to thrive as a cultural minority within his contemplated Utopia. (This denigration of tolerance was hardly fresh. He had argued in a lecture six years before that he "had no objection to being called a bigot.") In the same volume, replying to a certain Miss Bower, who had frowned on "one of the main tenets of the Nazi creed—the relegation of women to the sphere of the kitchen, the children, and the church," Eliot protested "the implication that what is Nazi is wrong, and need not be discussed on its own merits." Nine years afterward, when the fight against Germany was won, he published *Notes Toward the Definition of Culture*, again proposing the hegemony of a common religious culture. Here he wrote—at a time when Hitler's ovens were just cooled and the shock of the Final Solution just dawning—that "the scattering of Jews amongst peoples holding the Christian faith may have been unfortunate both for these peoples and for the Jews themselves," because "the effect may have been to strengthen the illusion that there can be culture without religion." An extraordinary postwar comment. And in an Appendix, "The Unity of European Culture," a radio lecture broadcast to Germany in 1946, one year after the Reich was dismantled, with Europe in upheaval, the death-camps exposed, and displaced persons everywhere, he made no mention at all of the German atrocities. The only reference to "barbarism" was hypothetical, a worried projection into a potentially barren future: "If Christianity goes, the whole of our culture goes," as if the best of European civilization (including the merciful tenets of Christianity) had not already been pulverized to ash throughout the previous decade. So much for where high art and traditional culture landed Eliot.

There is bad news, as it happens, even in the objective correlative. What was once accepted as an austere principle of poetics is suddenly decipherable as no more than a device to shield the poet from the raw shame of confession. Eliot is now unveiled as a confessional poet above all—one who was driven to confess, who *did* confess, whose subject was sin and guilt (his own), but who had no heart for the act of disclosure. That severe law of the impersonality of the poem—the masking technique purported to displace emotion from its crude source in the poet's real-life experience to its heightened incarnation in "a set of objects, a situation, a chain of events"—turns out to be motivated by something less august and more timorous than pure literary theory or a devotion to symbol. In the name of the objective correlative, Eliot had found a way to describe the wound without the embarrassment of divulging who held the knife. This was a conception far less immaculate than the practitioners of the New Criticism ever supposed; for thirty years or more Eliot's close readers remained innocent of—or discreet about—Eliot's private life. Perhaps some of them imagined that, like the other pope, he had none.

The assault on the masking power of the objective correlative—the breach in Eliot's protective wall—came about in the ordinary way: the biographies began. They began because time, which dissolves everything, at last dissolved awe. Although the number of critical examinations of Eliot, both book-length and in periodicals, is beyond counting, and although there are a handful of memoirs by people who were acquainted with him, the first true biography did not appear until a dozen years after his death. In 1977 Lyndall Gordon published *Eliot's Early Years*, an accomplished and informative study taking Eliot past his failed first marriage and through the composition of "The Waste Land." Infiltrated by the familiar worshipfulness, the book is a tentative hybrid, part dense critical scrutiny and part cautious narrative—self-conscious about the latter, as if permission has not quite been granted by the author to herself. The constraints of awe are still there. Nevertheless the poetry is advanced in the light of Eliot's personal religious development, and these first illuminations are potent. In 1984 a second biography arrived, covering the life entire; by now awe has been fully dispatched. Peter Ackroyd's *T. S. Eliot: A Life* is thorough, bold, and relaxed about its boldness—even now and then a little acid. Not a debunking job by any means, but admirably straightforward. The effect is to bring Eliot down to recognizably human scale—disorienting to a reader trained to Eliot-adulation and ignorant until now of the nightmare of Eliot's youthful marriage and its devastating evolution. Four years on, Eliot's centenary saw the publication of *Eliot's New Life*, Lyndall Gordon's concluding volume, containing augmented portraits—in the nature of discoveries—of two women Ackroyd had touched on much less intensively; each had expected Eliot to marry her after the death of his wife in a mental institution. Eliot was callous to both. Eleven years following her first study, Gordon's manner continues respectful and her matter comprehensive, but the diffidence of the narrative chapters is gone. Eliot has acquired fallibility, and Gordon is not afraid to startle herself, or the long, encrusted history of deferential Eliot scholarship. Volume Two is daring, strong, and psychologically brilliant. Finally, 1988 also marked the issuance of a fat book of letters, *The Letters of T. S. Eliot, Vol. I: 1898-1922*, from childhood to age thirty-five (with more to come), edited by Eliot's widow, Valerie Eliot, whom he married when she was thirty and he sixty-eight.

"The man who suffers and the mind which creates"—these inseparables, sundered long ago by Eliot himself, can now be surgically united.

If Eliot hid his private terrors behind the hedge of his poetry, the course of literary history took no notice of it. Adoration, fame, and the Nobel Prize came to him neither in spite of nor because of what he left out; his craft was in the way he left it out. And he had always been reticent; he had always hidden himself. It can even be argued that he went to live in England in order to hide from his mother and father.

His mother, Charlotte Stearns Eliot, was a frustrated poet who wrote religious verse and worked for the civic good. His father, Henry Ware Eliot, was an affluent businessman who ran a St. Louis brick-manufacturing company. Like any entrepreneur, he liked to see results. His father's father, an intellectual admired by Dickens, was good at results—though not the conventional kind. He had left the family seat in blueblood Boston to take the enlightenment of Unitarianism to the American West; while he was at it he established a university. Both of Eliot's parents were strong-willed. Both expected him to make a success of himself. Both tended to diminish his independence. Not that they wanted his success on any terms but his own—it was early understood that this youngest of six siblings (four sisters, one of whom was nineteen years older, and a brother almost a decade his senior) was unusually gifted. He was the sort of introspective child who is photographed playing the piano or reading a book or watching his girl cousins at croquet (while himself wearing a broad-brimmed straw hat and a frilly dress, unremarkable garb for upper-class nineteenth-century male tots). His mother wrote to the headmaster of his prep school to ensure that he would not be allowed to participate in sports. She wrote again to warn against the dangers of swimming in quarry ponds. She praised Eliot's schoolboy verse as better than her own, and guaranteed his unease. "I knew what her verses meant to her. We did not discuss the matter further," he admitted long afterward. At his Harvard commencement in 1910, the same year as the composition of "Portrait of a Lady" and a year before "Prufrock," he delivered the farewell ode in a style that may have been a secret parody of his mother's: "For the hour that is left us Fair Harvard, with thee, / Ere we face the importunate years . . ." His mother was sympathetic to his ambitions as a poet—too sympathetic: it was almost as if his ambitions were hers, or vice-versa. His father took a brisk view of Eliot's graduate studies in philosophy: they were the ticket to a Harvard professorship, a recognizably respectable career.

But Eliot would not stay put. To the bewilderment of his parents—the thought of it gave his mother a "chill"—he ran off to Paris, partly to catch the atmosphere of Jules Laforgue, a French poet who had begun to influence him, and partly to sink into Europe. In Paris he was briefly attracted to Henri Bergson, whose lectures on philosophy he attended at the Collège de France, but then he came upon Charles Maurras; Maurras' ideas—"*classique, catholique, monarchique*"—stuck to him for life, and were transmuted in 1928 into his own "classicist, royalist, Anglo-Catholic." In 1910 the word "fascist" was not yet in fashion, but that is exactly what Maurras was: later on he joined the pro-Nazi Vichy regime, and went to jail for it after World War II. None of this dented Eliot's enduring admiration; *Hommage à Charles Maurras* was written as late as 1948. When Eliot first encountered him, Maurras was the founder of an anti-democratic organization called Action Française, which specialized in student riots and open assaults on free-thinkers and Jews. Eliot, an onlooker on one of these occasions, did not shrink from the violence. (Ackroyd notes that he "liked boxing matches also.")

After Paris he obediently returned to Harvard for three diligent years, doing some undergraduate teaching and working on his doctoral degree. One of his courses was with Bertrand Russell, visiting from England. Russell saw Eliot at twenty-five as a silent young dandy, impeccably turned out, but a stick without "vigour or life—or enthusiasm." (Only a year later, in England, the diffident dandy—by then a new husband—would move with his bride right into Russell's tiny flat.) During the remainder of the Harvard period, Eliot embarked on Sanskrit, read Hindu and Buddhist sacred texts, and tunneled into the investigations that would culminate in his dissertation, *Experience and the Objects of Knowledge in the Philosophy of F. H. Bradley*. Screened by this busy academic program, he was also writing poetry. When Harvard offered him a traveling scholarship, he set off for Europe, and never again came back to live in the country of his birth. It was the beginning of the impersonations that were to become transformations.

He had intended an extensive tour of the Continent, but, in August of 1914, when war broke out, he retreated to England and enrolled at Oxford, ostensibly to continue his studies in philosophy. Oxford seemed an obvious way station for a young man headed for a professorial career, and his parents, shuttling between St. Louis and their comfortable New England summer house, ineradicably American in their habits and point of view, could not have judged otherwise, or suspected a permanent transatlantic removal. But what Eliot was really after was London: the literary life of London, in the manner of Henry James's illustrious conquest of it three decades before. He was quiet, deceptively passive, always reserved, on the watch for opportunity. He met Ezra Pound almost immediately. Pound, a fellow expatriate, was three years older and had come to London five years earlier. He had already published five volumes of poetry. He was idiosyncratic, noisy, cranky, aggressive, repetitively and tediously humorous as well as perilously unpredictable, and he kept an eye out for ways to position himself at the center of whatever maelstrom was current or could be readily invented. By the time he and Eliot discovered each other, Pound had been through Imagism and was boosting Vorticism; he wanted to shepherd movements, organize souls, administer lives. He read a handful of Eliot's Harvard poems, including "Portrait of a Lady" and "Prufrock," and instantly anointed him as the real thing. To Harriet Monroe in Chicago, the editor of *Poetry*, then the most distinguished—and coveted—American journal of its kind, he trumpeted Eliot as the author of "the best poem I have yet had or seen from an American," and insisted that she publish "Prufrock." He swept around

London introducing his new protégé and finding outlets for his poems in periodicals with names like *Others* and *BLAST* (a Vorticist effort printed on flamingo-pink paper and featuring eccentric typography).

Eliot felt encouraged enough by these successes to abandon both Oxford and Harvard, and took a job teaching in a boy's secondary school to support the poet he was now heartened to become. His mother, appalled by such recklessness, directed her shock not at Eliot but at his former teacher, Bertrand Russell (much as she had gone to the headmaster behind the teen-age Eliot's back to protest the risks of the quarry pond): "I hope Tom will be able to carry out his purpose of coming on in May to take his degree. The Ph.D. is becoming in America . . . almost an essential condition for an Academic position and promotion therein. The male teachers in our secondary schools are as a rule inferior to the women teachers, and they have little social position or distinction. I hope Tom will not undertake such work another year—it is like putting Pegasus in harness." Eliot's father, storming behind the scenes, was less impressed by Pegasus. The appeal to Russell concluded, "As for 'The *BLAST*,' Mr. Eliot remarked when he saw a copy he did not know there were enough lunatics in the world to support such a magazine."

Home, in short, was seething. Within an inch of his degree, the compliant son was suddenly growing prodigal. A bombardment of cables and letters followed. Even the war conspired against the prodigal's return; though Pound was already preparing to fill Eliot's luggage with masses of Vorticist material for a projected show in New York, the danger of German U-boats made a journey by sea unsafe. Russell cabled Eliot's father not to urge him to sit for his exams "UNLESS IMMEDIATE DEGREE IS WORTH

RISKING LIFE." "I was not greatly pleased with the language of Prof. Russell's telegram," Eliot's father complained in a letter to Harvard. "Mrs. Eliot and I will use every effort to induce my son to take his examinations later. Doubtless his decision was much influenced by Prof. Russell." Clearly the maternal plea to Russell had backfired. Meanwhile Harvard itself, in the person of James H. Woods, Eliot's mentor in the philosophy department, was importuning him; Woods was tireless in offering an appointment. Eliot turned him down. Three years on, the family campaign to lure him home was unabated: the biggest gun of all was brought out—Charles W. Eliot, eminent educational reformer, recently President of Harvard, architect of the "five-foot shelf" of indispensable classics, and Eliot's grandfather's third cousin once removed. "I conceive that you have a real claim on my attention and interest," he assured his wayward young relative.

> It is, nevertheless, quite unintelligible to me how you or any other young American scholar can forego the privilege of living in the genuine American atmosphere—a bright atmosphere of freedom and hope. I have never lived long in England—about six months in all—but I have never got used to the manners and customs of any class in English society, high, middle, or low. After a stay of two weeks or two months in England it has been delightful for me to escape . . .
>
> Then, too, I have never been able to understand how any American man of letters can forego the privilege of being of use primarily to Americans of the present and future generations, as Emerson, Bryant, Lowell, and

> Whittier were. Literature seems to me highly climatic and national . . . You mention in your letter the name of Henry James. I knew his father well, and his brother William very well; and I had some conversation with Henry at different times during his life. I have a vivid remembrance of a talk with him during his last visit to America. It seemed to me all along that his English residence for so many years contributed neither to the happy development of his art nor to his personal happiness.
>
> . . . My last word is that if you wish to speak through your work to people of the "finest New England spirit" you had better not live much longer in the English atmosphere. The New England spirit has been nurtured in the American atmosphere.

What Eliot thought—three years before the publication of "The Waste Land"—of this tribal lecture, and particularly of its recommendation that he aspire to the mantle of the author of "Thanatopsis," one may cheerfully imagine. In any case it was too late, and had long been too late. The campaign was lost before the first parental shot. Eliot's tie to England was past revocation. While still at Oxford he was introduced to Vivien Haigh-Wood, a high-spirited, high-strung, artistic young woman, the daughter of a cultivated upper-class family; her father painted landscapes and portraits. Eliot, shy and apparently not yet relieved of his virginity, was attracted to her rather theatrical personality. Bertrand Russell sensed in her something brasher, perhaps rasher, than mere vivaciousness—he judged her light, vulgar, and adventurous. Eliot married her only weeks after they met. The marriage, he knew, was the seal on his determination to stay in England, the seal his parents could not break and against which they would be helpless. After the honeymoon, Russell (through pure chance Eliot had bumped into him on a London street) took the new couple in for six months, from July to Christmas—he had a closet-size spare room—and helped them out financially in other ways. He also launched Eliot as a reviewer by putting him in touch with the literary editor of the *New Statesman*, for whom Eliot now began to write intensively. Probably Russell's most useful service was his arranging for Eliot to be welcomed into the intellectual and literary circle around Lady Ottoline Morrell at Garsington, her country estate. Though invitations went to leading artists and writers, Garsington was not simply a salon: the Morrells were principled pacifists who provided farm work during the war for conscientious objectors. Here Eliot found Aldous Huxley, D. H. Lawrence, Lytton Strachey, Katherine Mansfield, the painter Mark Gertler, Clive Bell, and, eventually, Leonard and Virginia Woolf. Lady Ottoline complained at first that Eliot had no spontaneity, that he barely moved his lips when he spoke, and that his voice was "mandarin." But Russell had carried him—in his arms, as it were—into the inmost eye of the most sophisticated whorl of contemporary English letters. The American newcomer who had left Harvard on a student fellowship in 1914 was already, by the middle of 1915, at the core of the London literary milieu he had dreamed of. And with so many models around him, he was working on disposing of whatever remnants of St. Louis remained lodged in his mouth, and perfecting the manner and accent of a high-born Englishman. (If he was grateful to Russell for this happy early initiation into precisely the society he coveted, by 1931—in "Thoughts After Lambeth," an essay on the idea of a national English church—he was sneering, in italics, at Russell's "*gospel of happiness*.")

Meanwhile his parents required placating. A bright young man in his twenties had gone abroad to augment his studies; it was natural for him to come home within a reasonable time to get started on real life and his profession. Instead, he had made a precipitate marriage, intended to spend the rest of his days in a foreign country, and was teaching French and arithmetic in the equivalent of an American junior high school. Not surprisingly, the brick manufacturer and his piously versifying wife could not infer the sublime vocation of a poet from these evidences. Eliot hoped to persuade them. The marriage to Vivien took place on June 26, 1915; on June 28 Ezra Pound wrote a very long letter to Eliot's father. It was one of Eliot's mother's own devices—that of the surrogate pleader. As his mother had asked Russell to intervene with Eliot to return him to Harvard, so now Eliot was enlisting Pound to argue for London. The letter included much information about Pound's own situation, which could not have been reassuring, since—as Pound himself remarked—it was unlikely that the elder Eliot had ever heard of him. But he sweetened the case with respectable references to Edgar Lee Masters and Robert Browning, and was careful to add that Robert Frost, another American in London, had "done a book of New England eclogues." To the heartbroken father who had looked forward to a distinguished university career for his son, Pound said, "I am now much better off than if I had kept my professorship in Indiana"—empty comfort, considering it was Fair Harvard that was being mourned; what Pound had relinquished was Wabash College in a place called Crawfordsville. What could it have meant to Eliot's father that this twenty-nine-year-old contributor to the lunatic *BLAST* boasted of having "engineered a new school of verse now known in England, France and

America," and insisted that "when I make a criticism of your son's work it is not an amateur criticism"? "As to his coming to London," Pound contended,

> anything else is a waste of time and energy. No one in London cares a hang what is written in America. After getting an American audience a man has to begin all over again here if he plans for an international hearing . . . The situation has been very well summed up in the sentence: "Henry James stayed in Paris and read Turgenev and Flaubert, Mr. Howells returned to America and read Henry James." . . . At any rate if T.S.E. is set on a literary career, this is the place to begin it and any other start would be very bad economy.

"I might add," he concluded, "that a literary man's income depends very much on how rigidly he insists on doing exactly what he himself wants to do. It depends on his connection, which he makes himself. It depends on the number of feuds that he takes on for the sake of his aesthetic beliefs. T.S.E. does not seem to be so pugnacious as I am and his course should be smoother and swifter."

The prediction held. The two-year eruption that was Vorticism waned, and so did Pound's local star; he moved on to Paris—leaving London, as it would turn out, in Eliot's possession. Pound's letter to the elder Eliot was not all bluster: he may have been a deft self-promoter, but he was also a promoter of literary ideas, and in Eliot's work he saw those ideas made flesh. The exuberance that sent Pound bustling through London to place Eliot here and there was the enthusiasm of an inventor whose thingamajig is just beginning to work in the world at large, in the break-through spirit of Alexander Graham Bell's "Mr. Watson, come here." In Pound's mind Eliot was Pound's invention. Certainly the excisions he demanded in "The Waste Land" radically "modernized" it in the direction of the objective correlative by keeping in the symbols and chopping out context and narrative, maneuvering the poem toward greater obliqueness and opacity. He also maneuvered Eliot. A determined literary man must go after his own "connection," he had advised Eliot's father, but the boisterous Pound served the reticent Eliot in a network of useful connections that Eliot would not have been likely to make on his own—including John Quinn, a New York literary philanthropist who became his (unpaid) agent in America and shored him up from time to time with generous money contributions.

Eliot was dependent on Pound's approval, or for a long while behaved as if he was. It was Pound who dominated the friendship, periodically shooting out instructions, information, scalawag counsel and pontification. "I value his verse far higher than that of any other living poet," Eliot told John Quinn in 1918. Gradually, over a span of years, there was a reversal of authority and power. Eliot rose and Pound sank. Under the pressure of his marriage (Vivien never held a job of any kind, nor could she have, even if it had been expected of her), Eliot ascended in the pragmatic world as well. He gave up teaching secondary school—it required him to supervise sports—and tried evening adult extension-course lecturing. The preparation was all-consuming and the remuneration paltry. Finally he recognized—he was, after all, his father's son—that this was no way to earn a living. A friend of Vivien's family recommended him to Lloyds Bank, where he turned out to be very good at the work—he had a position in the foreign department—and was regularly praised and advanced. Eventually he joined Faber & Gwyer, the London publishing house (later Faber & Faber) and remained associated with it until the end of his life. And then it was Pound who came to Eliot with his manuscripts. Eliot published them, but his responses, which had once treated Pound's antics with answering foolery, became heavily businesslike and impatient. As founder and editor of a literary journal Vivien had named *The Criterion*, Eliot went on commissioning pieces from Pound, though he frequently attempted to impose coherence and discipline; occasionally he would reject something outright. In 1922 Pound had asserted that "Eliot's *Waste Land* is I think the justification of the 'movement,' of our modern experiment, since 1900," but by 1930 he was taunting Eliot for having "arrived at the supreme Eminence among English critics largely through disguising himself as a corpse." Admiration had cooled on both sides. Still, Eliot's loyalty remained fundamentally steadfast, even when he understood that Pound may have been approaching lunacy. After the Second World War, when Pound was a patient in St. Elizabeth's Federal Hospital for the Insane in Washington, D.C.—the United States government's alternative to jailing him for treason—Eliot signed petitions for his release and made sure to see him on visits to America. Eliot never publicly commented on the reason for Pound's incarceration: Pound had supported the Axis and had actively aided the enemy. On Italian radio, in Mussolini's employ, he had broadcast twice-weekly attacks on Roosevelt, Churchill, and the Jews (whom he vilified in the style of Goebbels).

Though in the long run the friendship altered and attenuated—especially as Eliot grew more implicated in his Christian commitment and Pound in his self-proclaimed paganism—Eliot learned much from Pound. He had already learned from Laforgue the technique of the ironically illuminated persona. The tone of youthful ennui, and the ageless though precocious recoil from the world of phenomena, were Eliot's own. To these qualities of negation Pound added others: indirection, fragmentation, suggestibility, the force of piebald and zigzag juxtaposition —what we have long recognized as the signs of modernism, that famous alchemy of less becoming more. But even as he was tearing down the conventional frame of art, Pound was instructing Eliot in how to frame a career: not that Eliot really needed Pound in either sphere. Poets and critics may fabricate "movements," but no one can invent the Zeitgeist, and it was the Zeitgeist that was promulgating modernism. Eliot may well have been headed there with or without Pound at the helm. That Pound considered Eliot a creature of his own manufacture—that he did in fact tinker with the design—hardly signifies, given that Eliot's art was anyhow likely to fall into the rumbling imperatives of its own time. As for Eliot's advancement into greater and greater reputation, even pushy Pound could not push a miracle into being. Still, it was evident early on that Pound's dictates were in full operation. "Now I am going to ask you to do something for me," Eliot informs his brother Henry in 1915,

> in case you are in Boston or New York this summer. These are suggestions of Ezra Pound's, who has a very shrewd head, and has taken a very great interest in my prospects. There will be people to be seen in Boston and New York, editors with whom I might have some chance . . . As you are likeliest to be in Boston, the first thing is the *Atlantic Monthly*. Now Pound considers it important, whenever possible, to secure

> introductions to editors from people of better social position than themselves,

and he goes on to propose that Isabella Stewart Gardner, an influential blueblood connection of his, be dragooned into sending a note to the editor of the *Atlantic* on Eliot's behalf. A few days later he is writing to Mrs. Gardner herself, announcing the imminent arrival of his brother, "in order that he may get your advice." To Henry he admits he has only a handful of poems to show, including "some rather second rate things," but anyhow he asks him to try for an opening at *Harper's, Century, Bookman,* and the *New Republic.* "Nothing needs to be done in Chicago, I believe."

Thus, Pound's training in chutzpah. Yet much of it was native to Eliot, picked up at the parental knee. Not for nothing was he the offspring of a mother who was a model of the epistolary maneuver, or of a father who demanded instant success. He had been reared, in any event, as one of the lords of creation in a conscious American aristocracy that believed in its superior birthright—a Midwestern enclave of what Cousin Charles Eliot had called "the finest New England spirit." In the alien precincts of London, where his credentials were unknown or immaterial, the top could not be so easily guaranteed; it would have to be cajoled, manipulated, seduced, dared, commanded, now and then dodged; it would have to be pressed hard, and cunningly. All this Eliot saw for himself, and rapidly. Reserve shored up cunning. It scarcely required Pound to teach him how to calculate the main chance, or how to scheme to impose his importance. He was actually better at it than Pound, because infinitely silkier. Whereas Pound had one voice to assault the barricades with—a cantankerous blast in nutty frontiersman spelling ("You jess set and hev a quiet draw at youh cawn-kob") that was likely to annoy, and was intended to shake you up—Eliot had dozens of voices. His early letters—where he is sedulously on the make—are a ventriloquist's handbook. To Mrs. Gardner he purrs as one should to a prominent patroness of the arts, with friendly dignity, in a courteously appreciative tone, avoiding the appearance of pursuit. Addressing the irascibly playful Pound, he is irascibly playful, and falls into identical orthographical jokiness. To his benefactor John Quinn he is punctiliously—though never humbly—grateful, recording the state of his literary barometer with a precision owed to the chairman of the board; nor does he ever fail to ask after Quinn's health. To his father he writes about money, to his mother about underwear and overcoats. Before both of them, anxiety and dutifulness prevail; he is eager to justify himself and to tot up his triumphs. He means to show them how right he was in choosing a London life; he is not a disappointment after all. "I am staying in the bank," he reports (he had been offered an editorship on a literary journal)—this alone will please his father, but there is much more:

> As it is, I occupy rather a privileged position. I am out of the intrigues and personal hatreds of journalism, and everyone respects me for working in a bank. My social position is quite as good as it would be as editor of a paper. I only write what I want to—now—and everyone knows that anything I do write is good. I can influence London opinion and English literature in a better way. I am known to be disinterested. Even through the *Egoist* I am getting to be looked up to by people who are far better known to the general public than I. There is a small and select public which regards

me as the best living critic, as well as the best living poet, in England. I shall of course write for the *Ath.* [*The Athenaeum*] and keep my finger in it. I am much in sympathy with the editor, who is one of my most cordial admirers. With that and the *Egoist* and a young quarterly review which I am interested in, and which is glad to take anything I will give, I can have more than enough power to satisfy me. I really think that I have far more *influence* on English letters than any other American has ever had, unless it be Henry James. I know a great many people, but there are many more who would like to know me, and I can remain isolated and detached.

All this sounds very conceited, but I am sure it is true, and as there is no outsider from whom you would hear it, and America really knows very little of what goes on in London, I must say it myself. Because it will give you pleasure if you believe it, and it will help to explain my point of view.

This was surely the voice of a small boy making his case to his skeptical parents: *it will give you pleasure if you believe it.* He was thirty years old. The self-assurance—or call it, as others did, the arrogance—was genuine, and before his father and mother he was unashamed of speaking of the necessity of power. Such an aspiration was axiomatic among Eliots. What he had set himself to attain was the absolute pinnacle—a place inhabited by no one else, where he could "remain isolated and detached." Fate would give him his wish exactly and with a vengeance, though not quite yet. If he was puffing London to St. Louis, and representing himself there as "the best living critic, as well as the best living poet, in England," two months later he was telling Lytton

Strachey that he regarded "London with disdain," and divided "mankind into supermen, termites, and wire-worms. I am sojourning among the termites."

In all this there is a wonder and an enigma: the prodigy of Eliot's rocketlike climb from termite to superman. London (and New York and Boston) was swarming with young men on a course no different from Eliot's. He was not the only one with a hotly ambitious pen and an appetite for cultivating highly-placed people who might be useful to him. John Middleton Murry and Wyndham Lewis, for example, both of whom were in Eliot's immediate circle, were equally striving and polished, and though we still know their names, we know them more in the nature of footnotes than as the main text. All three were engaged in the same sort of essayistic empire-building in the little magazines, and at the same time. Lewis published Eliot in *BLAST*, Murry published him in the *Athenaeum*, and later Eliot, when he was editing the *Criterion*, published Lewis. Yet Eliot very quickly overshadowed the others. The disparity, it can be argued, was that Eliot was primarily a poet; or that Eliot's talent was more robust. But even if we believe, as most of us do, that genius of its own force will sooner or later leap commandingly out (Melville's and Dickinson's redemption from obscurity being our sacred paradigms), the riddle stands: why, for Eliot, so soon? His termite days were a brevity, a breath; he was superman in an instant. What was it that singled Eliot out to put him in the lead so astoundingly early? That he ferociously *willed* it means nothing. Nearly all beginning writers have a will for extreme fame; will, no matter how resilient, is usually no more efficacious in the marketplace than daydream.

If there is any answer to such questions—and there may not be—it may lie hidden in one of Eliot's most well-appointed impersonations: the voice he employed as essayist. That charm of intimacy and the easy giving of secrets that we like to associate with essayists—Montaigne, Lamb, Hazlitt, George Orwell, Virginia Woolf when the mood struck her—was not Eliot's. As in what is called the "familiar" essay, Eliot frequently said "I"—but it was an "I" set in ice cut from the celestial vault: uninsistent yet incontestable, serenely sovereign. It seemed to take its power from erudition, and in part it did; but really it took it from some proud inner figuration or incarnation—as if Literature itself had been summoned to speak in its own voice:

> I am not considering whether the language of Dante or Shakespeare is superior, for I cannot admit the question: I readily affirm that the differences are such as make Dante easier for a foreigner. Dante's advantages are not due to greater genius, but to the fact that he wrote when Europe was still more or less one. And even had Chaucer or Villon been exact contemporaries of Dante, they would still have been farther, linguistically as well as geographically, from the center of Europe than Dante.

Who could talk back to that? Such sentences appear to derive from a source of knowledge—a congeries of assumptions—indistinguishable from majesty. In short, Eliot would not *permit* himself to be ignored, because it was not "himself" he was representing, but the very flower of European civilization. And there may have been another element contributing to the ready acceptance of his authority: as a foreigner, he was drawn to synthesizing and summarizing in a way that insiders, who take their context for granted, never do. He saw principles where the natives saw only phenomena. Besides, he had a clear model for focused ascent: Henry James. Knowing what he meant to become, he was immune to distraction or wrong turnings. "It is the final perfection, the consummation of an American," Eliot (in one of his most autobiographical dicta) wrote of James, "to become, not an Englishman, but a European—something which no born European, no person of any European nationality, can become."

So much for the larger trajectory. He had mapped out an unimpeded ideal destination. In the lesser geography of private life, however, there was an unforeseen impediment. Henry James had never married; Eliot had married Vivien. In 1915 she was twenty-seven, slender, lively, very pretty, with a wave in her hair and a pleasant mouth and chin. By 1919, Virginia Woolf was describing her as "a washed out, elderly and worn looking little woman." She complained of illness from the very first, but otherwise there were few immediate hints of the devastation to come. She was absorbed in Eliot's career. He brought his newest work to her for criticism; she read proofs; she assisted in preparing the *Criterion*. She also did some writing of her own—short stories, and prose sketches that Eliot admired and published in the *Criterion*. She had energy enough at the start: there were excursions, dinners, visits to Garsington, dance halls, dance lessons, theater, opera; even a flirtation with Bertrand Russell that turned into a one-night stand. ("Hellish and loathsome," Russell called it.) A month after the wedding she told Russell that she had married Eliot because she thought she could "stimulate" him, but that it could not be done. She began to suffer from headaches, colitis, neuralgia, insomnia. "She is a person who lives on a knife edge," Russell said. Eliot himself often woke at night feeling sick. He was plagued by colds, flu, bronchial problems; he smoked too much and he consistently drank too much, though he held it well. Retreating from Vivien, he threw himself into the work at the bank and into developing his literary reputation. Vivien had nowhere to go but into resentment, ill-will, hysteria. In the mornings the bed linens were frequently bloody—she menstruated excessively, and became obsessed with washing the sheets. She washed them herself even when they stayed in hotels. Morphine was prescribed for her various symptoms; also bromides and ether (she swabbed her whole body with ether, so that she reeked of it), and mercilessly bizarre diets—a German doctor combined starvation with the injection of animal glands. She collapsed into one nervous illness after another. Eliot repeatedly sent her to the country to recuperate while he remained in town. When his mother, now an elderly widow, and one of his sisters came on a visit from America, Vivien was absent, and Eliot was obliged to manage the complications of hospitality on his own. Anxiety over Vivien crept into all his business and social correspondence: "my wife has been very ill"; "she is all right when she is lying down, but immediately she gets up is very faint"; "wretched today—another bad night"; "Have you ever been in such incessant and extreme pain that you felt your sanity going, and that you no longer knew reality from delusion? That's the way she is. The doctors have never seen so bad a case, and hold out no definite hope, and have so far done her no good. Meanwhile she is in screaming agony . . ."

She brought out in him all his responsibility, vigilance, conscientiousness, troubled concern; in brief, his virtue. Her condition bewildered him; nothing in his experience, and certainly nothing in his upbringing, had equipped him for it; her manifold sicknesses were unpredictable, and so was she. Her sanity was in fact going. Daily she made him consider and reconsider his conduct toward her, and her ironic, clever, assaultive, always embarrassing responses ran tumbling over his caution. He dreaded dinner parties in her company, and went alone or not at all. It became known that Eliot was ashamed of his wife. But he was also ashamed of his life. Little by little he attempted to live it without Vivien, or despite Vivien, or in the few loopholes left him by Vivien. She was in and out of sanitoria in England, France, and Switzerland; it was a relief to have her away. What had once been frightened solicitude was gradually transmuted into horror, and horror into self-preservation, and self-preservation into callousness, and callousness into a kind of moral brutality. She felt how, emotionally and spiritually, he was abandoning her to her ordeal. However imploringly she sought his attention, he was determined to shut her out; the more he shut her out, the more wildly, dramatically, and desperately she tried to recapture him. He was now a man hunted—and haunted—by a mad wife. He saw himself transmogrified into one of the hollow men of his own imagining, that scarecrow figure stuck together out of "rat's coat, crowskin, crossed staves":

> The eyes are not here
> There are no eyes here
> In this valley of dying stars
> In this hollow valley
> This broken jaw of our lost kingdoms

He carried this Golgothan self-portrait with him everywhere; his lost kingdoms were in the stony looks he gave to the world. Virginia Woolf was struck by "the grim marble face . . . mouth twisted and shut; not a single line free and easy; all caught, pressed, inhibited." "Humiliation is the worst thing in life," he told her. Vivien had humiliated him. Torment and victimization—she of him, and he of her—had degraded him. Bouts of drink depleted him. At times his behavior was as strange as hers: he took to wearing pale green face powder, as if impersonating the sickly cast of death. Virginia Woolf thought he painted his lips. In 1933, after eighteen years of accelerating domestic misery, he finally broke loose: he went to America for a series of angry lectures (published later as *After Strange Gods: A Primer of Modern Heresy*) in which he attacked Pound, D. H. Lawrence, liberalism, and "free-thinking Jews," complaining that the United States had been "invaded by foreign races" who had "adulterated" its population. In London, meanwhile, a remorseful Vivien was refurbishing the flat for his homecoming; she even offered to join him overseas. In the black mood of his lectures her letter shocked him into a quick cruel plan. Writing from America, he directed his London solicitors to prepare separation documents and to deliver them to Vivien in his absence. When he arrived back in England, the deed was done. Vivien in disbelief continued to wait for him in the reupholstered flat. He moved instead into the shabby guest rooms of the parish house of St. Stephen's, an Anglican congregation with a high-church bent. There, subdued and alone among celibate priests, he spent the next half-dozen years in penance, suffering the very isolation and detachment he had once prized as the influential poet's reward.

Yet Vivien was in pursuit. Though he kept his lodgings secret from her, with fearful single-mindedness she attempted to hunt him down, turning up wherever there might be a chance of confronting him, hoping to cajole or argue or threaten him into resuming with her. He contrived to escape her time after time. By now he had left the bank for Faber; she would burst into the editorial offices without warning, weeping and pleading to be allowed to talk to him. One of the staff would give some excuse and Eliot would find a way of sneaking out of the building without detection. She carried a knife in her purse—it was her customary flamboyance—to alarm him; but it was a theater knife, made of rubber. She sent Christmas cards in the name of "Mr. and Mrs. T. S. Eliot," as if they were still together, and she advertised in *The Times* for him to return. She called herself sometimes Tiresias, and sometimes Daisy Miller, after the doomed Jamesian heroine. In a caricature of what she imagined would please him, she joined the newly formed British Union of Fascists. One day she actually caught him; she went up to him after a lecture, handed him books to sign as if they were strangers, and begged him to go home with her. He hid his recoil behind a polite "How do you do?" When she got wind of a scheme to commit her to a mental hospital, she fled briefly to Paris. In 1938 she was permanently institutionalized, whether by her mother or her brother, or by Eliot himself, no one knows; but Eliot had to have been consulted, at the very least. When her brother visited her in 1946, a year before her death, he reported that she seemed as sane as he was. She had tried on one occasion to run away; she was captured and brought back. She died in the asylum a decade after her commitment. Eliot never once went to see her.

Out of this brutalizing history of grieving and loss, of misalliance, misfortune, frantic confusion, and recurrent panic, Eliot drew the formulation of his dream of horror—that waste land where

> . . . I Tiresias have foresuffered all
> . . . and walked among the lowest of the dead

Here is no water but only rock . . .
If there were only water amongst the rock
Dead mountain mouth of carious teeth that cannot
spit

. . . blood shaking my heart
The awful daring of a moment's surrender
Which an age of prudence can never retract
By this, and this only, we have existed
Which is not to be found in our obituaries
Or in memories draped by the beneficent spider
Or under seals broken by the lean solicitor
In our empty rooms

He might have regarded his marriage and its trials as a regrettable accident of fallible youth—the awful daring of a moment's surrender—compounded by his initial sense of duty and loyalty. But he was shattered beyond such realism, and finally even beyond stoicism. He felt he had gazed too long on the Furies. The fiery brand he had plucked out of his private inferno seemed not to have been ignited in the ordinary world; it blackened him metaphysically, and had little to do with fractured expectations or the social difficulties of mental illness. What he knew himself to be was a sinner. The wretchedness he had endured was sin. Vivien had been abused—by doctors and their scattershot treatments, and by regimens Eliot could not have prevented. The truth was she had been drugged for years. And he had abused her himself, perhaps more horribly, by the withdrawal of simple human sympathy. It was she who had smothered his emotional faculties, but reciprocal humiliation had not earned reciprocal destinies. Vivien was confined. He was freed to increase his fame. Nevertheless—

as if to compensate her—he lived like a man imprisoned; like a penitent; like a flagellant. He was consumed by ideas of sin and salvation, by self-loathing. The scourge that was Vivien had driven him to conversion: he entered Christianity seriously and desperately, like a soul literally in danger of damnation, or as though he believed he was already half-damned. The religiosity he undertook was a kind of brooding medieval monkishness: ascetic, turned altogether inward, to the sinful self. Its work was the work of personal redemption. In "Ash Wednesday" he exposed the starting-point, the beginning of abnegation and confession:

> Because these wings are no longer wings to fly
> But merely vans to beat the air
> The air which is now thoroughly small and dry
> Smaller and dryer than the will
> Teach us to care and not to care
> Teach us to sit still.

And in a way he did learn to sit still. He was celibate. He was diligent and attentive in his office life while conducting an orderly if lonely domestic routine. He was at Mass every morning, and frequently went on retreat. During the night blitz of London in 1939, he served for a time as an air raid warden, often staying up till dawn. Then, to escape the exhausting bombings, like so many others he turned to commuting from the far suburbs, where he became the paying guest of a family of gentlewomen. In 1945, at the war's end, he made another unusual household arrangement, one that also had its spiritual side: he moved in with John Hayward, a gregarious wit and bookish extrovert whom disease had locked in a wheelchair. Eliot performed the necessary small personal tasks for his companion, wheeled him to the park on pleasant afternoons, and stood vigilantly behind his chair at the parties Hayward liked to preside over—Eliot reserved and silent under the burden of his secret wounds and his eminence, Hayward boisterous, funny, and monarchically at ease. In the evenings, behind the shut door of the darkest room at the back of the flat, Eliot recited the rosary, ate his supper from a tray, and limited himself to a single game of patience. This odd couple lived together for eleven years, until Eliot suddenly married his young secretary, Valerie Fletcher. She offered him the intelligent adoration of an infatuated reader who had been enchanted by his poetry and his fame since her teens; she had come to Faber & Faber with no other motive than to be near him. Vivien had died in 1947; the marriage to Valerie took place in 1957. After the long discipline of penance, he opened himself to capacious love for the first time. As he had known himself for a sinner, so now he knew himself for a happy man.

But the old reflex of recoil—and abandonment—appeared to have survived after all. From youth he had combined ingrained loyalty with the contrary habit of casting off the people who seemed likely to impede his freedom. He had fled over an ocean to separate himself from his demanding parents—though it was his lot ultimately to mimic them. He was absorbed by religion like his mother, and ended by writing, as she did, devotional poetry. Like his father, he was now a well-established businessman, indispensable to his firm and its most influential officer. (It developed that he copied his father even in trivia. The elder Eliot was given to playful doodlings of cats. The son—whose knack for cartooning exceeded the father's—wrote clever cat verses. These, in the form of the long-running Broadway musical, are nearly the whole sum of Eliot's current American renown: if today's undergraduates take spontaneous note of Eliot at all, it will be "Cats" on their tape cassettes, not "The Waste Land.") Still, despite these evolving reversions, it was the lasting force of his repudiations that stung: his scorn for the family heritage of New England Unitarianism, his acquisition in 1927 of British citizenship. He had thrown off both the liberal faith of his fathers—he termed it a heresy—and their native pride of patriotism. He had shown early that he could sever what no longer suited. The selfless interval with John Hayward was cut off overnight: there is a story that Eliot called a taxi, told Hayward he was going off to be married, and walked out. After so prolonged a friendship—and a dependence—Hayward felt cruelly abandoned. He never recovered his spirit. Eliot was repeatedly capable of such calculated abruptness. His abandonment of Vivien—the acknowledged sin of his soul, the flaming pit of his exile and suffering—was echoed in less theological tones in his careless dismissal of Emily Hale and Mary Trevelyan, the wounded women whose loving attachment he had welcomed for years. When Vivien died, each one—Emily Hale in America and Mary Trevelyan close at hand in London—believed that Eliot would now marry her.

Miss Hale—as she was to her students—was a connection of the New England cousins; Eliot had known her since her girlhood. Their correspondence, with its webwork of common associations and sensibilities, flourished decade after decade—she was a gifted teacher of drama at various women's colleges and private schools for girls, with a modest but vivid acting talent of her own. Eliot's trips to America always included long renewing visits with her, and she in turn traveled to England over a series of summer vacations to be with him. One of their excursions was to the lavish silent gardens of Burnt Norton, the unoccupied country mansion of an earl. (That single afternoon of sunlight and roses was transformed by "a grace of sense, a white light still and moving," into the transcendent incantations of "Burnt Norton," the first of the "Quartets.") In America she waited, in tranquil patience and steady exultation, for the marriage that was never to come: generations of her students were informed of her friendship with the greatest of living poets. Eliot found in her, at a distance, unbodied love, half-elusive nostalgia, the fragility of an ideal. When she threatened, at Vivien's death, to become a real-life encumbrance, he diluted their intimacy; but when he married Valerie Fletcher he sloughed Emily off altogether—rapidly and brutally. Stunned and demoralized—they had been friends for fifty years—she gave up teaching and spiralled into a breakdown. She spent the rest of her life in the hope that her importance to Eliot would not go unrecognized. Her enormous collection of his letters (more than a thousand) she donated to Princeton University, and—Eliot-haunted and Eliot-haunting—she asked him to return hers. He did not reply; he had apparently destroyed them. The "man I loved," she wrote to Princeton, "*I* think, did not respond as he should have to my long trust, friendship and love." She stipulated that the Princeton repository not be opened until 2019; she looked to her vindication then. Having been patient so long, she was willing to be patient even beyond the grave. Eliot may have bestowed his infirm old age on Miss Fletcher, but the future would see that he had loved Miss Hale in his prime.

As for Mary Trevelyan, she was a hearty pragmatist, a spunky activist, a bold managerial spirit. For nineteen years she was a prop against Eliot's depressions, a useful neighbor—she drove him all over in her car—and, to a degree, a confidante. From the beginning of Vivien's incarceration until his marriage to Valerie—i.e., from 1938 until 1957—Eliot and Mary were regularly together at plays, at parties, and, especially, at church. Their more private friendship centered on lunches and teas, domestic evenings cooking and listening to music in Mary's flat, her matter-of-fact solicitude through his illnesses and hypochondria. They made a point of mentioning each other in their separate devotions. Mary was at home in the pieties Eliot had taken on—she came of distinguished High Anglican stock, the elite of government, letters, and the cloth, with a strong commitment to public service. Her father was a clergyman who erected and administered churches; the historian G. M. Trevelyan was a cousin; her relatives permeated Oxford and Cambridge. (Humphrey Carpenter, author of a remarkably fine biography of Ezra Pound—fittingly published in Eliot's centenary year—represents the newest generation of this family.)

With Mary, Eliot could unbutton. He felt familiar enough to indulge in outbursts of rage or contemptuous sarcasm, and to display the most withering side of his character, lashing out at the people he despised. Through it all she remained candid, humorous, and tolerant, though puzzled by his unpredictable fits of withdrawal from her, sometimes for three months at a time. He drew lines of conduct she was never permitted to cross: for instance, only once did he agree to their vacationing together, and that was when he needed her—and the convenience of her driving—to help entertain his sister, visiting from America. Mary was accommodating but never submissive. During the war she organized a rest hostel in Brussels for soldiers on leave from the front; in 1944 she nursed hundreds of the wounded. After the war she traveled all over Asia for UNESCO, and founded an international house in London for foreign students. Plainly she had nothing in common with the wistful and forbearing Miss Hale of Abbot Academy for girls. But her expectations were the same. When Vivien died, Mary proposed marriage to Eliot—twice. When he refused her the first time, he said he was incapable of marrying anyone at all; she thought this meant his guilt over Vivien. The second time, he told her about his long attachment to Emily Hale, and how he was a failure at love; she thought this meant psychological exhaustion. And then he married Valerie. Only eight days before the wedding—held secretly in the early morning at a church Eliot did not normally attend—he and Mary lunched together for hours; he disclosed nothing. On the day of the wedding she had a letter from him commemorating their friendship and declaring his love for Valerie. Mary sent back two notes, the earlier one to congratulate him, the second an unrestrained account of her shock. Eliot responded bitterly, putting an end to two decades of companionship.

But all this—the years of self-denial in the parish house, the wartime domesticity among decorous suburban ladies, the neighborly fellowship with John Hayward and Mary Trevelyan, the break with Hayward, the break with Emily Hale, the break with Mary Trevelyan, the joyous denouement with Valerie Fletcher—all this, however consecrated to quietism, however turbulent, was aftermath and postlude. The seizure that animated the poetry had already happened—the seizure was Vivien. Through Vivien he had learned to recognize the reality of sin in all its influences and phases; she was the turning wind of his spiritual storm. Vivien herself understood this with the canniness of a seer: "As to Tom's *mind*," she once said, "I am his mind." The abyss of that mind, and its effect on Eliot as it disintegrated, led him first through a vortex of flight, and then to tormented contemplation, and finally to the religious calm of "Burnt Norton":

> Time present and time past
> Are both perhaps present in time future.
> And time future contained in time past.

Time past marked the psychological anarchy of his youthful work, that vacuous ignorance of sin that had produced "Prufrock," "Gerontion," "The Hollow Men," "The Waste Land." Not to acknowledge the real presence of sin is to be helpless in one's degradation. Consequently Prufrock is a wraith "pinned and wriggling on the wall," uncertain how to "spit out all the butt-ends of my days and ways"; Gerontion is "a dry brain in a dry season"; the hollow men "filled with straw" cannot falter through to the end of a prayer—"For Thine is / Life is / For Thine is the"; the voice of "The Waste Land"—"burning burning burning burning"—is unable to imagine prayer. And the chastening "future contained in time past" is almost surely the inferno that was Vivien: what else could that earlier hollowness have arrived at if not a retributive burning? The waste land —a dry season of naked endurance without God—had earned him the ordeal with Vivien; but the ordeal with Vivien was to serve both time past and time future. Time past: he would escape from the formless wastes of past metaphysical drift only because Vivien had jolted him into a sense of sin. And time future: only because she had jolted him into a sense of sin would he uncover the means to future absolution—the genuine avowal of himself as sinner. To the inferno of Vivien he owed clarification of what had been. To the inferno of Vivien he owed clarification of what might yet be. If Vivien was Eliot's mind, she had lodged Medusa there, and Medusa became both raging muse and purifying savior. She was the motive for exorcism, confession, and penitence. She gave him "Ash Wednesday," a poem of supplication. She gave him "Four Quartets," a subdued lyric of near-forgiveness, with long passages of serenely prosaic lines (occasionally burned out into the monotone of philosophic fatigue), recording the threshold of the shriven soul:

> . . . music heard so deeply
> That it is not heard at all, but you are the music
> While the music lasts. These are only hints and
> guesses,
> Hints followed by guesses; and the rest
> Is prayer, observance, discipline, thought and action.
> The hint half guessed, the gift half understood, is
> Incarnation.

What makes such "reading backward" possible, of course, is the biographies. (I have relied on Peter Ackroyd and Lyndall Gordon for much of the narrative of Eliot's life.) Knowledge of the life interprets—decodes—the poems: exactly what Eliot's theory of the objective correlative was designed to prevent. Occasionally the illuminations cast by reading backward provoke the uneasy effect of looking through a forbidden keyhole with a flashlight:

> "My nerves are bad tonight. Yes, bad. Stay with
> me.
> "Speak to me. Why do you never speak? Speak.

"What are you thinking of? What thinking? What?
"I never know what you are thinking. Think."

I think we are in rats' alley
Where the dead men lost their bones.

That, wailing out of a jagged interval in "The Waste Land," can only be Vivien's hysteria, and Eliot's recoil from it. But it hardly requires such explicitness (and there is little else that is so clearly explicit) to recognize that his biographers have broken the code of Eliot's reticence—that programmatic reticence embodied in his doctrine of impersonality. The objective correlative was intended to direct the reader to a symbolic stand-in for the poet's personal suffering—not Vivien but Tiresias. Secret becomes metaphor. Eliot's biographers begin with the metaphor and unveil the secret. When the personal is exposed, the objective correlative is annihilated.

And yet the objective correlative has won out, after all, in a larger way. If "The Waste Land" can no longer hide its sources in Eliot's private malaise, it has formidably sufficed as an "objective equivalence" for the public malaise of generations. Its evocations of ruin, loss, lamentation, its "empty cisterns and exhausted wells," are broken sketches of the discontents that remain when the traditional props of civilization have failed: for some (unquestionably for Eliot), a world without God; for others, a world without so much as an illusion of intelligibility or restraint. In 1867, contemplating the Victorian crisis of faith, Matthew Arnold saw "a darkling plain . . . where ignorant armies clash by night," but in Eliot's echoing "arid plain" there is nothing so substantial as even a clash—only formlessness, "hooded hordes swarming," "falling towers"; hallucination succeeds hallucination, until all the crowns of civilization—"Jerusalem Athens Alexandria / Vienna London"—are understood to be "unreal."

In 1922 (a postwar time of mass unemployment, economic disintegration and political uncertainty), "The Waste Land" fell out upon its era as the shattered incarnation of dissolution, the very text and texture of modernism—modernism's consummate document and ode. In the almost seventy years since its first publication, it has taken on, as the great poems do (but not the very greatest), a bloom of triteness (as ripe truth can over-mature into truism). It is no more "coherent" to its newest readers than it was to its astonished earliest readers, but it is much less difficult: tone and technique no longer startle. Post-Bomb, post-Holocaust, post-moonwalk, it may actually be too tame a poem to answer to the mindscape we now know more exhaustively than Eliot did. Professor Harry Levin, Harvard's eminent pioneer promulgator of Proust, Joyce, and Eliot, quipped a little while ago—not altogether playfully—that modernism "has become old-fashioned." "The Waste Land" is not yet an old-fashioned poem, and doubtless never will be. But it does not address with the same exigency the sons and daughters of those impassioned readers who ecstatically intoned it, three and four decades ago, in the belief that infiltration by those syllables was an aesthetic sacrament. Even for the aging generation of the formerly impassioned, something has gone out of the poem—not in "The Waste Land" proper, perhaps, but rather in that parallel work Eliot called "Notes on 'The Waste Land.'" This was the renowned mock-scholarly apparatus Eliot tacked on to the body of the poem, ostensibly to spell out its multiple allusions—a contrivance that once seemed very nearly a separate set of modernist stanzas: arbitrary, fragmented, dissonant, above all solemnly erudite. "The whole passage from Ovid," drones the sober professorial persona of the "Notes," "is of great anthropological interest." There follow nineteen lines of Latin verse. The procession of brilliantly variegated citations—Augustine, the Upanishads, Verlaine, Baudelaire, Hermann Hesse, Shakespeare, Tarot cards, the Grail legend—suggests (according to Professor Levin) that context was to Eliot what conceit was to the metaphysical poets. A fresh reading of the "Notes" admits to something else—the thumbed nose, that vein in Eliot of the practical joker, released through Macavity the Mystery Cat and in masses of unpublished bawdy verses (nowadays we might regard them as more racist than bawdy) starring "King Bolo's big black bassturd kween." In any case, whatever pose Eliot intended, no one can come to the "Notes" today with the old worshipful gravity. They seem drained of austerity—so emphatically serious that it is hard to take them seriously at all.

The same with the plays. With the exception of the first of the five, "Murder in the Cathedral"—a major devotional poem of orchestral breadth—the plays are all collapsed into curios. From our perspective, they are something worse than period pieces, since that is what they were—Edwardian drawing room dramas—when they were new. They hint at (or proclaim) a failure of Eliot's public ear. His aim was to write popular verse plays for the English stage—an aim worthy (though Eliot never had the hubris to say this) of Shakespeare. George Bernard Shaw had been content with prose—and the majestically cunning prose speeches in "Murder in the Cathedral" are reminiscent of nothing so much as Shaw's "Saint Joan," including Shaw's preface to that play. The dialogue of enjambment that is the style and method of "The Cocktail Party," "The

Confidential Clerk," and "The Elder Statesman," never attains the sound of verse, much less poetry. That was precisely Eliot's hope: he considered "Murder in the Cathedral" too blatantly poetic, a "dead end." His goal was to bury the overt effects of poetry while drawing out of ordinary speech and almost ordinary situations a veil of transcendence—even, now and then, of mystical horror, as when (in "The Family Reunion") the Furies suddenly appear, or when (in "The Cocktail Party") a character we are meant to imagine as a saint and a martyr goes off to be a missionary among the "natives" and is eaten by ants. (Having first been crucified, it ought to be added. And though there are farcical moments throughout, the devouring anthill is not intended as one of them.) Nevertheless nothing transcendent manages to rise from any printed page of any of the last four plays—almost nothing suggestive of poetry, in fact, except an occasional "wisdom" patch in the semi-lyrical but largely prosy manner of the philosophical lines in "Four Quartets." Possibly this is because the printed page is perforce bare of technical stagecraft, with its color and excitement. Yet—similarly unaccoutered—Shakespeare, Marlowe, and Shaw, in their greater and lesser written art, send out language with presence and power enough to equal absent actors, sets, lighting, costumes. Much of Eliot's dialogue, rather than achieving that simplicity of common speech he aspired to, plummets to the stilted, the pedestrian, the enervated:

Oh, Edward, when you were a little boy,
I'm sure you were always getting yourself measured
To prove how you had grown since the last holidays.
You were always intensely concerned with yourself;
And if other people grow, well, you want to grow too.

Given only the text and nothing else, a reader of "The Cocktail Party," say, will be perplexed by its extravagant performing history: in London and New York in the fifties, it filled theaters and stunned audiences. Read now, these later plays are unmistakably dead, embalmed, dated beyond endurance—dated especially in the light of the vigorous fifties, when the energetic spokesmen of the Angry Young Men were having their first dramatic hearing. As playwright, Eliot inexplicably eschewed or diluted or could not pull off his theory of demarcation between "the man who suffers and the mind which creates," so the plays are surprisingly confessional—the Furies harbor Vivien, a character is tormented by thinking he has killed his wife, Valerie turns up as a redemptive young woman piously named Monica, etc. Since Eliot's private life was not only closed but unguessed-at in those years, gossip could not have been the lure for theater-goers. The lure was, in part, skillful production: on the page, the Furies when they pop up seem as silly as the news of the hungry anthill, but their theatrical embodiment was electrifying. Fine performances and ingenious staging, though, were at bottom not what brought overflowing audiences to see Eliot's plays. They came because of the supremacy of Eliot's fame. They came because verse drama by T. S. Eliot was the most potent cultural vitamin of the age.

Inevitably we are returned to the issue (there is no escaping it at any point) of Eliot's renown. As a young man, he had hammered out the prestige of a critical reputation by means of essay after essay. By the time of the later plays he had become a world celebrity, an international feature story in newspapers and magazines. But neither the essays by themselves, nor (certainly) the plays—always excepting "Murder in the Cathedral," which ought to count among the most lastingly resonant of the poems—could have won for Eliot his permanent place in English letters. The fame belongs to the poems. The rest, however much there might be of it, was spinoff. Yet the body of poems is amazingly small in the light of Eliot's towering repute. In 1958, for example, invited to Rome for an honorary degree, he was driven through streets mobbed with students roaring "*Viva* Eliot!" Mass adulation of this sort more often attaches to Presidents and monarchs—or, nowadays, to rock stars. What did that roar rest on? Leaving aside the early Bolo ribaldry (which in any case never reached print), the fourteen cat verses, and the contents of a little posthumous collection called "Poems Written in Early Youth" (from ages sixteen to twenty-two), but not omitting two unfinished works—"Sweeney Agonistes" and "Coriolan"—Eliot's entire poetic oeuvre comes to no more than fifty-four poems. England, at least, is used to more abundant output from the poets it chooses to mark with the seal of permanence. My copy of Wordsworth's *Poetical Works* adds up to nine hundred and sixty-six pages of minuscule type, or approximately a thousand poems. The changes in the written culture between, say, the "Ode on Intimations of Immortality," published in 1807, and Eliot's "Waste Land," published one hundred and fifteen years later, speak for themselves. Still, granting the impertinence of measuring by number, there remains something extraordinary—even uncanny—about the torrent of transoceanic adoration that, for Eliot, stemmed from fifty-four poems.

Eliot may have supposed himself a classicist, but really he is in the line of the Romantics: subjective, anguished, nostalgic, mystical, lyrical. The critic Harold Bloom's mild view is that he "does not derive from Dante and Donne, as he thought, but from Tennyson and Whitman"

—a judgment that might have stung him. For Eliot to have believed himself an offspring of the cosmic Dante and the precision-worker Donne, and to end, if Professor Bloom is correct, as a descendant of the softer, lusher music of Tennyson, is no serious diminishment (Tennyson is permanent too)—though it *is* a diminishment. Lord Tennyson, the British Empire's laureate, may have seemed a weighty and universal voice to the Victorians. For us he is lighter and more parochial. It is in the nature of fame to undergo revision: Eliot appears now to be similarly receding into the parochial, even the sectarian (unlike the all-embracing Whitman, with whom he shares the gift of bel canto). His reach—once broad enough to incorporate the Upanishads—shrank to extend no farther than the neighborhood sacristy, and to a still smaller space: the closet of the self. His worship was local and exclusionary not simply in the limited sense that it expressed an astringent clerical bias, or that he observed the forms of a narrow segment of the Church of England—itself an island church, after all, though he did his best to link it with what he termed "the Universal Church of the World." What made Eliot's religiosity local and exclusive was that he confined it to his personal pain and bitterness: he allowed himself to become estranged from humanity. Feeling corrupt in himself, he saw corruption everywhere: "all times are corrupt," he wrote; and then again, "the whole of modern literature is corrupted by what I call Secularism." Demanding that faith—a particular credo—be recognized as the foundation of civilization, he went on to define civilization as extraneous to some of its highest Western manifestations—the principles of democracy, tolerance, and individualism. Despite his youthful study of Eastern religion and his poet's immersion in Hebrew scripture, he was finally unable to imagine that there might be rival structures of civilization not grounded in the doctrine of original sin, and yet intellectually and metaphysically exemplary. Even within the familial household of Christendom, he was quick to cry heretic. In any event, the style of his orthodoxy was, as Harry Levin put it, "a literary conception." As a would-be social theorist he had a backward longing for the medieval hegemony of cathedral spires—i.e., for a closed society. It was a ruefulness so poignant that it preoccupied much of the prose and seeped into the melancholy cadences of the poetry. As a modernist, Eliot was the last of the Romantics.

In the end he could not disengage the mind that created from the man who suffered; they were inseparable. But the mind and the man—the genius and the sufferer—had contributed, in influence and authority, more than any other mind and man (with the exception perhaps of Picasso) to the formation of the most significant aesthetic movement of the twentieth century. It was a movement so formidable that its putative successor cannot shake off its effects and is obliged to carry on its name; helplessly, we speak of the "postmodern." Whether postmodernism is genuinely a successor, or merely an updated variant of modernism itself, remains unresolved. Yet whichever it turns out to be, we do know for certain that we no longer live in the literary shadow of T. S. Eliot. 'Mistah Kurtz—he dead"—the celebrated epigraph Eliot lifted from Conrad's "Heart of Darkness" and affixed to "The Hollow Men"—applies: the heart has gone out of what once ruled. High art is dead. The passion for inheritance is dead. Tradition is equated with obscurantism. The wall that divided serious high culture from the popular arts is breached; anything can count as "text." Knowledge—saturated in historical memory—is displaced by information, or memory without history:

data. Allusiveness is crosscultural in an informational and contemporary way (from, say, beekeeping to film-making), not in the sense of connecting the present with the past. The relation of poets to history is that they can take it or leave it, and mostly they leave it, whether in prosody or in the idea of the venerable. If it is true that "The Waste Land" could not be written today because it is too tame for the savagery we have since accumulated, there is also a more compelling truth: because we seem content to live without contemplation of our formal beginnings, a poem like "The Waste Land," mourning the loss of an integral tradition, is for us inconceivable. For the modernists, the center notoriously did not hold; for us (whatever *we* are), there is no recollection of a center, and nothing to miss, let alone mourn.

Was it the ever-increasing rush to what Eliot called "Secularism" that knocked him off his pinnacle? Was it the vague nihilism of "modern life" that deposed modernism's prophet? Was Eliot shrugged off because his pessimistic longings were ultimately judged to be beside the point? The answer may not be as clearcut as any of that. The changes that occurred in the forty years between the Nobel award in 1948 and Eliot's centennial in 1988 have still not been assimilated or even remotely understood. The Wordsworth of the "Ode to Duty" (composed the same year as "Intimations of Immortality") has more in common with the Eliot of "Four Quartets"—the differing idioms of the poetry aside—than Eliot has with Allen Ginsberg. And yet Ginsberg's "Howl," the single poem most representative of the break with Eliot, may owe as much, thematically, to "The Waste Land" as it does to the bardic Whitman, or to the opening of the era of anything-goes. Ginsberg belongs to the generation that knew Eliot as sanctified, and, despite every irruption into indiscipline, Eliot continues alive in Ginsberg's ear. For the rest, a look at the condition of most poetry in America today will disclose how far behind we have left Eliot. William Carlos Williams, a rival of Eliot's engaged in another vein of diction and committed to sharply contrasting aesthetic goals ("no ideas but in things"), said of the publication of "The Waste Land" that he "felt at once it had set me back twenty years," largely because of its European gravity of erudition. The newest generation in the line of descent from Williams, though hardly aware of its own ancestry, follows Williams in repudiating Eliot: music is not wanted, history is not wanted, idea is not wanted. Even literature is not much wanted. What *is* wanted is a sort of verbal snapshot: the quick impression, the short flat snippet that sounds cut from a sentence in a letter to a friend, the casual and scanty "revelation." As Eliot in his time spurned Milton's exalted epic line as too sublime for his need, so now Eliot's elegiac fragments appear too arcane, too aristocratic, and too difficult, for contemporary ambition. Ironic allusiveness—Eliot's inspired borrowing—is out of the question: there is nothing in stock to allude to. Now and then there are signs—critical complaints and boredom—that the school of pedestrian verse-making is nearly exhausted, and more and more there are poets who are venturing into the longer line, the denser stanza, a more intense if not a heightened diction.

But the chief elements of the Age of Eliot are no longer with us, and may never return: the belief that poetry can be redemptive, the conviction that history underlies poetry. Such notions may still be intrinsic to the work of Joseph Brodsky and Czeslaw Milosz—Europeans resident in America. Eliot was an American resident in Europe. Even as he was exacting from both poetry and life a perfected impersonation of the European model, he was signing himself, in letters, *Metoikos*, the Greek word for resident alien. He knew he was a contradiction. And it may simply be that it is in the renunciatory grain of America to resist the hierarchical and the traditional. Eliot's "high culture" and its regnancy in and beyond the American university may have been an unsuccessful transplant that "took" temporarily, but in the end would be rejected by the formation of natural tissue. Or, as Eliot himself predicted in the "Dry Salvages" section of "Four Quartets,"

> We had the experience but missed the meaning.

For the generation for whom Eliot was once a god (my own), the truth is that we had the experience and were irradiated by the meaning. Looking back over the last forty years, it is now our unsparing obligation to disclaim the reactionary Eliot. What we will probably go on missing forever is that golden cape of our youth, the power and prestige of high art.

Justice (Again) to Edith Wharton

NEARLY FORTY YEARS ago, Edmund Wilson wrote a little essay about an underrated American novelist and called it "Justice to Edith Wharton." She was in need of justice, he claimed, because "the more commonplace work of her later years had had the effect of dulling the reputation of her earlier and more serious work." During this last period—a stretch of about seventeen years, from (roughly) 1920 to her death in 1937—Edith Wharton's novels were best sellers, her short stories commanded thousands of dollars; but both in mode and motivation she remained, like so many others in the twenties and thirties, a nineteenth-century writer. She believed in portraying character, her characters displayed the higher values, her prose was a platform for her own views. In 1937, when Wilson undertook to invigorate her reputation, the machinery of nineteenth-century fiction was beginning to be judged not so much as the expression of a long tradition, or (as nowadays we seem to view it) as the exhausted practice of a moribund convention, but more bluntly as a failure of talent. Wilson accounted for that apparent failure in Edith Wharton by speculating on the psychological differences between male and female writers:

> It is sometimes true of women writers—less often, I believe, of men—that a manifestation of something like genius may be stimulated by some exceptional emotional strain, but will disappear when the stimulus has passed. With a man, his professional, his artisan's life is likely to persist and evolve as a partially independent organism through the vicissitudes of his emotional experience. Henry James in a virtual vacuum continued to possess and develop his *métier*. But Mrs. Wharton had no *métier* in this sense.

What sort of "justice" is this? A woman typically writes best when her emotions are engaged; the barren female heart cannot seize the writer's trade? Only a decade ago, such a declaration would have been derided by old-fashioned feminists as a passing insolence. But even the satiric reader, contending in one fashion or another with this passage, would have been able, ten years ago, to pluck the offending notion out as a lapse in the texture of a measured and generally moderating mind.

No longer. Wilson's idea returns only to hold, and it holds nowhere so much as among the literary proponents of the current women's movement: Wilson's lapse is exalted to precept. The idea of Edith Wharton as a "woman writer" in need of constantly renewable internal stimuli, whose gifts are best sustained by "exceptional emotional strain"—all this suits the newest doctrine of sexual exclusiveness in literature. Indeed, one of the outstanding tenets of this doctrine embraces Wilson unrelentingly. "Rarely in the work now being written by women," according to an article called "Toward a Definition of the Female Sensibility,"

> does one feel the presence of writers genuinely penetrating their own experience, risking emotional humiliation and the facing-down of secret fears, unbearable wisdoms . . . There are works, however, . . . in which one feels the heroic effort stirring,*

and there follow numerous examples of women writing well because of the stimulus of some exceptional emotional strain.

Restitution, then (one supposes), is to come to Edith Wharton not from the old-fashioned feminists, but from the newer sort, who embrace the proposition that strong emotion in women, emotion uniquely female, is what will best nourish a female literature. What we are to look for next, it follows, is an ambitious new-feminist critical work studying Wharton's "vicissitudes of . . . emotional experience" and correlating the most fevered points with the most accomplished of the fictions.

Such a work, it turns out, more extensive and more supple than Wilson's pioneer brief would suggest, has just made its appearance: Ellen Moers's *Literary Women*. Like other new feminists, Moers believes that there is such an entity as the "history of women," that there are poetic images uniquely female, and even "landscapes charged with female privacy." She writes of "how much the freedom and tactile sensations of near-naked sea bathing has meant to modern women," and insists that a scene recounting the sensation of walking through a field of sea-like grass provides that "moment when Kate Chopin reveals herself most truly a woman writer." Edith Wharton's life—a buried life—ought, properly scrutinized, to feed such a set of sympathies, and to lure the attention of restitution. *Literary Women*, after all, is conceived of in part as a rescue volume,

* Vivian Gornick, *The Village Voice*, May 31, 1973.

as a book of rehabilitation and justice: a number of writers, Moers explains, "came to life for me as women writers as they had not done before. Mrs. Gaskell and Anne Brontë had once bored me; Emily Dickinson was an irritating puzzle, as much as a genius; I could barely read Mary Shelley and Mrs. Browning. Reading them anew as women writers taught me how to get excited about these five, and others as well."

Others as well. But Edith Wharton is omitted from *Literary Women*. Her name appears only once, as an entry in an appendix. Only *The House of Mirth* is mentioned there, along with a reference, apparently by way of explanation of the larger omission, to the chapter on Edith Wharton in Alfred Kazin's *On Native Grounds*. Pursuing the citation, one discovers that Kazin, like Wilson, like the new feminists, speaks of "the need that drove her to literature." Whatever the need, it does not engage Moers; or Kazin. He advances the notion that "to Edith Wharton, whose very career as a novelist was the tenuous product of so many personal maladjustments, the novel became an involuted expression of self." Unlike the new feminists, Kazin will not celebrate this expression; it represents for him a "failure to fulfill herself in art." Wharton, he concludes, "remains not a great artist but an unusual American, one who brought the weight of her personal experience to bear upon a modern American literature to which she was spiritually alien."

Justice to Edith Wharton: where, then, is it to come from? Not taken seriously by the dominant criticism, purposefully ignored by the radical separatist criticism of the new feminists*—she represents an antagonism.

* Though, to be fair, I have heard of at least one new-feminist literature class that has studied *The House of Mirth* – evidently because it is so easy to interpret its heroine as the ideal victim.

The antagonism is not new. Wharton describes it herself in her memoir, *A Backward Glance:*

> My literary success puzzled and embarrassed my old friends far more than it impressed them, and in my own family it created a kind of constraint which increased with the years. None of my relations ever spoke to me of my books, either to praise or blame—they simply ignored them; and among the immense tribe of my cousins, though it included many with whom I was on terms of affectionate intimacy, the subject was avoided as if it were a kind of family disgrace, which might be condoned but could not be forgotten. Only one eccentric widowed cousin, living a life of lonely invalidism, turned to my novels for occasional distraction, and had the courage to tell me so.

She continues: "At first I felt this indifference acutely; but now I no longer cared, for my recognition as a writer had transformed my life."

So it is here—in this uplifting idea, "my life," this teleological and novelistic idea above all—that one will finally expect to look for Wharton's restitution "as a writer." The justice that criticism perversely fails to bring, biography will achieve.

Perhaps. The biography of a novelist contains a wonderful advantage: it accomplishes, when well executed, a kind of mimicry. A good biography is itself a kind of novel. Like the classic novel, a biography believes in the notion of "a life"—a life as a triumphal or tragic story with a shape, a story that begins at birth, moves on to a middle part, and ends with the death of the protagonist.

Despite the reliable pervasiveness of birth and death,

hardly any "real" life is like that. Most simply unfold, or less than that, dream-walk themselves out. The middle is missing. What governs is not pattern but drift. Most American lives, moreover, fail to recognize that they are sticks in a stream, and are conceived of as novels-of-progress, as purposeful *Bildungsromane* saturated with an unending hopefulness, with the notion of infinite improvement on the way toward a salubrious goal; the frontier continues to inhabit the American mentality unfailingly.

And most American biographies are written out of this same source and belief. A biography that is most like a novel is least like a life. Edith Wharton's life, though much of it was pursued outside of America, is an American life in this sense: that, despite certain disciplines, it was predicated on drift, and fell out, rather than fell into place. If other American lives, less free than hers, drift less luckily between the Scylla and Charybdis of obligation and crisis, hers drifted in a setting all horizon, in a perpetual non-circumstance clear of external necessity. She had to invent her own environment and its conditions, and while this may seem the reverse of rudderlessness, what it signifies really is movement having to feign a destination. A life with a "shape" is occasioned by what is present in that life; drift grows out of what is absent. For Edith Wharton there was—outside the writing—no destination, and no obligation to get there. She had houses, she had wealth; she chose, rather than "had," friends. She had no family (she was estranged from her brothers, and we hear nothing further about the affectionate cousins), she had no husband (though she was married to one for more than half her life), she had no children. For a long time she resented and disliked children, and was obsessed by a love for small dogs. She was Henry James's ideal American heroine: she was indeed his very heiress of all the ages, she was "free," she was cultivated both in the conventional and the spiritual sense, she was gifted, acute, mobile; she appeared to be mistress of her destiny.

The destiny of such freedom is drift, and though her life was American in this, it was European in its resignation: she had no illusion that—outside the writing—she was doing more than "filling in." Her one moment of elevated and secure purpose occurred when, inspired by the model of Walt Whitman in the hospitals of the Civil War, she founded war relief agencies in France during the First World War. She supervised brilliantly: she supervised her friendships, her gardeners, her guests, the particulars of her dinner parties, her households; she even, to a degree, supervised the insurmountable Henry James—she took him for long rides in her car, she demanded hours in London and tea at Lamb House, she finagled with his publisher to provide him with a handsome advance (she herself was the secret philanthropist behind the scenes), she politicked to try and get him the Nobel Prize for Literature. She supervised and commanded, but since no one demanded anything of *her* (with a single exception, which, like the Gorgon's head, was not to be gazed at), she was captain, on an uncharted deep, of a ship without any imaginable port. She did everything on her own, to no real end; no one ever asked her to accommodate to any pressure of need, she had no obligations that she did not contrive or duty that she did not devise. Her necessities were self-imposed. Her tub went round and round in a sea of self-pleasing.

All this was outside the writing. One learns it from R. W. B. Lewis's prize-winning biography,* which is,

* *Edith Wharton: A Biography* (Harper & Row, 1975). The prizes are the Pulitzer, the National Book Critics Circle Award, and Columbia University's Bancroft Prize.

like a posthumously uncovered Wharton novel, sustained by the idea of "a life." It has the fecund progression, the mastery of incident, the affectionate but balanced devotion to its protagonist, the power of suspenseful development, even the unraveling of a mysterious love story, that the "old" novel used to deliver—the novel before it became a self-referring "contemporary" art-object. In its own way it is a thesis novel: it is full of its intention to bring justice to Edith Wharton. A massive biography, almost by its weight, insists on the importance of its subject. Who would dare pass that writer by to whom a scholar-writer has dedicated, as Lewis has, nearly a decade of investigation and discovery? "They are among the handsomest achievements in our literature," he remarks of her major fictions. And adds: "I have wondered, with other admirers of Edith Wharton, whether her reputation might today stand even higher if she had been a man."

If the last statement has overtones of the new feminism—glory but for the impediment of sex—the book does not. Lewis sets out to render the life of an artist, not of a "woman artist." Unexpectedly, though it is the artist he is after, what he succeeds chiefly in giving us is the life of a woman. The "chiefly" is no small thing: it is useful to have a documented narrative of an exceptional upper-class woman of a certain American period. Still, without romanticizing what is meant by the phrase "an artist's life," there is a difference between the biography of a writer and the mode of living of a narrow American class.

Can the life justify the writer then? Or, to put it otherwise, can biography take the place of literary judgment? Lewis's book is a straightforward "tale," not a critical biography. Nor is it "psychobiography": though it yields new and revealing information about Edith Wharton's sexual experience, it does not propose to illumine the hidden chambers of the writer's sentience—as, for example, Ruby V. Redinger's recent inquiry into George Eliot's relationship to her brother Isaac, with its hunches and conjectures, purports to do, or Quentin Bell's half-study, half-memoir of Virginia Woolf. Lewis has in common with these others the revelation of a secret. In the case of Quentin Bell, it is the exact extent of Virginia Woolf's insanity; in the volume on George Eliot, the secret is the dense burden of humiliation imposed by an adored brother more cruel and rigid than society itself. And in Lewis, the secret is an undreamed-of, now minutely disclosed, adulterous affair with a journalist. In all three accounts, the writer is on the whole not there. It is understandable that the writer is mainly absent for the psychobiographer; something else is being sought. It is even more understandable that the writer should be absent for a nephew-biographer, whose preoccupation is with confirming family stories.

But if, for Lewis, the writer is not there, it is not because he fails to look for her but because she is very nearly invisible. What, through luck and diligence, he causes to become visible is almost not the point, however unpredictable and startling his discoveries are. And they are two: the surprising place of Morton Fullerton in Edith Wharton's middle years, and the appearance of a candid manuscript, written in her seventies, describing, with the lyrical explicitness of an enraptured anatomist, a fictional incestuous coupling. The manuscript and the love affair are so contrary to the established Wharton legend of cold propriety that they go far to make us look again—but only at the woman, not at the writer.

The real secret in Lewis's biography is devoid of sex, lived or imagined, though its centerpiece is a bed; and it concerns not the woman but the writer. The secret is divulged on page 353, when Wharton is fifty-one, and occupies ten lines in a volume of nearly six hundred pages. The ten lines recount a perplexing incident—"a minor fit of hysterics." The occasion is mysterious: Edith Wharton and Bernard Berenson, touring the great cities and museums of Europe together, arrive at the Hotel Esplanade in Berlin. They check into their respective rooms, and Edith Wharton, ignoring the view of the city though she has never been there before, begins to rage

> because the bed in her hotel room was not properly situated; not until it had been moved to face the window did she settle down and begin to find Berlin "incomparable." Berenson thought this an absurd performance; but because Edith never harped upon the physical requirements of her literary life, he did not quite realize that she worked in bed every morning and therefore needed a bed which faced the light. It had been her practice for more than twenty years; and for a woman . . . who clung so tenaciously to her daily stint, the need was a serious one.

The fit and its moment pass; the ensuing paragraphs tell of German politics snubbed and German music imbibed—we are returned, in short, to the life of an upper-class American expatriate tourist, privileged to travel in the company of a renowned connoisseur. But the plangent moment—an outcry over the position of a bed—dominates the book: dominates what has gone before and what is to come, and recasts both. Either the biographer can stand up to this moment—the woman revealed *as writer*—or the book falls into the drifting ash of "a life."

It falls, but it is not the biographer's fault; or not his fault alone. Edith Wharton—as writer—is to blame. She put a veil over the bed that was her workplace, and screened away the real life that was lived in it. What moves like a long afterimage in the wake of reading Lewis is a procession of stately majesties: Edith Wharton always standing, always regal, always stiffly dressed and groomed, standing with her wonderfully vertical spine in the hall of one of her great houses, or in the drawing room of her Paris apartment, with her fine hand out to some equally resplendent guest, or in her gardens, not so much admiring her flowers as instructing or reprimanding the servants of her flowers; or else "motoring" through the dust of some picturesque lane in the French countryside, her chauffeur in peaked hat and leather goggles, like blinders, on a high seat in front of her, indistinguishable from the horse that still headed most vehicles on the road.

If this is the Wharton myth, she made it; she wove it daily. It winds itself out like a vivid movie, yet darkly; it leaves out the window-lit bed. What went on outside the bed does not account for what went on in it. She frequented literary salons, and on a smaller scale held them (after dinner, Henry James reading aloud in the library); she talked bookishly, and with fervor; she was an intellectual. But she was not the only brilliant woman of her time and status; all of that, in the biography of a writer, weighs little.

Visualize the bed: she used a writing board. Her breakfast was brought to her by Gross, the housekeeper, who almost alone was privy to this inmost secret of the bedchamber. (A secretary picked up the pages from the floor for typing.) Out of bed, she would have had to be, according to her code, properly dressed, and this meant stays. In bed, her body was free, and freed her pen.

There is a famous photograph of Edith Wharton seated at a desk; we know now, thanks to the "minor fit of hysterics" at the Hotel Esplanade, how the camera lies—even though it shows us everything we might want to know about a way of life. The time is in the 1890s, the writer is in her early thirties. The desk is vast, shining, with a gold-tooled leather top; at the rear of its far surface is a decorated rack holding half a dozen books, but these are pointless—not only because anyone using this desk would need an impossibly long reach, but because all the volumes are faced away from the writer, with their backs and titles to the open room. Two tall electrified candlestick-lamps (the wire drags awkwardly) stand sentinel over two smaller candlesticks; there is a single letter, already stamped; otherwise the desk is clear, except for a pair of nervous ringed hands fiddling with a bit of paper.

The hands belong to a young woman got up, to our eyes, as theatrically as some fanciful notion of royalty: she is plainly a lady of fashion, with a constricted waist and a constricting tall collar; her dress is of the whitest fabric, all eyeleted, embroidered, sashed; her hair is elaborately rolled and ringleted; an earring makes a white dot below the high dark eave of her hair; her back is straight, even as she leans forward with concentrated mouth and lost eyes, in the manner of a writer in trance. Mellifluous folds hide her feet; a lady has no legs. She is sitting on a graceful chair with whorled feet—rattan framed by the most beautiful carved and burnished wood. (A rattan chair with not a single hole? No one could ever have *worked* in such a chair; the photographer defrauds us—nothing more important than a letter will ever be written at this desk.) The Oriental carpet, with its curious and dense figures, is most explicitly in focus, and over the edge of it a tail of skirt spills, reflected white on a floor as sleek as polished glass. In the background, blurred to the camera's lens but instructive to ours: a broad-shouldered velvet chair, a marble bust on an ebony pedestal, a table with a huge porcelain sculpture, a lofty shut oak or walnut door. —In short, an "interior," reminding us that the woman at the unused desk has undertaken, as her first writing venture, a collaborative work called *The Decoration of Houses*.

There are other portraits in this vein, formal, posed, poised, "intellectual" (meaning the subject muses over a seeming letter or book), all jeweled clips and chokers and pearls in heavy rows, pendants, feathered hats, lapdogs, furs, statuesque burdens of flounced bosom and grand liquescent sleeve, queenly beyond our bourgeois imaginings. And the portraits of houses: multiple chimneys, balconies, cupolas, soaring Romanesque windows, immense stone staircases, summer awnings of palatial breadth, shaped ivy, topiary like over-sized chess pieces, walks, vistas, clouds of flower beds.

What are we (putting aside Marxist thoughts) to make of this avalanche of privilege? It is not enough to say: money. The class she derived from never talked of money; the money was invisible, like the writing in bed, and just as secret, and just as indispensable. The "love of beauty," being part of class habit, does not explain it; perhaps the class habit does. It was the class habit that kept her on the move: the class habit that is restlessness and drift. She wore out houses and places, or else her spirit wore out in them: New York, Newport, Lenox—finally America. In France there was the Paris apartment in the Rue de Varenne, then a small estate in St. Brice-sous-Forêt, in the country north of Paris, then an old chateau in Hyères, on the warm Mediterranean coast. Three times in her life she supervised the total renovation of a colossal mansion and its grounds, in effect building and furnishing and landscaping from scratch; and once, in Lenox, she bought a piece of empty land and really did start from scratch, raising out of the earth an American palace called The Mount. All of this exacted from her the energy, attentiveness, and insatiable governing impulses of a corporation chief executive; or the head of a small state.

In an architectural lull, she would travel. All her life she traveled compulsively, early in her marriage with her husband, touring Europe from February to June, afterward with various male companions, with the sense, and with the propriety, of leading a retinue. Accumulating "scenes" —hotels, landscapes, seascapes, museums, villages, ruins —she saw all the fabled cities of Europe, the islands of the Aegean, Tunis, Algiers, Carthage, the Sahara.

And all the while she was surrounded by a crowd. Not simply while traveling: the crowd was part of the daily condition of her houses and possessions. She had a household staff consisting of maids ("housemaids" and "chambermaids"—there appears to be a difference), a chief gardener and several under-gardeners, cook, housekeeper, majordomo, chauffeur, personal maid, "traveling" maid, secretary, "general agent," footmen. (One of the latter, accompanying her to I Tatti, the Berenson villa in Italy, inconveniently fell in love with a Berenson maid, and had to be surrendered.) These "establishments," Lewis remarks, "gave her what her bountiful nature desired: an ordered life, a carefully tended beauty of surroundings, and above all, total privacy." The "above all" engenders skepticism. Privacy? Surveying that mob of servants, even imagining them crossing silent carpets on tiptoe, one takes the impression, inevitably, of a hive. Her solitude was the congested solitude of a monarch; she was never, like other solitary-minded American writers (one thinks of Poe, or of course Emily Dickinson, or even Scott Fitzgerald), completely alone in the house. But these hectic movements of the hive were what she required; perhaps she would not have known how to do without them. Chekhov could sit at a table in the middle of the din of a large impoverished family, ignoring voices and footsteps in order to concentrate on the scratch of his pen. Edith Wharton sat up in bed with her writing board, in the middle of the active business of a house claiming her attention, similarly shutting out the only family she had. A hired family, an invented one. When she learned that her older brother Freddy, living not far away in Paris, had suffered a stroke, she was "unresponsive"; but when Gross, her housekeeper of long standing, and Elise, her personal maid, both grew fatally ill within a short space, she wrote in her diary, "All my life goes with those two dying women."

Nicky Mariano, in her memoir of her life as secretary-companion to Berenson, recalls how Edith Wharton treated her with indifference—until one day, aboard a yacht near Naples, she happened to ask after Elise. She was at once dispatched to the cabin below to visit with the maid. "From then on I became aware of a complete change in Edith's manner to me. There was a warmth, a tone of intimacy that I had never heard before." And again, describing how Wharton "looked after her servants with affectionate zeal and took a lively interest in all their joys and sorrows," she produces another anecdote:

> I remember how once during one of our excursions with her, she was deeply hurt and angry when on leaving a villa near Siena after a prolonged visit she discovered that neither her maid nor her chauffeur had been asked into the house.

What is the effect on a writer of being always encircled by servants? What we are to draw from this is not so much the sadness of purchased affections, or even the parasitism (once, left without much help for a brief period, she was bewildered about her daily survival), but something more perplexing: the moment-by-moment influence of continuous lower-class companionship. Room ought to be given to considering this; it took room in Wharton's life: she was with her servants all the time, she was with her friends and peers only some of the time. E. M. Forster sought out the common people in the belief that too much education atrophies the senses; in life and in art he went after the lower orders because he thought them the embodiment of the spontaneous gods of nature. In theory, at least —perhaps it was only literary theory—Forster wanted to become "instinctual," and instinct was with the working class. But Edith Wharton kept her distance even as she drew close; she remained mistress always. It made her a kind of double exile. As an expatriate settled in France, she had cut herself off from any direct infusion of the American sensibility and the American language. Through her attachment to her servants, she became intimately bound to illiterate lives remote from her mentality, preoccupations, habitual perceptions—a second expatriation as deliberate as the more obvious one. Nor did her servants give her access to "ordinary" life (she was no Lady Chatterley, there was no gamekeeper for her)—no one is "ordinary" while standing before the monarch of the house. Still, she fussed over her army of hirelings; it was a way of inventing claims. For her servants she provided pensions; she instituted a trust fund as a private charity for three Belgian children; she sent regular checks to her sister-in-law, divorced from her brother a quarter of a century and therefore clearly not to be taken for family. For family, in short, she substituted claims indisputably of her own making. She could feel responsible for servants and acquired dependents as others feel responsible for parents, brothers, children: but there was a tether made of money, and the power-end of the tether was altogether in her hand. With servants, there is no murkiness—as there sometimes is in friendship—about who is beholden to whom.

With her friends it was more difficult to invent claims; friendship has a way of resisting purchase, and she had to resort to ruses. When she wanted to release Morton Fullerton from the entangling blackmail of his former French mistress, she arranged with Henry James to make it seem as if the money were coming impersonally from a publisher. Fullerton having been, however briefly, her lover, it was hardly possible to hand over one hundred pounds and call it a "pension"; the object was not so much to keep Fullerton's friendship free as to establish the illusion of such freedom. It was enough for the controlling end of the money tether to know the tether was there; and anyhow the tether had a witness and an accomplice. "Please consider," James wrote, entering into the plot, "that I will play my mechanical part in your magnificent combination with absolute piety, fidelity, and punctuality."

But when it was James himself who came to be on the receiving end of the golden tether, he thundered against the tug of opulence, and the friendship was for a while impaired. The occasion was a proposal for his seventieth birthday: Edith Wharton, enlisting about forty moneyed Americans, thought to raise "not less than $5000," the idea being "that he should choose a fine piece of old furniture, or something of the kind"—but to James it all smelled blatantly of charity, meddling, pity, and cash. Once he got wind of the plan he called it a "reckless and indiscreet undertaking," and announced in a cable that he was beginning "instant prohibitive action. Please express to individuals approached my horror. Money absolutely returned."

It was returned, but within a few months James was hooked anyhow on that same line—hooked like Morton Fullerton, without being aware of it. This time the accomplice was Charles Scribner, who forwarded to James a phoney "advance" of eight thousand dollars intended to see him through the writing of *The Ivory Tower*—but the money was taken out of Wharton's own advance, from another publisher, of fifteen thousand dollars. The reluctant agent of the scheme, far from celebrating "your magnificent combination," saw it rather as "our fell purpose." "I feel rather mean and caddish and must continue so to the end of my days," Charles Scribner grumbled. "Please never give me away." In part this sullenness may have been guilt over not having himself volunteered, as James's publisher, to keep a master artist free from money anxiety, but beyond that there was a distaste for manipulation and ruse.

This moral confusion about proprieties—whom it is proper to tip, and whom not—expressed itself in other strange substitutions. It was not only that she wanted to pay her lover and her friend for services rendered, sexual or literary—clearly she had little overt recognition of the *quid pro quo* uses of philanthropy. It was not only that she loved her maid Gross more than her mother, and Arthur White her "man" more than her brother—it is understood that voluntary entanglements are not really entanglements at all. But there were more conspicuous replacements. Lacking babies, she habitually fondled small dogs: there is an absurd photograph of Edith Wharton as a young woman of twenty-eight, by then five years into her marriage, with an angry-looking Pekingese on each mutton-leg shoulder; the animals, pressed against her cheeks, nearly obscure her face; the face is cautious and contemplative, as of one not wanting to jar precious things. A similar photograph shows her husband gazing straight out at us with rather empty pale eyes over a nicely trimmed mustache and a perfect bow tie —on his lap, with no special repugnance, he is holding three small dogs, two of them of that same truculent breed, and though the caption reads "Teddy Wharton with his dogs," somehow we know better whose dogs they are. His body is detached; his expression, very correct and patient, barely hides—though Lewis argues otherwise—how he is being put upon by such a pose.

Until late in life, she never knew a child. Effie, the little girl in *The Reef*, is a child observed from afar—she runs, she enters, she departs, she is sent, she is summoned, at one moment she is presented as very young, at another she is old enough to be having lessons in Latin. She is a figment of a child. But the little dogs, up to the end of Edith Wharton's life, were always understood, always thought to have souls, always in her arms and in her bed; they were, Lewis says, "among the main joys of her being." Drawing up a list of her "ruling passions" at forty-four, she put "Dogs" second after "Justice and Order." At sixty-two she wrote in her journal of "the *us*ness" in the eyes of animals, "with the underlying *not-us*ness which belies it," and meditated on their "eternal inarticulateness and slavery. Why? their eyes seem to ask us."

The fellow feeling she had for the *not-us*ness of her Pekingese she did not have for her husband, who was, from her point of view, also "*not-us*." He too was inarticulate and mired in the slavery of a lesser intellect. He was a good enough man, interested (like his wife) in being perfectly clothed, vigorous and humorous and kind and compliant (so compliant that he once actually tried to make his way through James's *The Golden Bowl*)—undistinguished in any jot, the absolute product of his class. He had no work to do, and sought none. One of Edith Wharton's friends—a phrase instantly revealing, since her friends were practically never his; the large-hearted Henry James was nearly the only one to cross this divide—observed that Teddy Wharton's "idleness was busy and innocent." His ostensible employment was the management of his wife's trust funds, but he filled his days with sports and hunting, and his glass with fine wine. Wine was the one thing he had a connoisseur's familiarity with; and, of all the elegant good things of the world, wine was the one thing his wife disliked. When he was fifty-three he began to go mad, chiefly, it would seem, because he had married the wrong wife, with no inkling that she would turn out to be the wrong wife. Edith Newbold Jones at twenty-three was exactly what Edward Wharton, a dozen years older, had a right to expect for himself: she had heritage (her ancestor, Ebenezer Stevens, was an enterprising artillery officer in the Revolutionary War), she had inheritance (the Joneses owned the Chemical Bank of New York and much of the West Side). In brief, family and money. The dominant quality—what he had married her for, with that same idle innocence that took note only of the pleasantly obvious—was what Edith Wharton was afterward to call "tribe." The Whartons and the Joneses were of the same tribe—old Protestant money—and he could hardly predict that his wife would soon replace him in the nuptial bed with a writing board. At first he was perplexed but proud: Louis Auchincloss quotes a description of Teddy Wharton from Consuelo Vanderbilt's memoirs as "more of an equerry than an equal, walking behind [his wife] and carrying whatever paraphernalia she happened to discard," and once (Lewis tells us), walking as usual behind her, Teddy exclaimed to one of her friends, "Look at that waist! No one would ever guess that she had written a line of poetry in her life." She, meanwhile, was driven to writing in her journal, "Oh, Gods of derision! And you've given me over twenty years of it!" This outcry occurred immediately after she had shown her husband, during a wearying train journey, "a particularly interesting passage" in a scientific volume called *Heredity and Variation*. His response was not animated. "I heard the key turn in my prison-lock," she recorded, in the clear metaphorical style of her fiction.

A case can be made that it was she who turned the key on him. His encroaching madness altered him—he began to act oddly, out of character; or, rather, more in character than he had ever before dared. The equerry of the paraphernalia undertook to behave as if he were master of the paraphernalia—in short, he embezzled a part of the funds it had been his duty to preserve and augment. And, having been replaced in bed by a writing board, he suddenly confessed to his wife (or perhaps feverishly bragged) that he had recently gone to live with a prostitute in a Boston apartment, filling its remaining rooms with chorus girls; the embezzled funds paid for the apartment. The story was in the main confirmed. His madness had the crucial sanity of needs that are met.

His wife, who—granted that philanthropy is not embezzlement—was herself capable of money ruse, and who had herself once rapturously fallen from merely spiritual friendship, locked him up for it. Against his protestations, and those of his sister and brother, he was sent to a sanitorium.

Teddy had stolen, Teddy had fallen; he was an adulterer. She had never stolen (though there is a robust if mistaken critical tradition that insists she stole her whole literary outlook from Henry James); but she had fallen, she was an adulteress. Teddy's sexual disgrace was public; hers went undivulged until her biographer came upon it more than three decades after her death. But these sardonic parallels and opposites illumine little beyond the usual ironies of the pot and the kettle. What had all at once happened in Edith Wharton's life was that something *had* happened. Necessity intervened, her husband was irrefutably a manic-depressive. He had hours of excitement and accusation; more often he was in a state of self-castigation. He begged her for help, he begged to be taken back and to be given a second chance. " . . . when you came back last year," she told him, "I was ready to overlook everything you had done, and to receive you as if nothing had happened." This referred to the Boston apartment; she herself had been in a London hotel with Fullerton at nearly the same time. In the matter of her money she was more unyielding. Replying to his plea to be allowed to resume the management of her trusts and property, she took the tone of a mistress with a servant who has been let go, and who is now discovered still unaccountably loitering in the house. "In order that no further questions of this kind should come up, the only thing left for me to do is to suggest that you should resign your Trusteeship . . . Your health unfortunately makes it impossible for you to take any active part in the management of my affairs." Gradually, over months, she evolved a policy: she did everything for him that seemed sensible, as long as it was cold-hearted. He was removed, still uncured, from the sanitorium, and subjected to a regime of doctors, trips, traveling companions, scoldings. In the end, when he was most sick and most desperate, she discarded him, handing him over to the doctors the way one hands over impeding paraphernalia to an equerry. She discarded him well before she divorced him; divorce, at that period and in her caste, took deliberation. She discarded him because he impeded, he distracted, he was a nuisance, he drained her, he wore her out. As a woman she was contemptuous of him, as a writer she fought off his interruptions. The doctors were more polite than Henry James, who characterized Teddy Wharton as able to "hold or follow no counter-proposal, no plan of opposition, of his own, for as much as a minute or two; he is immediately *off*—irrelevant and childish . . . one's pity for her is at the best scarce bearable."

She too pitied herself, and justly, though she forgot to pity *him*. He had lost all trust in himself, whatever he said he timidly or ingratiatingly or furiously took back. He was flailing vainly after the last flashes of an autonomy his wife had long ago stripped from him. And during all that angry space, when she was bitterly engaged in fending off the partisan ragings of his family, and coldly supervising his medical and traveling routines, she, in the stern autonomy of her morning bed, was writing *Ethan Frome*, finishing *The Reef*, bringing off short stories. She could do all this because she did not look into her husband's eyes and read there, as she had read in the eyes of her little dogs, the helpless pathos of "Why?" It was true that she did not and could not love him, but her virtue was always according to principle, not passion. Presumably she also did not love the French soldiers who were sick with tuberculosis contracted in the trenches of the First World War; nevertheless for them she organized a cure program, which she termed "the most vital thing that can be done in France now." Whatever the most vital thing for Teddy might have been—perhaps there was nothing—she relinquished it at last. The question of the tubercular soldiers was, like all the claims on her spirit that she herself initiated, volitional and opportune. She had sought out these tragedies, they were not implicated in the conditions of her own life, that peculiar bed she had made for herself—"such a great big uncompromising 4-poster," James called it. For the relief of tubercular soldiers and other good works, she earned a French medal, and was made a Chevalier of the Legion of Honor. An arena of dazzling public exertion. But in the lesser frame of private mess she did nothing to spare her husband the humiliation of his madness. It is one thing to go mad, it is another to be humiliated for it. The one time in her life drift stopped dead in its trackless spume, and a genuine claim made as if to seize her—necessity, redder in tooth and claw than any sacrifice one grandly chooses for oneself—she turned away. For her, such a claim was the Gorgon's head, to gaze on which was death.

Writer's death. This is something most writers not only fear but sweat to evade, though most do not practice excision with as clean a knife-edge as cut away "irrelevant and childish" Teddy from Edith Wharton's life. "Friend, client, child, sickness, fear, want, charity, all knock at once at thy closet door and say—'Come out unto us.' But keep thy state," Emerson advised, "come not into their confusion." And Mann's Tonio Kröger declaims that "one must die to life to be utterly a creator." This ruthless romantic idea—it cannot be lived up to by weaklings who succumb to conscience, let alone to love—is probably at bottom less romantic than pragmatic. But it is an idea very nearly the opposite of Wilson's and Kazin's more affecting view of Edith Wharton: that joylessness was her muse, that her troubles energized her for fiction—the stimulus of "some exceptional emotional strain," according to Wilson, "so many personal maladjustments," according to Kazin, which made the novelist possible. If anything made the novelist possible, it was the sloughing off of the sources of emotional strain and personal maladjustment. As for the parallel new-feminist opinion that a woman writes best when she risks "unbearable wisdoms," it does not apply: what wisdom Edith Wharton found unbearable she chose not to bear.

The rest was chatter. Having turned away from the Gorgon's head, she spent the remainder of her life—indeed, nearly the whole of it—in the mainly insipid, sometimes inspired, adventure of elevated conversation. She had her friends. There were few women—whether because she did not encounter her equals among women, or because she avoided them, her biographer yields no hint. The majority were men (one should perhaps say "gentlemen")—Lapsley, Lubbock, Berenson, Fullerton, Simmons, James, Bourget, D'Humières, Berry, Sturgis, Hugh-Smith, Maynard, Gregory, Grant, Scott . . . the list is longer still. Lewis fleshes out all these names brilliantly, particularly Berry and Fullerton; the great comic miraculous James needs no fleshing out. James was in a way afraid of her. She swooped down on him to pluck him away for conversation or sightseeing, and he matched the "commotion and exhaustion" of her arrivals against the vengeance of Bonaparte, Attila, and Tamerlane. "Her powers of devastation are ineffable," he reported, and got into the habit of calling her the Angel of Devastation. She interrupted his work with the abruptness of a natural force (she might occur at any time) and at her convenience (she had particular hours for her work, he had all hours for his). He read her novels and dispatched wondrous celebrating smokescreens of letters ("I applaud, I mean I value, I egg you on") to hide the insufficiency of his admiration. As for her "life," it was a spectacle that had from the beginning upset him: her "desolating, ravaging, burning and destroying energy." And again: "such a nightmare of perpetually renewable choice and decision, such a luxury of bloated alternatives." "*What* an incoherent life!" he summed it up. Lewis disagrees, and reproaches James for partial views and a probable fear of strong women; but it may be, on all the lavish evidence Lewis provides, that the last word will after all lie with drift, exactly as James perceived it in her rushing aimlessness aimed at him.

Before Lewis's landmark discovery of the Wharton-Fullerton liaison, Walter Van Rensselaer Berry—Wharton's distant cousin, an international lawyer and an aristocrat—was commonly regarded as the tender center and great attachment of her life. Lewis does not refute this connection, though he convincingly drains it of sexual particularity, and gives us the portrait of a conventionally self-contained dry-hearted lifelong bachelor, a man caught, if not in recognizable drift, then in another sort of inconclusiveness. But Walter Berry was Edith Wharton's first literary intellectual—a lightning bolt of revelation that, having struck early, never lost its electrical sting. Clearly she fed on intellectuals—but in a withdrawn and secretive way: she rarely read her work aloud, though she rejoiced to hear James read his. She brooded over history and philosophy, understood everything, but was incapable in fiction or elsewhere of expressing anything but the most commonplace psychology. This was, of course, her strength: she knew how human beings behave, she could describe and predict and surprise. Beyond that, she had a fertile capacity for thinking up stories. Plots and permutations of plots teemed. She was scornful of writers who agonized after subject matter. Subjects, she said, swarmed about her "like mosquitoes," until she felt stifled by their multiplicity and variety.

The truth is she had only one subject, the nineteenth century's unique European literary subject: society. Standard American criticism, struggling to "place" Edith Wharton in a literary environment unused to her subject, has contrived for her the role of a lesser Henry James. This has served to indict her as an imitative figure. But on no significant level is the comparison with James pertinent, except to say that by and large they wrote about the same kinds of people, derived from the same class. Otherwise the difference can be seized in a breath: James was a genius, Wharton not. James invented an almost metaphysical art, Wharton's insights lay close against their molds: what she saw she judged. James became an American in the most ideal sense, Wharton remained an estranged New Yorker. James was an uncanny moralist, Wharton a canny realist. James scarcely ever failed—or, at least, his few failures when they occurred were nevertheless glorious in aspiration and seamless in execution. When Wharton failed, she fell into an embarrassing triteness of language and seeing.

It is a pity that her name is attached so unrelentingly—thanks to the American high school—to *Ethan Frome*, a desolate, even morbid, narrow, soft-at-the-center and at the last unsurprising novella not at all typical of her range. It is an outdoor book that ends mercilessly indoors; she was an indoor novelist. She achieved two permanent novels, one –*The House of Mirth*—a spoiled masterpiece, a kind of latterday reverse *Scarlet Letter*, very direct yet eerie, the other *The Age of Innocence*, a combination of ode and elegy to the New York of her childhood, affirmation and repudiation both. A good many of her short stories and some of the novellas ("The Old Maid," for instance) are marvels of shapeliness and pointedness. This applies also to stories written during her late period, when she is widely considered to have debased her gift. The common accusation —Wilson makes it—is that her prose finally came to resemble women's-magazine fiction. One can venture that she did not so much begin to sound like the women's magazines, as that they began to sound like her, a condition that obtains until this moment. No one has explored Wharton's ongoing subliminal influence on current popular fiction (see almost any issue of *Redbook*); such an investigation would probably be striking in its disclosure of the strength of her legacy. Like any hokey imitation long after the model is lost to consciousness, it is not a bad compliment, though it may be awkward to admit it. (One of the least likely tributes to the Roman Empire, after all, is the pervasiveness of nineteenth-century American civic architecture.) But *The House of Mirth* and *The Age of Innocence* are, like everything unsurpassable because deeply idiosyncratic, incapable of spawning versions of themselves; in these two novels she is in command of an inwardness commensurate with structure. In them she does not simply grab hold of society, or judge it merely; she turns society into an exulting bird of prey, with blood on its beak, steadily beating its wings just over our heads; she turns society into an untamable *idea*. The reader, apprehensive, yet lured by the bird's lyric form, covers his face.

She could do all that; she had that power. Lewis, writing to justify and defend, always her sympathetic partisan, nevertheless hedges. Having acknowledged that she had "begun to locate herself—with a certain assurance, though without vanity—in the developing course of American literature," he appends a doubt:

> But in another part of her, there remained something

> of the conviction drilled into her in old New York that it was improper for a lady to write fiction. One could do so only if one joked about it—if one treated it, to borrow Lubbock's word, as "an amusement." She sometimes sounded as if her writing were her entertainingly guilty secret, and in her memoirs she referred to it (borrowing the title of a popular children's book of her own New York youth) as her "secret garden."
>
> But in the winter of 1911 [she was then at work on *The Reef*], as on perhaps half a dozen other occasions, it was the believing artist that was in the ascendancy during the hard-driving morning hours.

Somehow it is easy to doubt that she had this doubt—or, if she once had it, that she held it for long. To believe in her doubt is to make the bad case of the orthodox critics who, unlike Lewis, have shrunk from taking her seriously as an artist because as an American aristocrat she was born shockingly appurtenanced, and therefore deserves to be patronized for her sorrows. To believe in her doubt is to make the bad case of the new feminists, for whom female sex is, always and everywhere, an impediment difficult to transcend—even when, for an obsessed writer of talent, there is nothing to transcend. To believe in her doubt is to reverse the terms of her life and her work. Only "half a dozen other occasions" when Wharton was a "believing artist"? Only so few? This would mean that the life outside her bed—the dressed life of conversation and travel, the matchstick life of drift—was the primary life, and the life with her writing board—the life of the believing artist—the deviation, the anomaly, the distraction.

But we know, and have always known (Freud taught us

only how to reinforce this knowledge), that the secret self is the true self, that obsession is confession. For Edith Wharton that is the only acceptable evaluation, the only possible justice. She did not doubt her allegiance. The writing came first. That she kept it separate from the rest was a misrepresentation and a mistake, but it may also have been a species of holy instinct — it was the one uncontaminated zone of her being: the place unprofaned. Otherwise she can be defined only by the horrific gyrations of "a life" — by the spiraling solipsism and tragic drift that led her to small dogs instead of babies, servants instead of family, high-minded male distance instead of connubial friendship, public virtue instead of private conscience, infatuation instead of the love that sticks. Only the writing board could justify these ugly substitutions. And some would say — myself not among them — that not even the writing board justified them.

What Henry James Knew

I. The Horrible Hours

AS MODERNISM SINKS IN, or fades out—as it recedes into a kind of latterday archaism, Cubism turned antiquated, the old literary avant-garde looking convincingly moth-eaten—certain writers become easier to live with. It is not only than they seem more accessible, less impenetrable, simpler to engage with, after decades of familiarity: the quality of mystery has (mysteriously) been drained out of them. Joyce, Proust, Woolf, surely Pound and Eliot—from all of these, and from others as well, the veil draws back. One might almost say, as the twentieth century shuts down, that they are objectively less "modern" than they once were. Their techniques have been absorbed for generations. Their idiosyncrasies may not pall, but neither do they startle. Their pleasures and their stings, while far from humdrum, nevertheless open out into psychological references that are largely recognizable. What used to be revelation (Proust's madeleine, the world that ends not with a bang but a whimper) is reduced to reflex. One reads these masters now with satisfaction—they have been ingested—but without the fury of early avarice.

Yet one of the great avatars of modernism remains immune to this curious attrition: in the ripened Henry James, and in him almost alone, the sensation of mysteriousness does not attenuate; it thickens. As the years accumulate, James becomes, more and more compellingly, our contemporary, our urgency.

The author of *Daisy Miller* (1878), and of *Washington Square* (1880), and even of *The Portrait of a Lady* (1881), was a nineteenth-century writer of felicitous nuance and breadth. The earlier stories and novels are meant to be rooms with a view, thrown open to the light. If mysteries are gathered there, they are gathered to be dispelled. The entanglements of human nature, buffeted by accident, contingency, mistaken judgment, the jarrings of the social web, the devisings of the sly or the cruel, are in any event finally transparent, rational. Isabel Archer's long meditation, in *The Portrait of a Lady*, on her marriage to Gilbert Osmond leads her to the unraveling—the clarification—of her predicament. "They were strangely married," she perceives, "and it was a horrible life"—directly seen, understood, stated, in the manner of the fiction of realism. Like Catherine Sloper, the heroine of *Washington Square*, Isabel has known too little and now knows more. For the James of this mainly realist period, it is almost never a case of knowing too much.

After 1895, the veil thickens. Probably the most celebrated example of a darkening texture is the interpretive history of "The Turn of the Screw" (1898); what was once read wholly in the light of its surfaces can no longer sustain the innocence, or the obtuseness, of its original environment. The tale's first readers, and James himself, regarded this narrative of a frightened governess and her unusual young charges as primarily a ghost story, suitably shadowed in eerie riddle. In his Notebook sketch of 1895, James speaks of "apparitions," of "evil presences," of hauntings and their "strangely gruesome effect." In the Preface to "The Turn of the Screw" for the 1906 New York Edition of his work, he appears light-handedly to toss out the most conventional of these rumblings. "I cast my lot with pure romance," he insists, and calls "this so full-blown flower of high fancy" a "fairy-tale pure and simple." But also, and contradictorily, he assigns his apparitions "the dire duty of causing the situation to reek with the air of Evil," the specifications of which James admits he has left it to the reader to supply. "Make him *think* the evil, make him think it for himself," he asserts.

Since then, under the tutelage of Freud, later readers *have* thought it for themselves, and have named, on James's behalf, a type of horror he could not or would not have brought to his lips. What was implicit in James became overt in Freud. With time, and with renewed critical speculation, James's ghosts in "The Turn of the Screw" have swollen into the even more hideous menace of eros corrupted, including the forbidden, or hidden, sexuality of children. Whether James might have conceived explicitly of these images and hints of molestation is beside the point. There is, he contends in the Preface, "from beginning to end of the matter not an inch of expatiation," and evil's particulars are, on purpose, "positively all blanks," the better to delegate the imagination of terror to anyone but the author himself. Still, is it likely that the privacy of James's own imagination can be said to hold positively all blanks? Imagination works through exactitudes of detail, not through the abdication of its own authority. Whatever it was James thought, he thought *some*thing. Or, rather, he felt something: that gauzy wing that brushes the very pit of the mind even as the mind declares nothing is there. James is one of that handful of literary proto-inventors—ingenious intuiters—of the unconscious; it is the chief reason we count him among the imperial moderns.

The pivotal truth about the later Henry James is not that he chooses to tell too little—that now and then he deliberately fires blanks—but that he knows too much, and much more than we, or he, can possibly take in. It is as if the inklings, inferences, and mystifications he releases in his maturest fictions (little by little, like those medicinal pellets that themselves contain tinier pellets) await an undiscovered science to meet and articulate them. The Freud we already have may be insufficient to the James who, after 1895, became the recondite conjurer whom the author of *Daisy Miller* might not have recognized as himself.

In the fiction of realism—in the Jamesian tale before the 1895 crux—knowledge is the measure of what can be rationally ascertained, and it is almost never a case of knowing too much—i.e., of a knowledge beyond the reach not only of a narrative's dramatis personae but also of the author himself. The masterworks of modernism, however, nearly always point to something far more subterranean than simple ascertainment. *The Castle*, for example, appears to know more than Kafka himself knows—more about its own matter and mood, more about its remonstrances and motives, more about the thread of Kafka's mind. In the same way, "The Turn of the Screw" and other Jamesian works of this period and afterward—*The Awkward Age* above all, as we shall see—vibrate with cognitions that are ultimately not submissive to their creator. It is as if from this time forward, James will write nothing but ghost stories—with the ghosts, those shadows of the unconscious, at the controls. Joyce in particular sought to delineate whatever demons beat below, to bring them into the light of day—to explain them by playing them out, to incarnate them in recognizable forms, or (as in *Finnegans Wake*) to re-incubate them in the cauldron of language. This was what the modernists did, and it is because they succeeded so well in teaching us about the presence of the unconscious that we find them more and more accessible today. But the later James—like Kafka, a writer seemingly as different from James as it is possible to be—is overridden by a strangeness that is beyond his capacity to domesticate or explicate. James, like Kafka, enters mazes and penetrates into the vortex of spirals; and, again like Kafka, the ghost in the vortex sometimes wears his own face.

The 1895 crux, as I have called it, was James's descent into failure and public humiliation. The story of that humiliation—a type of exposure that damaged James perhaps lastingly, and certainly darkened his perspectives—is brilliantly told in Leon Edel's consummate biography: a biography so psychologically discriminating that it has drawn generations of its readers into a powerful but curious sympathy with James. Curious, because an admirable genius is not nearly the same as a sympathetic one, an instruction James himself gives us in, to choose only two, Hugh Vereker and Henry St. George, the literary luminaries of a pair of tales ("The Figure in the Carpet," "The Lesson of the Master") bent on revealing the arrogance of art. Yet to approach James through Edel is, if not practically to fall in love with James, to feel the exhilarations of genius virtually without flaw. James, for Edel, is sympathetic and more; he is unfailingly and heroically civilized, selfless for art, gifted with an acuity of insight bordering on omniscience. He is—in James's own celebrated words—one of those upon whom nothing is lost. Edel's is a portrait that breaks through the frame of immaculate scholarship into generous devotion, a devotion that in the end turns on a poignant theory of James's fragility of temperament—and never so much as on the night of January 5, 1895, when James's play, *Guy Domville*, opening that evening, was jeered at and its author hissed.

Too nervous to sit through the rise of the curtain, James had gone down the street to attend Oscar Wilde's new work, *An Ideal Husband*. When it was over, scorning Wilde as puerile even as he made his way out through a wash of delighted applause, he returned to *Guy Domville* just as the closing lines were being spoken. Though the clapping that followed was perilously mixed with catcalls, the theater manager, misjudging, brought James out on the stage. "All the forces of civilization in the house," James described it afterward, "waged a battle of the most gallant, prolonged and sustained applause with the hoots and jeers and catcalls of the roughs, whose roars (like those of a cage of beasts at some infernal zoo) were only exacerbated by the conflict." George Bernard Shaw, who was in the audience as a reviewer, wrote of the "handful of rowdies" and "dunces" who sent out "a derisive howl from the gallery." James stumbled off the stage and walked home alone, brooding on "the most horrible hours of my life." The catastrophe of public rejection, James's biographer concludes, "struck at the very heart of his self-esteem, his pride and sovereignty as an artist."

It *had* been a sovereignty. In fact it had been an impregnability. He would not have been so damaged had he not had so far to fall. Literary embarrassment, to be sure, was familiar enough to James; it depressed him, as he grew older, that his novels were no longer widely read, and that his sales were often distressingly puny. But the assault on *amour-propre* that rocked James in the wake of his theater debacle was something else. It was a vulnerability as unprecedented as it was real—feelings of jeopardy, the first faint cracks of existential dread, the self's enfeeblement. He was unused to any of that; he had never been fragile, he had never been without the confidence of the self-assured artist, he had never been mistrustful. What he had been all along was magisterial. Admirers of Leon Edel's James may be misled by Edel's tenderness into imagining that some psychological frailty in James himself is what solicits that tenderness—but sovereign writers are not commonly both artistically vulnerable *and* sovereign.

And James's record of sovereignty—of tough impregnability—was long. He was fifty-two when the rowdies hissed him; he was twenty-one when he began publishing his Olympian reviews. To read these early essays is to dispel any notion of endemic hesitancy or perplexity. In 1866, at twenty-three, reviewing a translation of Epictetus, he speculates on the character of this philosopher of Stoicism with oracular force: "He must have been a wholesome spectacle in that diseased age, this free-thinking, plain-speaking old man, a slave and a cripple, sturdily scornful of idleness, luxury, timidity, false philosophy, and all power and pride of place, and sternly reverent of purity, temperance, and piety—one of the few upright figures in the general decline." This has the tone not simply of a prodigy of letters, but of large command, of one who knows the completeness of his powers. If anything can be said to be implicit in such a voice, it is the certainty of success; success on its own terms—those terms being the highest imaginable exchange between an elite artist and his elite readership. And the earlier these strenuous yet ultimately serene expectations can be established, the stronger the shield against vulnerability; mastery in youth arms one for life.

Or nearly so. On the night of January 5, 1895, when the virtuoso's offering was received like a fizzled vaudeville turn, the progress of unquestioned fame came to a halt. What was delicacy, what was wit, what was ardor, what was scrupulous insight? What, in brief, was the struggle for art if its object could be so readily blown away and trodden on? James might wrestle with these terrors till dawn, like that other Jacob, but his antagonist was more likely a messenger from Beelzebub than an angel of the Lord. Failure was an ambush, and the shock of it led him into an inescapable darkness.

He emerged from it—if he ever emerged from it at all—a different kind of writer. Defensively, he began to see in doubles. There was drama, and there was theater. And by venturing into the theater, he had to live up to—or down to—the theater's standards and assumptions. "I may have been meant for the Drama—God knows!—but I certainly wasn't meant for the Theater," he complained. And another time: "Forget not that you write for the stupid—that is, that your maximum of refinement must meet the minimum of intelligence of the audience—the intelligence, in other words, of the biggest ass it may contain. It is a most unholy trade!" Yet in 1875, twenty years before the *Guy Domville* calamity, he exalted what had then seemed the holiest of trades, one that "makes a demand upon an artist's rarest gifts." "To work successfully beneath a few grave, rigid laws," he reflected, "is always a strong man's highest ideal of success." In 1881 he confided to his journal that "beginning to work for the stage" was "the most cherished of my projects."

The drama's attraction—its seductiveness—had its origin in childhood theater-going; the James children were introduced first to the New York stage, and then to the playhouses of London and Paris, of which they became habitués. But the idea of the *scene*—a passion for structure, trajectory, and relevation that possessed James all his life—broke on him from still another early source: the transforming ecstasy of a single word. On a summer night in 1854, in the young Henry's presence, a small cousin his own age (he was then eleven) was admonished by her father that it was time to go to bed, and ran crying to her mother for a reprieve. "Come now, my dear; don't make a scene—I *insist* on your not making a scene," the mother reproved, and at that moment James, rapturously taking in the sweep of the phrase, fell irrevocably in love with the "witchcraft," as he called it, of the scene's plenitude and allure. "The expression, so vivid, so portentous," he said in old age, "was one I had never heard—it had never been addressed to us at home . . . Life at these intensities clearly became 'scenes': but the great thing, the immense illumination, was that we could make them or not as we chose."

That, however, was the illumination of drama, not the actuality of theater managers, actors, audiences. The ideal of the stage—as a making, a kneading, a medium wholly subject to the artist's will—had become infected by its exterior mechanisms. "The dramatic form," he wrote in 1882, "seems to me the most beautiful thing possible; the misery of the thing is that the baseness of the English-speaking stage affords no setting for it." By 1886 he was driven to confess that the "very dear dream . . . had faded away," and that he now thought "less highly of the drama, as a form, a vehicle, than I did—compared with the novel which can do and say so much more." In James's novel of the theater, *The Tragic Muse*, begun in 1888, a character bursts out, "What crudity compared to what the novelist does!" And in 1894, in a letter to his brother William, James speculated that "unless the victory and the spoils have not . . . become more proportionate than hitherto to the humiliations and vulgarities and disgusts, all the dishonor and chronic insult," he intended "to 'chuck' the whole intolerable experiment and return to more elevated and independent courses. I have come to *hate* the whole theatrical subject."

It was a gradual but steady repudiation, repeatedly contradicted by James's continuing and zigzag pursuit of managers and productions. In the end, the theater repudiated *him*; but the distinction he insisted on between theater, that low endeavor, and drama, that "highest ideal," went on to serve him in what would become one of his strangest fictions. After *Guy Domville*, he undertook to imagine a novel which would have all the attributes of a theatrical production. The reader would be supplied with dialogue, sets, grand and ingenious costuming, gestures of the head and hand; there would be entrances and exits; there would be drawing rooms and wit. The "few grave, rigid laws" of the drama would wash away all the expository freedoms and flexibilities of the traditional novel—above all the chance to explain the action, to comment and interpret, to speak in metaphor. Narrative, and the narrator's guiding hum, would give way to the bareness of talk unaccoutered and unconstrued, talk deprived of authorial amplification; talk as *clue*.

The work that was to carry the burden of this lucidly calculated experiment was conceived on March 4, 1895, three months after the failure of *Guy Domville*. On that day James entered into his Notebook "the idea of the little London girl who grows up to 'sit with' the free-talking modern young mother . . . and, though the conversation is supposed to be expurgated for her, inevitably hears, overhears, guesses, follows, takes in, becomes acquainted with, horrors." The Notebook recorded nothing about any intention to mimic the form of a play. But in his Preface to the New York Edition (1908) of *The Awkward Age*, James stressed that, from the start, the story and its situation had presented itself to him "on absolutely scenic lines, and that each of these scenes in itself . . . abides without a moment's deflexion by the principle of the stage-play." Speaking of the "technical amusement" and "bitter-sweetness" arising from this principle, he reflected on the rich novelistic discursiveness he had early determined to do without: "Exhibition may mean in a 'story' twenty different ways, fifty excursions, alternatives, excrescences, and the novel, as largely practiced in English, is the perfect paradise of the loose end." The play, by contrast, "consents to the logic of but one way, mathematically right, and with the loose end as gross an impertinence on its surface, and as grave a dishonour, as the dangle of a snippet of silk or wool on the right side of a tapestry." Moreover, he pointed out, the play is committed to "objectivity," to the "imposed absence of that 'going behind,'" to eschewing the "storyteller's great property-shop of aids to illusion."

In choosing to write a novel confined to dialogue and scene; in deciding to shape *The Awkward Age* according to self-limiting rules of suppression and omission; in giving up the brilliant variety of the English novel's widest and lushest potential, an art of abundance that he had long ago splendidly perfected—what was James up to? What system of psychological opposition had he fallen into? On the one hand, a play in the form of a novel, or a novel in the form of a play, was a response to "the most horrible hours of my life." What the stage would not let him do, he would do in any case—on his own venerable turf, with no possibility of catcalls. An act of triumph, or contempt, or revenge; perhaps a reward for having endured so much shame. And on the other hand, a kind of penance: he was stripping himself clean, reducing a luxuriant craft to a monkish surrender of its most capacious instruments.

But penance for what? *The Awkward Age* represents an enigma. Though it intends unquestionably to be a comedy—a social comedy, a comedy of manners (as "The Turn of the Screw" unquestionably sets out to be a ghost story)—some enormous grotesquerie, or some grotesque enormity, insinuates itself into this ultimately mysterious work. Having straitjacketed his tale with the "few grave, rigid laws" of the stage, James resolved not to "go behind" its scenes with all those dozens of canny analyses and asides that are possible for the novel; yet on the whole it is as if proscenium and backdrop, and all the accouterments between them, have melted away, and nothing is left but what is "behind"—a "behind" any ordinary novelistic explication would not be equal to and could not touch. Paradoxically, the decision *not* to "go behind" put James squarely backstage, in the dark of the wings, in ill-lit and untidy dressing rooms among discarded makeup jars and their sticky filth—in the very place where there can be no explanation of the world on stage, because the world on stage is an invention and an untruth. James descended, in short, into an interior chaos; or to say it otherwise, with the composition of *The Awkward Age* he became, finally and incontrovertibly, a modernist. Like the modernists, he swept past the outer skin (the theater and its stage, the chatter of counterfeit drawing rooms, the comings and goings of actors and audiences, the coherent conscious machinery of things) to the secret life behind—glimmers of buried truths, the undisclosed drama of hint and inference.

The facade of comedy and the horror behind. And the penalty for "going behind"—while rigging up, via those "few grave, rigid laws," every obstacle to it—was the impenetrable blackness, the blankness, the *nox perpetua*, that gathered there, among the ropes and pulleys, where it is inevitable that one "hears, overhears, guesses, follows, takes in, becomes acquainted with, horrors." (The condition, one might note, of K. in *The Castle*.) And the horrors themselves? They cannot be named. It is their namelessness that defines them as horrors.

Yet James did give them a name—amorphous, suggestive, darkened by its imperial Roman origins, reminiscent of ancient clerical pageantry, more a riddle than a name: "the sacred terror." A translation, or, more likely a transmutation, of *sacro terrore:* the awe one feels in the presence of sacred or exalted personages, Pope or emperor, before whom one may not speak; the dread one feels before the divine mysteries, or the head of Medusa. The face of a knowledge that is beyond our knowledge—intimations that cannot be borne. In the Preface to "The Turn of the Screw," James referred (handling it lightly so as not to be burned) to "the dear old sacred terror" as "the withheld glimpse" of "dreadful matter." The glimpse is withheld; to be permitted more than the glimpse would be to know too much. The sacred terror is, in fact, the sensation—not simply fright, but a kind of revulsion—that comes when glimpse perilously lengthens into gaze.

II. The Sacred Terror

In 1894, the year before the idea of *The Awkward Age* materialized in his Notebook, and not long before *Guy Domville* went into rehearsals, two electrifying personal events brought James close to the sacred terror, far closer than he wished to be. In both instances he stopped at glimpse and contrived to shut himself away from gaze. The first event was the suicide, in Italy, of Constance Fenimore Woolson. A relation of James Fenimore Cooper, Fenimore (as she was called) was an American novelist who settled successively in Florence, Venice and Rome. Bent on homage, she had first approached James in 1880, in Florence, with a letter of introduction from America. James found her intelligent and moderately engaging, and offered his assistance as an acutely sophisticated guide to Florentine art. But what was a cautious friendship on his part became, on hers, a worshipful love. James could not reciprocate. She was middle-aged, unmarried, deaf in one ear—an admirable companion whom he was learning to be wary of. He worried that she might mistake occasional camaraderie for an encouragement of the affections. The news of her death in 1894, after nearly a decade and a half of correspondence (her letters were very long, his very short) bewildered and initially misled him. He had the impression she had died of "pneumonia supervening on influenza," and prepared to journey from London to her funeral in Rome. "Poor isolated and fundamentally tragic being!" he summed her up. "She was intrinsically one of the saddest and least happy natures I have ever met; and when I ask myself what I *feel* about her death the only answer that comes to me is from what I felt about the melancholy, the limitations and the touching loneliness of her life. I was greatly attached to her and valued exceedingly her friendship." All that, however, was glimpse, not gaze. The moment James learned it was suicide that had removed Fenimore—she had leaped from a second-story window—he retreated quickly and decided against attending her burial. Leon Edel speculates that James felt some responsibility for the hopelessness that had led to what James termed her "suicidal mania." Whether that is so or not, it is certainly true that James came to rest in a conventional, and distancing, judgment—"fundamentally tragic being!"—and averted his eyes from any connection he might have had with Fenimore's dread, or her destruction. He would not seek to know too much. He would evade the sacred terror. He would not "go behind": the preparation for going behind—the horrible hours—had not yet occurred.

Two years before Fenimore's death, James's sister Alice died in London. The cause was breast cancer, but she had been strangely invalided since girlhood, and was in the care of a young woman companion, Katharine Loring. Alice had followed James to London, or had at least followed his inclination to extract himself from America. Hers was an activist temperament (she interested herself in the hot politics of Irish Home Rule) that had chosen, for reasons neither her physicians nor her family could fathom, to go to bed for life. An 1889 photograph of her lodgings at Leamington survives: a capacious sick-room, high-ceilinged, with a single vast window, curtained and draperied; pictures dropped on long wires from the wainscoting; a chandelier sprouting fat globes; a tall carved mirror over a black fireplace; a round table with lamp, vase, flowers, books, magnifying glass. The effect is of Victorian swathing—layers of cloth over every flat and vertical surface: the mantel hung with cloth, the table, the back of a chair.

Lamps, jugs, flowers, photos parade across the mantel. The Persian hearthrug smothers still another carpet, splotched with large flowers. Alice James herself seems swathed, almost swaddled, half-erect on a kind of sofa muffled in voluminously sprawling bedclothes, pillows propping her shoulder and neck. Next to her, nearer the window, holding a book, sits Miss Loring, her throat and bosom lost in a flurry of scarves. Both women are severely buttoned to the chin. It is a photograph that incites the lungs to gulp air; if it were possible to step into this scene, though the looking glass is polished and clear, one might feel choked by too many flower-patterns, the mistiness of light incarcerated, the stale smells of unrelieved enclosure.

William James, in his farewell letter to his sister, wrote that "if the tumor should turn out to be cancerous, . . . then goodbye to neurasthenia and neuralgia and headache, and weariness and palpitation and disgust all at one stroke." To this physician brother, Alice had all along suffered from "the inscrutable and mysterious character of the doom of nervous weakness which has chained you down for all these years." Alice's illness, in short, was—until the advent of cancer—what we nowadays call "psychological." The genius sister of two genius brothers, she was self-imprisoned, self-restricted. Engulfed by cushions and shawls and wrappings at Leamington, in 1889 she began a diary: "I think that if I get into the habit of writing a bit about what happens, or rather what doesn't happen, I may lose a little of the sense of loneliness and desolation which abides with me."

She had had a history of terrors and nightmares. At twenty she had her first nervous breakdown (if that is what it was), at thirty her second, whereupon she was launched into an infinite series of undiagnosable ailments and their dubious, sometimes bizarre, remedies. She talked of suicide, and kept lists of contemporary suicides. She struggled for intellectual autonomy in an age when young women submitted, through marriage or otherwise, to the limitations of the domestic. Invalidism was, obliquely, one manner of solution: it yielded up an escape from ordinary female roles and contexts. At rest on her sofa, surrounded by heaps of books on every table-top, Alice lived in her head. In her head she fought for Irish liberation; in her head she fought for her own. A famous sentence in her diary records a passionate revolution, in fantasy, of body and soul against a ruling class of one: "As I used to sit immovable reading in the library with waves of violent inclination suddenly invading my muscles, taking some one of their myriad forms such as throwing myself out of the window or knocking off the head of the benignant pater as he sat with his silver locks, writing at his table, it used to seem to me that the only difference between me and the insane was that I had not only all the horrors and suffering of insanity but the duties of doctor, nurse, and straitjacket upon me too."

In contrast to these dark recollections, Alice's diary offers a mellow view of Henry James, who often came to divert her and Miss Loring, bringing catty news and speculative gossip from his broader social world. "I have given him endless care and anxiety but notwithstanding this and the fantastic nature of my troubles I have never seen an impatient look upon his face or heard an unsympathetic or misunderstanding sound cross his lips. He comes at my slightest sign," she wrote, and spoke of a "pitch of brotherly devotion never before approached by the race." After Alice's death in 1892, Katharine Loring took away with her to Boston an urn containing Alice's ashes, and two thick notebooks; the latter were the pages of the diary. Two years later—in 1894, the year of Fenimore's suicide—Miss Loring arranged for the diary to be privately printed, and dispatched one copy to Henry, and another to William. Both brothers were impressed. Henry described his sister's literary claim—he recognized that the diary *was* a literary work—as "heroic in its individuality, its independence—its face-to-face with the universe for and by herself," and praised the "beauty and eloquence," the "rich irony and humor," of Alice's pen. William's own high pleasure—"a leaf in the family laurel crown"—was tempered by a graver evaluation: "personal power venting itself on no opportunity," he concluded.

But it was Henry who backed away from the diary—much as he had had second thoughts about going to Fenimore's funeral. To begin with, he insisted that the diary not be published in his lifetime; and then he burned his copy—motivated, he said, by Alice's habit of setting down his sometimes unseemly accounts of friends and acquaintances. (Years later he made a bonfire of all the thousands of letters in his possession, obliterating the revelations of decades.) Amusement had become, in his sister's hands, document. James found himself shaken by "so many names, personalities, hearsays (usually, on Alice's part, through *me!*)"; he informed William that Alice's exposures made him "intensely nervous and almost sick with terror about possible publicity, possible accidents, reverberation etc.," and that he "used to say everything to Alice (on system) that could *égayer* [entertain] her bedside and many things in confidence. I didn't dream she wrote them down . . . It is a 'surprise' that is too much of a surprise." There was more for James to grapple with, though, than the mortification of stumbling on his own remarks. It might be disconcerting that Alice mentioned a certain essayist's "self-satisfied smirk." Yet something else lay coiled at the bottom of his sister's diary, and James was unequipped to live with it.

He met there, in fact—side by side with the bits of raillery and the vehement Irish nationalism—terrifying resonances and reminiscent apparitions. After the death of the James paterfamilias at home in Massachusetts, the diary disclosed, Alice, desolate in an empty house, was assaulted by the vibrations of a voice: "In those ghastly days, when I was by myself in the little house on Mt. Vernon Street, how I longed to flee . . . and escape from the 'Alone, Alone!' that echoed thro' the house, rustled down the stairs, whispered from the walls, and confronted me, like a material presence, as I sat waiting, counting the moments." James himself, five years after the undoing of *Guy Domville*, grieved over "*the essential loneliness of my life*" (the emphasis is his own). "This loneliness," he put it, "what is it still but the deepest thing about one? Deeper, about *me*, at any rate, than anything else; deeper than my 'genius,' deeper than my 'discipline,' deeper than my pride, deeper, above all, than the deep counterminings of art."

Alice James's "Alone!" and Henry James's "deepest thing" had their antecedents in a phantasmagorical visitation endured by their father fifty years before. It was a vision, or a phantom, or an omen, so paralyzing to the spirit, so shocking in its horror, that Henry James Senior was compelled to give it a name (seemingly a fusion of "devastation," "visitation," "vast") out of Swedenborgian metaphysics: *vastation*. One spring day after dinner, he testified, "feeling only the exhilaration incident to a good digestion," he was all at once flooded by panic: "To all appearance it was a perfectly insane and abject terror, without ostensible cause, and only to be accounted for, to my perplexed imagination, by some damnèd shape squatting invisible to me within the precincts of the room, and raying out from his fetid personality influences fatal to life. The thing had not lasted ten seconds before I felt myself a wreck; that is, reduced from a state of firm, vigorous, joyful manhood to one of almost helpless infancy." And another time he described himself as "inwardly shriveled to a cinder," altered to a "literal nest of hell within my own entrails."

The younger Henry James had turned away from Fenimore's suicide. In nearly the same moment he had turned away from his sister's diary. The suicide intimated influences fatal to life from a fetid personality. The diary was fundamentally a portrait of infantile helplessness, a shriveled soul, hell within the entrails. The elder James, with his damnèd shape; Fenimore, flinging herself to the pavement; Alice, listening to the ghostly susurrations of her abandonment—each had dared to look into the abyss of knowing-too-much; James would not look with them. It was not until he had himself succumbed to his own vastation—eye to eye with the sacred terror on the stage of the St. James's Theater in 1895—that he was ready to exchange glimpse for gaze. The brawling pandemonium (it continued, in fact, for fifteen minutes) had not lasted ten seconds before he felt himself a wreck, reduced from a state of firm, vigorous, sovereign artistry to one of almost helpless infancy. Everything he had thought himself to be—a personage of majestic achievement—disintegrated in an instant. He could not go on as he had. Simply, he lost his nerve.

But he found, in the next work he put his hand to, not only a new way of imagining himself, but a new world of art. By paring away narrative rumination and exposition—by treating the novel as if it were as stark as a play-script—he uncovered (or invented) a host of labyrinthine depths and devices that have since been signally associated with literary modernism. For one thing, representation, while seeming to keep to its accustomed forms, took on a surreal quality, inscrutably off-center. For another, intent, or reason, gave way to the inchoate, the inexpressible. The narrative no longer sought to make a case for its characterizations; indirection, deduction, detection, inference, proliferated. An unaccountable presence, wholly unseen, was at last let in, even if kept in the tale's dark cellar: the damnèd shape, the sacred terror. The tale began to know more than the teller, the dream more than the dreamer; and Henry James began his approach to the Kafkan. In those "most horrible hours of my life" after his inward collapse on the stage of the St. James, the curtain was being raised for *The Awkward Age*.

III. *The Awkward Age*

The Awkward Age is, ostensibly, a comedy of manners, and resembles its populous class in that it concerns itself with the marriageability of a young woman. Nearly a hundred years after James wrote, no theme may appear so moribund, so obsolete, as the notion of "marrying off" a daughter. Contemporary daughters (and contemporary wives) enter the professions or have jobs, and do not sit on sofas, month after month, to be inspected by possibly suitable young men who are themselves to be inspected for their incomes. The difference between late Victorian mores and our own lies in female opportunity and female initiative, with freedom of dress and education not far behind. Yet the similarities may be stronger than the differences. It is still true that the term of marital eligibility for young women is restricted to a clearly specified span of years; it is still true that a now-or-never mentality prevails, and that young women (and often their mothers) continue to be stung by the risks of time. The gloves, parasols, boas, corsets, feathered hats, and floor-sweeping hems have vanished; the anxiety remains. A century ago, getting one's daughter appropriately married was a central social preoccupation, and, though marriage is nowadays not a young woman's only prescribed course in life, it is as much a gnawing preoccupation as it ever was. In this respect, no one can call the conditions of *The Awkward Age* dated.

In respect of sexual activity, those conditions are equally "modern." If sexual activity, in habit and prospect, defines manners, then—as a comedy of manners—*The Awkward Age* is plainly not a period piece. To be sure, society no longer pretends, as the Victorians did, to an ideal of young virgins kept from all normal understanding until the post-nuptial deflowering; but in *The Awkward Age*, which depicts a public standard of ineffable purity not our own, that standard is mocked with bawdy zest. (Henry James bawdy? Consider the scuffle during which little Aggie sets her bottom firmly down upon a salacious French novel.) *The Awkward Age*, as a matter of fact, teems with adultery and emblems of incest; what appears to be wholesome finally suggests the soiled and the despoiled.

Still, it is not sexual standards and their flouting that move this novel from its opening lightness toward the shadowed distortions that are its destination. Rather, it is the unpredictable allegiances of probity. Probity arrives in the shape of Mr. Longdon, who "would never again see fifty-five" but is rendered as an aged, even antediluvian, gentleman, complete with pince-nez, old-fashioned reticences, and touchy memories of his prime. In his prime, in a moral atmosphere he judges to be superior to that of the present, he (long ago) loved and lost Lady Julia. He has never married, and for years has lived away from London, in the country, in a house poignantly similar to James's own Lamb House in Rye. He is a meticulous watcher and silent critic, sensitive, upright, certainly elderly in his perception of himself; a man of the past. One might imagine at first that Mr. Longdon (he is always called "Mr.") is yet another incarnation of James's eager old gentlemen—the life-seeker Strether who, in *The Ambassadors*, opens himself to the seductions of Paris, or the thrill-thirsty John Marcher of "The Beast in the Jungle," who waits for some grand sensation or happening to befall him. Mr. Longdon, by contrast, is a backward-looker. Lady Julia was his Eden, and the world will never again be so bright or so right. "The more one thinks of it," he remarks, "the more one seems to see that society . . . can never have been anything but increasingly vulgar. The point is that in the twilight of time—and I belong, you see, to the twilight—it had made out much less how vulgar it *could* be."

He has come to London, then, as a kind of anthropologist (though his motives are never clarified), on the trail of Lady Julia's descendants, and is welcomed into the culture of the natives: the chief of the natives being Mrs. Brookenham, Lady Julia's daughter, who is at the hub of a fevered salon. All roads lead to Mrs. Brook's, and the travelers are encrusted with bizarre trappings. The Duchess, a callously opportunistic Englishwoman who is the widow of a minor Italian aristocrat, is rearing her Neapolitan ward, Agnesina ("little Aggie"), as a snow-white slate on which "the figures were yet to be written." The hugely rich Mr. Mitchett, known as Mitchy, rigged out in unmatched merry-andrew gear and tolerant to the point of nihilism, is the zany but good-hearted son of a shoemaker become shoe mogul. Vanderbank, or Van—a handsome, winning, self-protective, evasive young man of thirty-five, impecunious on a mediocre salary, whom Mr. Longdon befriends—is Mrs. Brook's (relatively) secret lover. In and out of Mrs. Brook's salon flow schemers, snobs, faithless wives and husbands, jesters, idlers, fantastic gossips; even a petty thief, who happens to be Mrs. Brook's own son, Harold. And at the tea table in the center of it all sits (now and then) her daughter, Lady Julia's granddaughter, Fernanda—Nanda—who smokes, runs around London "squeezing up and down no matter whose staircase," and chooses as an intimate a married woman with an absent husband.

Nanda is fully aware of the corrupted lives of her mother's circle. Her father is indifferent, negligent, a cipher; her brother sponges on everyone who enters the house, and on every house he enters; her parents live enormously beyond their means; all relationships are measured by what can be gotten out of them. "Edward and I," Mrs. Brook declares to the Duchess, "work it out between us to show off as tender parents and yet to get from you everything you'll give. I do the sentimental and he the practical." With her "lovely, silly eyes," Mrs. Brook at forty-one is youthfully attractive, but cuts two years off her daughter's age in order to snip two years from her own. There is no shame, no guilt, no conscience; the intrinsic has no value.

All these people (but for the blunt Duchess, who is plain Jane) have names that are cursory, like their lives: Mrs. Brook, Van, Mitchy, Aggie, Tishy, Carrie, even Nanda; it is as if only Mr. Longdon troubles to take a long breath. "I've been seeing, feeling, thinking," he admits. He understands himself to be "a man of imagination," an observer, with a "habit of not privately depreciating those to whom he was publicly civil." (A habit that James himself, on the evidence of the embarrassments of Alice's diary, did not always live up to.) Mrs. Brook's salon, by contrast, feeds on conspiracy, on sublimely clever talk, on plots and outrageous calculations, on malice and manipulation, on exploitation, on matchmaking both licit and illicit; everyone is weighed for cash worth. Mitchy rates high on the money scale, low on social background. Vanderbank, with his beauty and cultivated charm, is the reverse. Mr. Longdon has money, judiciousness, and an unappeased and unfinished love for Lady Julia, whose memory serves as a standard for fastidious decorum and civilized reciprocity—none of it to be found in present-day London, least of all in Mrs. Brook's drawing room. Mr. Longdon despises Mrs. Brook and is almost preternaturally drawn to Nanda. Though Lady Julia was beautiful and Nanda is not, he is overcome by what he takes to be a magical likeness. In Nanda, Lady Julia is nearly restored for him—except that Nanda is a modern young woman with access to the great world; she knows what Lady Julia in her girlhood would never have been permitted (or perhaps would never have wished) to know.

The ground on which *The Awkward Age* is spread—and woven, and bound, and mercilessly knotted—is precisely this: what a young woman ought or ought not to know, in a new London that "doesn't love the latent or the lurking, has neither time nor sense for anything less discernible than the red flag in front of the steam-roller," as Vanderbank cautions Mr. Longdon. "It wants cash over the counter and letters ten feet high. Therefore you see it's all as yet rather a dark question for poor Nanda—a question that in a way quite occupies the foreground of her mother's earnest little life. How *will* she look, what will be thought of her and what will she be able to do for herself?" Nanda at eighteen, having come of age (Mrs. Brook, for all her shaving of years, can no longer suppress this news), is ready to be brought down—from the schoolroom, so to speak—to mingle among the denizens and fumes of Mrs. Brook's nether realm. "I seem to see," James complained in his Notebook, ". . . English society before one's eyes—the great modern collapse of all the forms and 'superstitions' and respects, good and bad, and restraints and mysteries . . . decadences and vulgarities and confusions and masculinizations and femininizations—the materializations and abdications and intrusions, and Americanizations, the lost sense, the brutalized manner . . . the general revolution, the failure of fastidiousness." And he mourned the forfeiture "of nobleness, of delicacy, of the exquisite"—losses he connected with "the non-marrying of girls, the desperation of mothers, the whole alteration of manners . . . and tone, while our theory of the participation, the *presence* of the young, remains unaffected by it."

Nanda, in brief, still unmarried at twenty, becomes, by virtue (or, one might say, by vice) of her saturation in her mother's circle, unmarriageable. The Duchess has reared little Aggie on a different scheme—the strict continental preservation of her purity, mental and other. Little Aggie is consequently a marvel of protected innocence and ignorance, decorative and inutile, "like some wonderful piece of stitching." She is "really the sort of creature," Vanderbank offers, that Nanda "would have liked to be able to be." And Mrs. Brook lightly yet chillingly notes, "She couldn't possibly have been able . . . with so loose—or, rather, to express it more properly, so perverse—a mother."

Nanda's mother's looseness and perverseness is pointed enough: she knows her daughter is in love with Vanderbank, but means to keep hold of him for herself.

Vanderbank, in any event, is useless as a potential husband —he has no money. Mitchy has both money and hope, and is perpetually in pursuit of Nanda. But fond though she is of him, Mitchy—a free balloon, a whimsical cynic, dotingly unconcerned, endlessly kind, all without being rooted in serious discrimination—is for Nanda literally untouchable. She will not so much as allow him to kiss her hand. Mitchy, she tells Mr. Longdon, is "impossible." Who, then, will Nanda marry? In surroundings thickened by innuendo and conspiracy, Mr. Longdon, man of probity, himself descends to insinuation and plot—though he might think of these as inference and discretion. In combination with the Duchess, he cooks up the idea of inducing Vanderbank to marry Nanda. Despite the delicacy that veils his intent, it crudely comes down to money: Mr. Longdon will make it worth Vanderbank's while to propose to Nanda. After which, hearing of Mr. Longdon's scheme, Mitchy will relinquish Nanda (Nanda has herself urged Mitchy on Aggie), and the Duchess, finally, will have a clear field to sweep him up for her immaculate little ward. Shoemaker's offspring or no, Mitchy is a prize promising strings of pearls.

Aggie, wed to Mitchy, turns instantly wild. What was yesterday a *tabula rasa* grows hectic overnight with prurient scribblings. But under Mrs. Brook's reign (and London practice), a sullied Aggie is acceptable, predictable, even conventional. The Duchess is not simply calm. She is smug. Aggie, married, is promptly expected to know whatever there is to know of sexual heat, deceit, the denigration of husbands, the taking of lovers, the scufflings of wives. There is no surprise in any of it. English rules apply: abdications and intrusions, revolution and the failure of fastidiousness—as long as the wedding is past. Postnuptial contamination troubles no one.

Nanda's is a different case. She is tainted and unmarried. "If Nanda doesn't get a husband early in the business," the Duchess advises Mr. Longdon, "she won't get one at all. One, I mean, of the kind she'll take. She'll have been in it over-long for *their* taste." "Been in what?" Mr. Longdon asks. "Why in the air they themselves have infected for her!" the Duchess retorts. The infection is carried by the clever young men who, "with intellectual elbow-room, with freedom of talk," hang about Mrs. Brook's drawing room, putting their hostess "in a prodigious fix—she must sacrifice either her daughter or . . . her intellectual habits." And the Duchess crows: "You'll tell me we go farther in Italy, and I won't deny it, but in Italy we have the common sense not to have little girls in the room." Yet Nanda is far from being a little girl. "Of course she's supposedly young," the Duchess pursues, "but she's really any age you like: your London world so fearfully batters and bruises them."

In the end Vanderbank declines to marry Nanda, not even for profit. She delights him; he admires her; he may even adore her; and he is certainly not in love with her mother. Nanda, on her side, seemingly ignorant of Mr. Longdon's bribe (though she is ignorant of nothing else), longs for Vanderbank's proposal. On a lyrical summer afternoon, it appears about to come; finally it does not. Nanda is "infected": she knows too much. Superficially, one may protest fashionable London's double standard—excessive worldliness does not interfere, after all, with the marital eligibility of young men. And the argument can be made—it *is* made—that, if Vanderbank cannot marry without money, he cannot marry with it either: perhaps he scruples to wed on means not his own. But it is not Mr. Longdon's bribe that Vanderbank finds impossible. It is

Nanda herself, Nanda in her contamination. Nor is the infection he intuits in her merely social worldliness, however alarming that worldliness may be.

Nanda's infection is more serious than that. Her knowing pestilential things heard and seen in her mother's salon is not the whole source and sum of her malady. What might have stopped at taintedness through oversophistication has, since the arrival of Mr. Longdon—to whom she has passionately attached herself—deepened into another order of contagion. Behind the comedy, a seal lifts from over the void; the sacred terror is seeping into the tale. A gentleman of integrity, universally understood as such, Mr. Longdon begins to draw after him a gradual toxicity, screened by benevolence. Nanda speaks affectionately of his "curious infatuation." She is herself curiously infatuated: "I set him off—what do you call it?—I show him off," she tells Vanderbank, "by his going round and round as the acrobat on the horse in the circle goes round the clown." And she acknowledges that her conversations with Mr. Longdon explore "as far as a man and a woman can together." To her mother she explains, "I really think we're good friends enough for anything." "What do you call that then," Mrs. Brook inquires, "but his adopting you?" And another time Mrs. Brook wonders whether this "little fussy ancient man" is attempting to "make up to" her daughter.

But the bond between Mr. Longdon and Nanda is more mysterious than any December-May flirtation, and it is assuredly not an adoption. It is true that Mr. Longdon pursues, he courts, he possesses. He takes Nanda away to his country house for a long stay. And finally he takes her to live with him permanently. Still, it is not an adoption, not a liaison, not anything like a marriage. It may be intended as a salvation: Nanda must be removed from Mrs. Brook's polluting household; Nanda, infected, is not marriageable. Mrs. Brook is privy to the fact of Mr. Longdon's bribe (Vanderbank has tattled to her), and though it may (or may not) portend her losing Vanderbank as lover, nothing could gratify her more. "I can't help feeling," she observes, "that something possibly big will come of Mr. Longdon." "Big" means, in this lexicon, money; and when the bribe to Vanderbank fails, Nanda, for want of an alternative falling under Mr. Longdon's protection, decidedly *does* fall into money.

She also falls into a peculiar aura: the aura of James's post-*Guy Domville* mood. James endowed Mr. Longdon not only with his own house, but with his own age, and with his own intimations of mortality and loss. To Nanda Mr. Longdon bursts out: "Oh, you've got time—you can come round again; you've a margin for accidents, for disappointments and recoveries: you can take one thing with another. But I've only my last little scrap." Mr. Longdon, one surmises, is here a mirror for certain darkening aspects of James himself. And so, interestingly, is Nanda, whose early self-recognition—"I shall never marry"—is a version of James's own youthful announcement: "I am too good a bachelor to spoil." The price of being so good a bachelor was a latterday profundity of loneliness, and in his latter years—though there was no Lady Julia in James's past on which to hang a present attachment—there were sentimental yearnings toward a whole series of engaging and gifted young men. The journalist Morton Fullerton (who became Edith Wharton's lover for a time) was one of them; Hendrik Andersen, a sculptor, was another. A third, who struck James as especially endearing, was Jonathan Sturges. Sturges, crippled by polio in childhood, was an American residing in England, "full of talk and intelligence, and of the absence of prejudice, . . . saturated with London, and with all sorts of contrasted elements in it, to which he has given himself up." This account of Sturges, appearing in one of James's letters, might easily be a portrait of Nanda. During the course of composition of *The Awkward Age*, which James was just then serializing for *Harper's*, Sturges was received with tender hospitality in Lamb House, and remained for many weeks. Nanda's visit to Mr. Longdon in his house in Suffolk (Lamb House is in Sussex) similarly lasts a number of weeks. The charming young men who so much appealed to James in this desolate period may have turned up, in Nanda, as a kind of imagined solution to isolation and despair. In real life, the charming young men came and went. In the novel, Nanda will move in and stay forever.

But *The Awkward Age* offers no solution after all. Nanda's ultimately going to live with Mr. Longdon is—for James's time and for our own—a serious anomaly. Nanda has twice been the subject of a bribe—once with Vanderbank, and again with her parents, who are only too glad to see that Mr. Longdon, by taking her in, really *is* doing something "big" for her. There is nothing honorable in Vanderbank's refusal of Mr. Longdon's bribe, and there is nothing straightforward in that refusal, which is never directly spoken. Vanderbank, pleasing everyone and no one, simply drifts away. He has the carelessness of consummate indifference; what is too tangled, or too demanding, can have no claim on him. He will never come through. "There are things I ought to have done that I haven't," he reluctantly tells Nanda in their brief last meeting. "I've been a brute and I didn't mean it and I couldn't help it." Moments before this admission, he sums it all up: "The thing is, you see, that *I* haven't a conscience. I only want my fun."

Mr. Longdon himself, presumably a man of acute conscience, does not escape corruption. Entering a corrupt community—a bribable community—he uncovers in himself an inclination to offer bribes. For Nanda's parents, the thing is more flagrant than a bribe. Mrs. Brook has, beyond question, sold her daughter to a rich man who will undoubtedly make her his heir. Mrs. Brook's acquiescence in Nanda's removal confirms the smell of the marketplace: plainly she would have declared against Nanda's going off with a "little fussy ancient man" who was poor. Mr. Longdon, in consequence, has succeeded in buying for his empty house a young woman nearly a third his age—and no matter how benign, or rescuing, or salvational this arrangement may appear to him, it is at bottom a purchase transaction, intended to assuage his lonely need. The young woman he purposes to protect will be sequestered from society on the premise that she is anyhow unmarriageable; on his account (even if he supposes it to be on *her* account) she will be foreclosed from the turnings and chances of a life beyond his own elderly precincts.

But Nanda has been brought to Mr. Longdon's house for still another reason: the revenge of love and the revenge of hate. Love of Lady Julia, hatred of Mrs. Brook. If Lady Julia in all her loveliness once passed him by, two generations afterward he is in possession of her grandchild. "I'm a hater," he says bluntly, reflecting on the decline of the standard that once made a "lady." In secluding Nanda from her mother's reach, he is trumpeting his contempt for Mrs. Brook: private hatred becomes public scorn. Nanda, for her part, goes with him willingly. She is complicit in the anomaly of their connection: she is the instrument of her own retreat. It is not the money—the being provided for—that lures Nanda; it is the strangeness, and, above all, the surrender.

For Nanda, Mr. Longdon's house holds out a suicidal peace: renunciation, a radical swerving from hope. Agreeing to enter that house of relinquishment (and moribund refinement)—this time never again to leave it—she is hurtled into a final storm of grief. Long ago, Mr. Longdon lost Lady Julia. Now Nanda has lost Vanderbank. They are matched in desolation.

> It burst from her, flaring up in a queer quaver that ended in something queerer still—in her abrupt collapse, on the spot, into the nearest chair, where she choked with a torrent of tears. Her buried face could only after a moment give way to the flood, and she sobbed in a passion as sharp and brief as the flurry of a wild thing for an instant uncaged; her old friend meantime keeping his place in the silence broken by her sound and distantly—across the room—closing his eyes to his helplessness and her shame. Thus they sat together while their trouble both conjoined and divided them.

Here James, in suddenly "going behind," momentarily abandons his "few grave, rigid laws" of dramatic restraint. It is as if, in this outburst of bereavement, the idea of helplessness and shame cannot be prevented from pressing forward, willy-nilly, from the cobwebbed backstage dark. The sacred terror is at last flung straight in the face of the tale. Not only helplessness and shame, but corruption; callousness; revenge; sexual displacement. Nanda displaces (or replaces) Lady Julia; beyond the novel's enclosure she may displace—or mask—James's endearing young men who come and go. There are, besides, incestuous hints: the young woman who might have been her protector's grandchild is intimately absorbed into the days and nights of his house. Her parents have abdicated. Her mother has sold her. The man she hoped to marry will not have her, even for a fortune. The man who takes her in, troubled by secret fevers and unthreshed motives, is sunk in a web of confusion; the young woman represents for him half a dozen identities, relations, unwholesome resolutions. And she, in joining him, has gone to bed, in effect, for life—as a penalty, or perhaps in penance, for knowing too much.

A panicked scenario. How much of it did James know? Did the teller penetrate to the bowels of the tale? The tale, in any case, penetrates—or decodes—the teller. The mosaic fly-eye of the narrative assembles all the shards and particles of James's chronicle of crisis, glimpse after glimpse, and sweeps them up, and compiles and conflates them into one horrendous *seeing*—James in his aging forlornness, in a house devoid of companionship and echoing with his sister's "Alone!"; Fenimore's wild crash; Alice's burial-in-life; the return of his father's "damnèd shape" and its fatal influences. And what was that shape if not James himself, at the crest of a life delivered over wholly to art, helpless on the stage on the evening of January 5, 1895, the crown of his genius thrown brutally down? "Thus they sat together while their trouble both conjoined and divided them." Divided, because James in his domicile, unlike Mr. Longdon, is alone, and will always be alone. Conjoined, because James is at once both Mr. Longdon and Nanda. But surely more than either or both. These two have been dropped into a pit. James is the pit's master, its builder and evoker.

After the cataclysmic turning point of *Guy Domville*, hidden knowings are everywhere in James—notably in *What Maisie Knew* (1897) and "The Turn of the Screw," and culminating in the last great pair of conspiratorial works, *The*

Wings of the Dove (1902) and *The Golden Bowl* (1904). The recurrence, in his own sensibility, of the paternal vastation, the recognition of an immutable deprivation ("*the essential loneliness of my life*"), the nearby explosions of suicide and self-immolation, the "horrible hours" themselves—all these pitchforked James out of the Victorian and into the modern novel. He broke down both social and narrative forms and plummeted, sans the old fastidiousness (and optimism), into the smoldering detritus of exhausted ways. It is probable that *The Awkward Age* is a novel that knows far more than its author knew, and holds more secrets of panic, shame, helplessness, and chaos than James could candidly face. But it was this work that crucially and decisively pried open the inmost door to the void. After which, released from glimpse into gaze, James could dare as Conrad dared, and as Kafka dared.

At the climax of his powers Henry James looked freely into the Medusan truth, he snared the unconscious. "Make him *think* the evil," he said, soliciting the unprepared nineteenth-century reader as the twentieth came near (a century that was to supply unthinkable evil), "make him think it for himself." And in the end—anarchy loosed upon the world, and pitilessness slouching toward him—James thought it for himself.

Henry James's Unborn Child

HENRY JAMES IS the only American writer whom our well-ingrained democratic literary conventions have been willing to call Master. Not even Emerson, who as philosopher of individualism stands as a kind of Muse to all subsequent American culture and society, has been granted that title. It fell to James—this acknowledgment of magisterial illuminations—not simply because of his Balzacian amplitude, although that would have been reason enough. From the oceanic plenitude of James's imagination and genius there rode out, with the aristocratic majesty of great seagoing ships, a succession of novels (20 of these), short stories (112; some, by contemporary standards, the size of novels), biographies and autobiographies, critical and social essays (ranging from a book-length vision of Hawthorne to the 1905 Bryn Mawr College commencement speech), travel and museum impressions, a dozen plays, innumerable literary notebooks, dazzling letters bearing both difficult truths and what James himself termed "the mere twaddle of graciousness."

Like the Cunarders of his day, James's ambition was

intercontinental. An expatriate who came of age in Cambridge, Massachusetts, during the Civil War, he lived and wrote in hotels and lodgings in Rome, Venice, Florence, Paris. Eventually he took up residence in London, and finally he bought a house in the little English sea town of Rye. His themes too were international—Americans in Europe, Europeans in America. "Very special and very interesting," he once noted, "the state of being of the American who has bitten deep into the apple of 'Europe' and then been obliged to take his lips from the fruit." As it turned out, James never did take his lips from the fruit; he died an American bachelor who was also a patriotic British subject. Numbers of his short stories—like "Hugh Merrow"—are about English people in England.

Yet what marks James as Master is not his Europeanized cosmopolitan eye, or even the cornucopia of his cascading novels and tales—masterpiece after masterpiece. Well before the advent of what we now call modernism, James's prose began to exhale the most refined and secret psychological processes and nuances; and it is these exquisite techniques of insight that distinguish him from other late-nineteenth-century writers. Mysteriously, with the passing of each new decade, James becomes more and more our contemporary—it is as if our own sensibilities are only just catching up with his. We can recognize him now as a powerful symbolist, one of the supreme literary innovators of consciousness.

"Hugh Merrow," an unfinished short story written in the densely reverberating style of James's "late manner," was discovered in 1937 by Leon Edel, James's unsurpassed interpreter and biographer, in an old sea chest at the bottom of Harvard's Widener Library. It lay there "neatly tied with red and blue cotton strips" among the last of the Notebooks and in the company of several commercial pocket diaries (in one of which James could view the Jewish liturgical calendar for the year 5671 amid the eclipses and tides of 1911). A fragment had, of course, no place in Edel's twelve-volume definitive edition of James's *Tales*. For fifty years—though "Hugh Merrow" was there for the asking, catalogued, readily accessible—no one came forward to publish it, comment on it, or even marvel at its uniquely truncated condition. An unaccountable absence of scholarly curiosity, given the always bustling university industry represented by Jamesian studies. (A Jamesian wonderment: is it only artists who are lured by the inchoate, and never scholars?) In bringing out *The Complete Notebooks of Henry James*—the sea-chest residue of James's pen—Leon Edel and his collaborator, Lyall H. Powers, have put into our hands the text of an acute psychological riddle: why did James, whose brilliant consummations did not fail him in 112 completed stories, break off in the middle of this one?

That he could have been discouraged by any falling off in tone or brio is unlikely. The style of "Hugh Merrow" is James at his steadiest and most assured. The comedy is burnished and fully self-aware. The progression of the plot is as finely calculated as anything James ever wrote. And it was not his habit, as the output of half a century testifies, to leave work unfinished. Nor was there anything casual about the design of "Hugh Merrow"—the Notebooks reveal at least six separate foreshadowings of this eccentric tale.

The first appears in the fall of 1895, in the form of a subject James calls "The Child," a story about a painter told to him thirdhand by friends of the Italian novelist Luigi Gualdo. In May of 1898, James begins to imagine a "woman who wants to have *been* married—to *have become* a widow," who approaches a painter for a portrait of the husband she has never had. A tendril of this motif turned into

"The Tone of Time," chiefly about rival lovers—but what seems to have been brewing here, and to have kept on brewing, is the idea of the life never lived, the missed experience. (This was to become the reigning theme of *The Ambassadors*, a novel at the summit of James's art, also written during this period.) Two years later, in 1900, "the little 'Gualdo' notion" is still haunting James, and now he jots down the version he will finally pursue: "a young childless couple comes to a painter and asks him to *paint* them a little girl (or a child *quelconque*) whom they can have as their own —since they so want one and can't come by it otherwise. My subject is what I get out of *that*."

That same day, setting down a long row of names (over a hundred of them) for possible future use in stories, James lists "Archdean," which will emerge as Captain Archdean, the young would-be father in "Hugh Merrow." Two other names on that list—"Marcher" and "Bartram"—will empower one of James's most shocking psychological horror tales, "The Beast in the Jungle," published the following year: about a man whose life, tragically hollow, passes him by solely because he has wilfully missed the chance to live it. John Marcher does not marry May Bartram, and ends in devastating loneliness.

James was at this time preoccupied with his own loneliness. Not long after the names Archdean, Marcher, and Bartram were entered into his Notebook, he confessed, in a letter, to "*the essential loneliness of my life*"—the emphasis is his. "This loneliness," he inquired, "what is it still but the deepest thing about one? Deeper about *me*, at any rate, than anything else; deeper than my 'genius,' deeper than my 'discipline,' deeper than my pride, deeper, above all, than the deep counterminings of art." Loneliness, he said, was to be his final port. He was fifty-seven.

The bachelor painter Hugh Merrow is presented cheerfully as "our young man," and yet he too is described as ultimately solitary. "He was single, he was, behind everything, lonely, and it had been given him so little to taste of any joy of perfect union, that he was, as to many matters, not even at one with himself. The joy of perfect union, nevertheless, had hovered before him like a dream . . ." Again the theme of the missed experience. In the story's original scheme it was not to have been in the artist, this sense of the lost life, but rather in the childless couple. It is as if James had inadvertently sketched himself in: a fleeting self-portrait in a corner of the canvas.

On the other hand, James's self-scrutiny is everywhere on the canvas. Captain and Mrs. Archdean are hoping to commission a portrait of a child that doesn't exist, the child they cannot have. Adoption won't do; a real son or daughter will fall short of the ideal. "Hugh Merrow," from its confident start to its abrupt stop, is a meditation on the nature of imagination. How close to reality is the artist's invention? Can there be invention without at least partial grounding in actuality—some hint or model? Is there an ideal beauty that solid flesh can never duplicate? Can one live on fantasy just as well as on reality? Is there "such a drawback as [the artist's] having *too* free a hand?" Is imagination only a tricky disguise for the actual and the known? Is art the same as forgery?

But these questions point to only half the riddle of "Hugh Merrow." The other half may come nearer to the marrow of the self. (Is it unimportant, by the way, that "Hugh" can be heard as "you," and "Merrow" as "marrow"?) The other half is psychosexual. It is Mrs. Archdean's intelligence that Hugh Merrow draws close to; she asks him to combine with her in the making of her child. Looking around his studio at "things on easels, started, unfinished, but taking more or less the form of life," she vividly implores him to give birth to an imagined child on her account, in her place. And what is the sex of the child to be? Captain Archdean wants a boy who will look like his wife; Mrs. Archdean wants a girl in the image of her husband. Since they can't agree on which it is to be—*they* aren't a perfect union—they leave it up to Hugh Merrow: the sexual choice is his. Girl or boy? The painter must decide.

Here the fragment ends. There is no climax. "It was wonderful how he pleased them . . . If only he could keep it up!"

Yet James had often before made such choices. His novels and stories are full of little girls understood—and inhabited—from within. Sensitive little boys are somewhat fewer, but they are dramatically there. He continually chose one or the other—in effect he chose both. But in "Hugh Merrow" he was pressing the artist—himself—to give birth to pure imagining, roused from the artist's inmost being and equivalent to it. If the painting is the painter, then James was pressing the artist—he was pressing himself—to decide his own sex, a charge impossible to satisfy. James had never married; he had never achieved perfect union with anyone. He counted his solitude the deepest thing about him. As for sexual union, he was apparently wholly inexperienced, a true celibate. He was at various times attracted to artistic young men, and there has always been speculation about suppressed homoerotic inclinations. Some have even gone so far as to hint at a castrating accident, the notorious "obscure hurt" of James's youth.

James, for his part, burned all the papers and letters he wished to keep from us. He intended to close the door on his privacy. It is a door that we, out of respect for the Master, ought not to force. But "Hugh Merrow" may, after all, be a crack of light from under the door. If James did not go on with "Hugh Merrow," it may be that it required him to resolve, once and for all, the unspoken enigma of his sexual identity. And this, as protean artist, as imaginative tenant of the souls of both women and men, he could not do.

There is more. In the figurations of "Hugh Merrow," James put to himself in its most radical form the question of his own missed experience. In life he had chosen not to be husband or father. But "Hugh Merrow" demanded more than symbolic fatherhood. It demanded that the artist become, through the visionary organization of his art, a mother. It equated the artist with the embryo-bearing woman—while at the same time urging the substitution of art for life. The aesthetic birth was to be an explicit stand-in for an impossible biological fruition. And here the intrinsic contradictions may have grown too stressful for James; the metaphor burst and could not be sustained. He could not keep it up, he could not deliver. In "Hugh Merrow"—a tale seemingly easy and comic, and surely rich with the recognitions of its own bizarreness—James was flinging himself past the threshold of the erotic into the very birth canal itself. In the face of psychological pressure so plainly insupportable, he withdrew.

The question for us is whether *we* will withdraw. Given the enchantment of an unfinished story by Henry James brought to light almost a century after the Master first conceived "the little 'Gualdo' notion," how many writers and readers will be tempted to complete the artist's birth rites? Who now will dare to paint the unimaginable unborn Child?

Mrs. Virginia Woolf: A Madwoman and Her Nurse

NO RECENT BIOGRAPHY has been read more thirstily by readers and writers of fiction than Quentin Bell's account of the life of his aunt Virginia.* Reviewing it, Elizabeth Hardwick speaks of "the present exhaustion of Virginia Woolf," and compares the idea of Bloomsbury—it "wearies"—to a pond run out of trout. But for most American writers, bewildered by the instability of what passes for culture and literature, envious of the English sense of place and of being placed, conscious of separations that yet lack the respectability of "schools" or even the interest of alien perspectives, stuck mainly with the crudity of being either For or Against Interpretation, the legend of Bloomsbury still retains its inspiriting powers. Like any Golden Age, it promises a mimetic future: some day again, says Bloomsbury of 1905, there will be friends, there will be conversation, there will be moods, and they will all again *really matter*, and fall naturally, in the way of things that matter, into history.

* *Virginia Woolf: A Biography* by Quentin Bell, Harcourt Brace Jovanovich, 1972.

Part of the special history of the Bloomsbury of mood is pictorial—and this has nothing to do with the art critic Roger Fry, or the painter Duncan Grant. It is not what the painters painted or what the writers wrote about painting that hangs on: it is the photographs, most of them no more official than snapshots, of the side of a house, two people playing checkers on an old kitchen chair set out in the yard, three friends and a baby poking in the sand. The snapshots are all amateur. Goblets of brightness wink on eaves, fences, trees, and wash out faces in their dazzle; eyes are lost in blackened sockets. The hem of a dress is likely to be all clarity, but the heads escape—under hat brims, behind dogs, into mottled leaf-shade. And out of the blur of those hopeless poses, cigarettes, hands on knees, hands over books, anxious little pups held up to the camera, walking sticks, long grotesque nose-shadows, lapels, outdoor chairs and tables, there rises up—no, leaks down—so much tension, so much ambition, so much fake casualness, so much heartbreaking attention to the momentariness of the moment. The people in the snapshots knew, in a way we do not, who they were. Bloomsbury was self-conscious in a way we are not. It sniffed at its own perceptions, even its own perceived posterity. Somewhere early in the course of her diaries, Virginia Woolf notes how difficult it would be for a biographer to understand her—how little biographers can know, she said—only from the evidence of her journals. Disbelieving in the probity of her own biography, she did not doubt that she would have her own biographer.

She did not doubt; she knew; they knew. Hatched from the last years of the reign of Victoria, Bloomsbury was still a world where things—if not people, then ideas—could be said to reign. Though old authority might be sneered at (or something worse even than a sneer—Virginia Woolf declared her certainty that she could not have become a writer had her father lived), though proprieties might be outrageously altered ("Semen?" asked Lytton Strachey, noticing a stain on Vanessa Bell's skirt one afternoon), though sex was accessible and often enough homoerotic, though freedom might be proclaimed on Gordon Square, though livings were earned, there was nonetheless a spine of authority to support Bloomsbury: family, descent, class and community—the sense of having-in-common. Bloomsbury, after all, was an inheritance. Both E. M. Forster's and Virginia Woolf's people were associated with the liberal and intellectual Clapham Sect of the century before. Cambridge made a kind of cousinship—the staircase at Trinity that drew together Clive Bell, Saxon Sydney-Turner, and Virginia Woolf's brother Thoby Stephen was the real beginning of the gatherings at Gordon Square. Bloomsbury was pacifist and busy with gossip about what it always called "buggery," but it was not radical and it did not harbor rebels. Rebels want to make over; the Bloomsburyites reinforced themselves with their like. The staircase at Trinity went on and on for the rest of their lives, and even Virginia Woolf, thinking to make over the form of the novel, had to have each newly completed work ratified by Morgan Forster and sometimes Maynard Keynes before she could breathe at ease again. The authority of one's closest familiars is the unmistakable note of Bloomsbury. It was that sure voice she listened for. "Virginia Woolf was a Miss Stephen," Quentin Bell begins, in the same voice; it is an opening any outsider could have written, but not in that sharp cadence. He is not so much biographer as a later member of the circle—Virginia Woolf's sister's son, the child of Vanessa and Clive Bell. He knows, he does not doubt. It is the note of self-recognition; of confidence; of inheritance. Everything is in his grip.

And yet—as she predicted—Virginia Woolf's biographer fails her. He fails her, in fact, more mournfully than any outsider could. It is his grip that fails her. This is not only because, sticking mainly to those matters he has sure authority over, he has chosen to omit a literary discussion of the body of work itself. "I have found the work of the biographer sufficiently difficult without adventuring in other directions," he tells us, so that to speak of Quentin Bell's "sure authority" is not to insinuate that all his data are, perhaps, out of childhood memory or family reminiscence, or that he has not mined library after library, and collection after collection of unpublished papers. He is, after all, of the next generation, and the next generation is always in some fashion an outsider to the one before. But what *is* in his grip is something more precise, curiously, than merely data, which the most impersonal research can reliably throw up: it is that particular intimacy of perspective—of experience, really—which characterizes not family information, but family bias. Every house has its own special odor to the entering guest, however faint—it sticks to the inhabitants, it is in their chairs and in their clothes. The analogy of bias to scent is chiefly in one's unconsciousness of one's own. Bell's Woolf is about Virginia, but it has the smell of Vanessa's house. The Virginia Woolf that comes off these pages is a kind of emanation of a point of view, long settled, by now, into family feeling. Stephens, Pattles, Fishers—all the family lines—each has its distinct and legendary scent. The Stephens are bold, the Pattles are fair, the Fishers are self-righteous. And Virginia is mad.

She was the family's third case of insanity, all on the Stephen side. Leslie Stephen, Virginia Woolf's celebrated father—a man of letters whose career was marked not least by the circumstance that Henry James cherished him—was married twice, the second time to Julia Duckworth, a widow with children. Together they produced Vanessa and Virginia, Thoby and Adrian. A child of Leslie Stephen's first marriage, the younger of Virginia's two half-sisters, was born defective—it is not clear whether backward or truly insane—and was confined to an asylum, where she died old. Virginia's first cousin—the child of her father's brother—went mad while still a young man, having struck his head in an accident. But one wonders, in the retrograde and rather primitive way one contemplates families, whether there might not have been a Stephen "taint." In a family already accustomed to rumor of aberration, Virginia Woolf, in any case, was incontrovertibly mad. Her madness was distinguished, moreover, by a threatening periodicity: at any moment it could strike, disabling everyone around her. Vanessa had to leave her children and come running, nurses had to be hired, rest homes interviewed, transport accomplished. The disaster was ten times wider than its victim.

And just here is the defect in writing out of family authority. The odor is personal, hence partial. Proust says somewhere that the artist brings to the work his whole self, to his familiars only those aspects that accommodate them. The biographer close to his subject has the same difficulty; the aspect under which Quentin Bell chiefly views his aunt Virginia is not of accommodation but of a still narrower partiality: discommodity, the effect on family perspective of Virginia Woolf's terrible and recurrent insanity. It was no mere melancholia, or poetic mooning—as, reading Leonard Woolf's deliberately truncated edition of her diary, we used to guess. A claustrophilic though inspired (also self-inspiring) document, it made us resent the arbitrary "personal" omissions: was it the madness he was leaving out? Certainly we wanted the madness too, supposing it to be the useful artistic sort: grotesque moods, quirks—epiphanies really. But it was not that; it was the usual thing people get put away for, an insanity characterized by incoherent howling and by violence. She clawed her attendants and had to be restrained; she would not touch food; she was suicidal. Ah, that cutting difference: not that she longed for death, as poets and writers sometimes do for melancholy's sake, but that she wanted, with the immediacy of a method, to be dead.

Bell's Woolf, then, is not about the Virginia Woolf of the diaries, essays, and novels—not, in the Proustian sense, about the writer's whole self. And surely this is not simply because literary criticism is evaded. Bell's Woolf is not about a writer, in fact; it is about the smell of a house. It is about a madwoman and her nurse.

The nurse was Leonard Woolf. Upon him Quentin Bell can impose no family aspects, rumors, characteristics, old experience, inherited style. He does not trail any known house-scent, like Stephens, Pattles, Fishers. Though he shared the Cambridge stairs—Thoby Stephen, Saxon Sydney-Turner, Clive Bell, Lytton Strachey, and Leonard Woolf together briefly formed the Midnight Society, a reading club that met on Saturday evenings in Clive Bell's rooms—he was not an inheritor of Cambridge. Cambridge was not natural to him, Bloomsbury was not natural to him, even England was not natural to him—not as an inheritance; he was a Jew. Quentin Bell has no "authority" over Leonard Woolf, as he has over his aunt; Leonard is nowhere in the biographer's grip.

The effect is unexpected. It is as if Virginia Woolf escapes—possessing her too selectively, the biographer lets her slip—but Leonard Woolf somehow stays to become himself. Which is to say, Bell's Virginia Woolf can be augmented by a thousand other sources—chiefly by her own work—but we learn as much about Leonard Woolf here as we are likely to know from any other source. And what we learn is a strange historical judgment, strange but unfragmented, of a convincing wholeness: that Leonard Woolf was a family sacrifice. Without him—Quentin Bell's clarity on this point is ineffaceable—Virginia Woolf might have spent her life in a mental asylum. The elder Stephens were dead, Thoby had died at twenty- six, Adrian married a woman apparently indifferent to or incompatible with the Bloomsburyites; it was Vanessa on whom the grimness fell. Leonard Woolf—all this is blatant—got Vanessa off the hook. He was, in fact, deceived: he had no inkling he was being captured for a nurse.

> Neither Vanessa nor Adrian gave him a detailed and explicit account of Virginia's illnesses or told him how deadly serious they might be . . . Her insanity was clothed, like some other painful things in that family, in a jest . . . Thus, in effect if not in intention, Leonard was allowed to think of Virginia's illnesses as something not desperately serious, and he was allowed to marry her without knowing how fearful a care such a union might be. In fairness to all parties it must be said that, even if Virginia's brother and sister had been as explicit and circumstantial as they ought to have been, Leonard would certainly not have been deflected from his purpose of marrying Virginia . . . As it was, he learnt the hard way and one can only wonder, seeing how hard it was, and that he had for so long to endure the constant threat of her suicide, to exert constant

vigilance, to exercise endless persuasive tact at mealtimes, and to suffer the perpetual alternations of hope and disappointment, that he too did not go mad.

In fact he nearly did, although he does not mention it.

"He does not mention it." There was in Leonard Woolf an extraordinary silence, a containment allied to something like concealment, and at the same time open to a methodical candor. This is no paradox; candor is often the mode of the obtuse person. It is of course perilous to think of Leonard Woolf as obtuse: he was both activist and intellectual, worldly and introspective; his intelligence, traveling widely and serenely over politics and literature, was reined in by a seriousness that makes him the most responsible and conscientious figure among all the Bloomsburyites. His seriousness was profound. It was what turned a hand press "small enough to stand on a kitchen table" into the Hogarth Press, an important and innovative publishing house. It was what turned Leonard Woolf himself from a highly able agent of colonialism—at the age of twenty-four he was an official of the British ruling apparatus in Ceylon—into a convinced anti-imperialist and a fervent socialist. And it was what turned the Jew into an Englishman.

Not that Leonard Woolf is altogether without ambivalence on this question; indeed, the word "ambivalence" is his own. Soon after his marriage to Virginia Stephen, he was taken round on a tour of Stephen relations—among them Virginia's half-brother, Sir George Duckworth, in his large house in Dalingridge Place, and "Aunt Anny," who was Lady Ritchie, Thackeray's daughter, in St. George's Square. He suffered in these encounters from an "ambivalence in my attitude to the society which I found in

Dalingridge Place and St. George's Square. I disliked its respectability and assumptions while envying and fearing its assurance and manners." And: "I was an outsider to this class, because, although I and my father before me belonged to the professional middle class, we had only recently struggled up into it from the stratum of Jewish shop-keepers. We had no roots in it." This looks like candor—"we had no roots"—but it is also remarkably insensible. Aware of his not belonging, he gives no evidence anywhere that the people he moved among were also aware of it. It is true that his own group of self-consciously agnostic Cambridge intellectuals apparently never mentioned it to his face. Thoby Stephen in a letter to Leonard in Ceylon is quick enough to speak of himself, mockingly, as a nonbelieving Christian—"it's no good being dainty with Christians and chapel's obviously rot"—but no one seems ever to have teased Leonard about his being an agnostic Jew. In the atmosphere of that society, perhaps, teasing would have too dangerously resembled baiting; levity about being a Christian was clearly not interchangeable with levity about being a Jew. Fair enough: it never is. But Virginia, replying to a letter in which Leonard implores her to love him, is oddly analytical: " . . . of course, I feel angry sometimes at the strength of your desire. Possibly, your being a Jew comes in also at this point. You seem so foreign." Was he, like all those dark lubricious peoples whose origins are remote from the moderating North, too obscurely other? She corrects herself at once, with a kind of apology: "And then I am fearfully unstable. I pass from hot to cold in an instant, without any reason; except that I believe sheer physical effort and exhaustion influence me." The correction—the retraction—is weak, and fades off; what remains is the blow: "You seem so foreign."

We do not know Leonard's response to this. Possibly he made none. It would have been in keeping had he made none. Foreignness disconcerted him—like Virginia he was at moments disturbed by it and backed away—and if his own origins were almost never mentioned to his face, his face was nevertheless *there*, and so, in those striking old photographs, were the faces of his grandparents. Leonard Woolf is bemused in his autobiography by his paternal grandfather, "a large, stern, black-haired, and black-whiskered, rabbinical Jew in a frock coat." Again he speaks of this "look of stern rabbinical orthodoxy," and rather prefers the "round, pink face of an incredibly old Dutch doll," which was the face of his Dutch-born maternal grandmother—about whom he speculates that it was "possible that she had a good deal of non-Jewish blood in her ancestry. Some of her children and grandchildren were fair-haired and facially very unlike the 'typical' Jew." Her husband, however, was a different case: "No one could have mistaken him for anything but a Jew. Although he wore coats and trousers, hats and umbrellas, just like those of all the other gentlemen in Addison Gardens, he looked to me as if he might have stepped straight out of one of those old pictures of caftaned, bearded Jews in a ghetto . . . " Such Jews, he notes, were equipped with "a fragment of spiritual steel, a particle of passive and unconquerable resistance," but otherwise the character, and certainly the history, of the Jews do not draw him. "My father's father was a Jew," he writes, exempting himself by two generations. "I have always felt in my bones and brain and heart English and, more narrowly, a Londoner, but with a nostalgic love of the city and civilization of ancient Athens." He recognizes that his "genes and chromosomes" are something else; he is a "descendant" of "the world's official fugitives and scapegoats."

But a "descendant" is not the same as a member. A descendant shares an origin, but not necessarily a destiny. Writing in his eighties, Leonard Woolf recollects that as a schoolboy he was elected to an exclusive debating society under the thumb of G. K. Chesterton and his brother, and "in view of the subsequent violent anti-Semitism of the Chestertons" he finds this "amusing"; he reports that he was "surprised and flattered." Sixty-three years afterward he is still flattered. His description of the public school that flattered him shows it to be a detestable place, hostile to both intellect and feeling: "I got on quite well with the boys in my form or with whom I played cricket, football, and fives, but it would have been unsafe, practically impossible, to let them know what I really thought or felt about anything which seemed to me important." *Would have been unsafe.* It was a risk he did not take—unlike Morgan Forster, who, in the same situation in a similar school, allowed himself to be recognized as an intellectual and consequently to suffer as a schoolboy pariah. Leonard Woolf did not intend to take on the role of pariah, then or later. Perhaps it was cowardice; or perhaps it was the opposite, that "fragment of spiritual steel" he had inherited from the ghetto; or perhaps it was his sense of himself as exempt from the ghetto.

Certainly he always thought of himself as wholly an Englishman. In the spring of 1935 he and Virginia drove to Rome. "I was astonished then (I am astonished still)," Quentin Bell comments, "that Leonard chose to travel by way of Germany." They were on German soil three days; near Bonn they encountered a Nazi demonstration but were unharmed, and entered Italy safely. What prompted Leonard Woolf to go into Germany in the very hour Jews were being abused there? Did he expect Nazi street hoodlums to distinguish between an English Jewish face and a

German Jewish face? He carried with him—it was not needed and in the event of street hoodlumism would anyhow have been useless—a protective letter from an official of the German embassy in London. More than that, he carried—in his "bones and brain and heart"—the designation of Englishman. It was a test, not of the inherited fragment of spiritual steel, but of the strength of his exemption from that heritage. If Quentin Bell is twice astonished, it may be because he calculated the risk more closely than Leonard; or else he is not quite so persuaded of the Englishness of Leonard Woolf as is Leonard Woolf.

And, superficially at least, it is difficult to be persuaded of it. One is drawn to Leonard's face much as he was drawn to his grandfather's face, and the conclusion is the same. What Leonard's eyes saw was what the eyes of the educated English classes saw. What Leonard felt on viewing his grandfather's face must have been precisely what Clive Bell and Thoby Stephen would have felt. There is an arresting snapshot—still another of those that make up the pictorial history of Bloomsbury—of Leonard Woolf and Adrian Stephen. They are both young men in their prime; the date is 1914. They are standing side by side before the high narrow Gothic-style windows of Asham House, the Sussex villa Leonard and Virginia Woolf owned for some years. They are dressed identically (vests, coats, ties) and positioned identically—feet apart, hands in pockets, shut lips gripping pipe or cigarette holder. Their shoes are lost in the weedy grass, and the sunlight masks their faces in identical skull-shadows. Both faces are serene, holding back amusement, indulgent of the photographer. And still it is not a picture of two cultivated Englishmen, or not only that. Adrian is incredibly tall and Vikinglike, with a forehead as broad and flat as a chimney tile; he looks like some blueblood American banker not long out of Princeton; his hair grows straight up like thick pale straw. Leonard's forehead is an attenuated wafer under a tender black forelock, his nose is nervous and frail, he seems younger and more vulnerable than his years (he was then thirty-four) and as recognizably intellectual as—well, how does one put the contrast? Following Leonard, one ought to dare to put it with the clarity of a certain cultural bluntness: he looks like a student at the yeshiva. Leonard has the unmistakable face of a Jew. Like his grandfather—and, again like him, despite his costume—Leonard Woolf might have stepped out of one of those pictures of caftaned Jews in the ghetto.

The observation may be obvious and boring but it is not insignificant, if only because it is derived from Leonard himself; it is his own lesson. What can be learned from it is not merely that he was himself conscious of all that curious contrast, but that his fellows could not have been indifferent to it. In a 1968 review of the penultimate volume of Leonard Woolf's memoirs, Dan Jacobson wonders, "Did his being a Jew never affect . . . his career or social life in the several years he spent as a colonial officer in Ceylon, his only companions during that time being other colonial civil servants—not in general the most enlightened, tolerant, or tactful of British social groups? Did it not arise in the political work he carried out later in England, especially during the rise of Nazism?" On all these matters Leonard is mute; he does not mention it. Not so Virginia. "He's a penniless Jew," she wrote in a letter to a friend announcing her marriage, and we know that if she had married a poor man of her own set she would not have called him a penniless Englishman. She called Leonard a Jew not to identify or explain him, but because, quite simply, that is how she saw him; it was herself she was explaining. And if she wrote light-heartedly, making a joke of marriage without inheritance, it was also a joke in general about unaccoutered

Jews—from her point of view, Leonard had neither inheritance nor heritage. He was—like the Hogarth Press later on—self-created.

Of course, in thinking about Leonard Woolf, one is plainly not interested in the question of the acculturated Jew (" . . . nearly all Jews are both proud and ashamed of being Jews," Leonard writes—a model of the type); it is not on the mark. What *is* to the point is the attitude of the class Leonard aspired to join. "Virginia for her part," Quentin Bell notes—and it is unnecessary to remind oneself that he is her nephew –

> had to meet the Woolf family. It was a daunting experience. Leonard himself was sufficiently Jewish to seem to her disquietingly foreign; but in him the trait was qualified. He had become so very much a citizen of her world . . . But Leonard's widowed mother, a matriarchal figure living with her large family in Colinette Road, Putney, seemed very alien to Virginia. No place could have been less like home than her future mother-in-law's house.
>
> And how did the Woolfs regard her? Did they perceive that she thought their furniture hideous? Did she seem to them a haughty goy thinking herself too good for the family of their brilliant son? I am afraid that they probably did.
>
> [Here follows an account of Virginia's response—aloof and truculent—upon learning the character of the dietary laws, which Mrs. Woolf observed.]
>
> Virginia was ready to allow that Mrs. Woolf had some very good qualities, but her heart must have sunk as she considered what large opportunities she would have for discovering them.

"Work and love and Jews in Putney take it out of me," she wrote, and it was certainly true.

This aspect of Virginia Stephen's marriage to Leonard Woolf is usually passed over in silence. I have rehearsed it here at such length not to emphasize it for its own sake—there is nothing novel about upper-class English distaste for Jews—but to make a point about Leonard. He is commonly depicted as, in public, a saintly socialist, and, in private, a saintly husband. He was probably both; but he also knew, like any percipient young man in love with a certain segment of society, how to seize vantage ground. As a schoolboy he was no doubt sincerely exhilarated by the playing field, but he hid his intellectual exhilarations to make it look as if the playing field were all there was to esteem; it was a way, after all, of buying esteem for himself. And though he was afterward no doubt sincerely in love with Virginia Stephen (surely a woman less intelligent would not have satisfied him), it would be a mistake to suppose that Virginia herself—even given her brilliance, her splendid head on its splendid neck, the radiance of her first appearance in Thoby's rooms in Cambridge wearing a white dress and round hat and carrying a parasol, astonishing him, Leonard says, as when "in a picture gallery you suddenly come face to face with a great Rembrandt or Velasquez"—it would be ingenuous, not to say credulous, to think that Virginia alone was all there was to adore. Whether Leonard Woolf fell in love with a young woman of beauty and intellect, or more narrowly with a Stephen of beauty and intellect, will always be a formidable, and a necessary, question.

It is a question that, it seems to me, touches acutely on Leonard Woolf in his profoundly dedicated role as nurse.

He was dedicated partly because he was earnestly efficient at everything, and also because he loved his wife, and also because he was a realist who could reconcile himself to any unlooked-for disaster. He came to the situation of Virginia's health determinedly and unquestioningly, much as, years later, when the German bombings had begun, he joined up with the Local Defence Volunteers: it was what had to be done. But in the case of Virginia more than merely courage was at issue; his "background" had equipped him well to be Virginia Stephen's nurse. When things were going badly he could take on the burden of all those small code-jottings in his diary—"V.n.w.," "b.n.," "V.sl.h."—and all the crises "Virginia not well," "bad night," "Virginia slight headache" horrendously implied, for the simple reason that it was worth it to him. It was worth it because she was a genius; it was worth it because she was a Stephen.

The power and allure of the Stephen world lay not in its distance from the Jews of Putney—Bloomsbury was anyhow hardly likely to notice the Jews of Putney, and if Virginia did notice, and was even brought to tea there, it was through the abnormal caprice of a freakish fate—but in its illustriousness. Virginia was an illustrious young woman: had she had no gift of her own, the luster of her father's situation, and of the great circle of the aristocracy of intellect into which she was born, would have marked her life. It was additionally marked by her double fortune of genius and insanity, and though her primary fortune—the circle into which she was born—attracted, in the most natural way, other members of that circle, the biting and always original quality of her mind put the less vivid of them off. Her madness was not public knowledge, but her intellect could not be hidden. Her tongue had a fearful and cutting brilliance. "I was surprised to find how friendly she made herself appear," said Walter Lamb, another of Thoby Stephen's Cambridge friends, amazed on one occasion to have been undevoured. He courted her for a time, pallidly, asking frightened questions: "Do you want to have children and love in the normal way?"—as if he expected nothing usual from Virginia Stephen. "I wish," she wrote to Lytton Strachey, after reporting Lamb's visits, "that earth would open her womb and let some new creature out." The courtship was brief and ended in boredom. Lamb's offer was one of at least four proposals of marriage from differing sources; Strachey himself had tendered her one. Since he preferred stableboys to women, a fact they both understood very well, it was a strange mistake. Sydney Waterlow, still another Cambridge name, was a suitor; she regarded him as "amiable." Hilton Young, a childhood friend—cast, says Quentin Bell, from a "smooth and well-proportioned mould"—might have been an appropriate match, mixing politics with poetry and gaining a peerage; he was merely "admirable." Meanwhile, Virginia was thoughtfully flirting with her sister's husband. At twenty-nine, despite all these attentions, she was depressed at being still unmarried; she was despondent, as she would be for the rest of her life, over her childlessness. Not one of those triflings had turned to infatuation, on either side.

It was fortunate. There was lacking, in all these very intelligent men, and indeed in their type in general, the kind of sexual seriousness that is usually disparaged as uxoriousness. It was a trait that Leonard invincibly possessed and that Clive Bell despised as "provincial and puritanical, an enemy to all that was charming and amusing in life." Clive was occupied by a long-standing affair and lived apart from Vanessa, who, at various times, lived with Roger Fry and with Duncan Grant—who was (so closely was this group tied) Lytton Strachey's cousin, and who may have been (so Quentin Bell allows us to conjecture) the father of Quentin's sister, Angelica. Vanessa typed and distributed copies of Lytton Strachey's indecent verse; once at a party she did a topless dance; it was legendary that she had at another party fornicated with Maynard Keynes "*coram publico*"—the whole room looking on. It may have been in honor of these last two occasions that Virginia Woolf, according to Quentin Bell, pronounced human nature to have been "changed in or about December 1910."

It was not a change Leonard Woolf approved of. Four years after this crucial date in human history he published a novel critical of "unnatural cultured persons" given to "wild exaggerated talk" and frivolous behavior; it was clearly an assault on Vanessa and Clive Bell and their circle. The novel, called *The Wise Virgins*, was about *not* marrying Virginia. Instead the hero is forced to marry a Putney girl, and lives unhappily ever after—only because, having been infected with Bloomsbury's licentious notions, he has carelessly gotten her with child. The fictional Leonard loses the heroine who represents Virginia, and is doomed to the drabness of Putney; in the one act he both deplores Bloomsbury and laments his deprivation of it. The real Leonard tried to pick his way between these soul-cracking contradictions. He meant to have the high excitement of Bloomsbury—and certainly "frivolity" contributed to Bloomsbury's dash and éclat—without the frivolity itself. He meant to be master of the full brilliant breadth of all that worldliness, and at the same time of the more sober and limiting range of his native seriousness.

That he coveted the one while requiring the other was—certainly in her biographer's eyes—the salvation of Virginia. No one else in that milieu could have survived—surely not as husband—her illnesses. Roger Fry, for instance, put his own mad wife away and went to live with Vanessa. As for Lamb, Waterlow, Young—viewed in the light of what Virginia Woolf's insanity extracted from her caretaker, their possibilities wither. Of all her potential husbands, only Leonard Woolf emerged as fit. And the opposite too can be said: of Bloomsbury's potential wives, only Virginia emerged as fit for Leonard. He was fit for her because her madness, especially in combination with her innovative genius, demanded the most grave, minutely persevering and attentive service. She was fit for him not simply because she represented Bloomsbury in its most resplendent flowering of originality and luminousness; so, after all, did Vanessa, an accomplished painter active with other painters in the revolutionary vitality of the Post-Impressionists. But just as no marriage could survive Vanessa for long, so Leonard married to Vanessa would not have survived Bloomsbury for long. What Leonard needed in Virginia was not so much her genius as her madness. It made possible for him the exercise of the one thing Bloomsbury had no use for: uxoriousness. It allowed him the totality of his seriousness unchecked. It *used* his seriousness, it gave it legitimate occupation, it made it both necessary and awesome. And it made *her* serious. Without the omnipresent threat of disintegration, freed from the oppression of continuous vigil against breakdown, what might Virginia's life have been? The flirtation with Clive hints at it: she might have lived, at least outwardly, like Vanessa. It was his wife's insanity, in short, that made tenable the permanent—the secure—presence in Bloomsbury of Leonard himself. Her madness fed his genius for responsibility; it became for him a corridor of access to her genius. The spirit of Bloomsbury was not Leonard's, his temperament was against it—Bloomsbury could have done without him. So could a sane Virginia.

The whole question of Virginia's sexuality now came into Leonard's hands. And here too he was curiously ambivalent. The honeymoon was not a success; they consulted Vanessa, Vanessa the sexual creature—when had she had her first orgasm? Vanessa could not remember. "No doubt," she reflected, "I sympathised with such things if I didn't have them from the time I was 2." "Why do you think people make such a fuss about marriage & copulation?" Virginia was writing just then; " . . . certainly I find the climax immensely exaggerated." Vanessa and Leonard put their heads together over it. Vanessa said she believed Virginia "never had understood or sympathised with sexual passion in men"; this news, she thought, "consoled" Leonard. For further consolation the two of them rehearsed (and this was before England had become properly aware of Freud) Virginia's childhood trauma inflicted by her elder step-brother George Duckworth, who had, under cover of big-brotherly affection, repeatedly entered the nursery at night for intimate fondlings, the nature of which Virginia then hardly comprehended; she knew only that he frightened her and that she despised him. Apparently this explanation satisfied Leonard—the "consolation" worked—if rather too quickly; the ability to adjust speedily to disappointment is a good and useful trait in a colonial officer, less so in a husband. It does not contradict the uxorious temperament, however, and certainly not the nursing enterprise: a wife who is seen to be frigid as well as mad is simply taken for that much sicker. But too ready a reconcilement to bad news is also a kind of abandonment, and Leonard seems very early to have relinquished, or allowed Virginia to relinquish, the sexual gratifications of marriage. All the stranger since he repeatedly speaks of himself as "lustful." And he is not known to have had so much as a dalliance during his marriage.

On the other hand, Quentin Bell suggests—a little coyly, as if only blamelessly hinting—that Virginia Woolf's erotic direction was perhaps toward women rather than men. The "perhaps" is crucial: the index to the first volume lists "passion for Madge Vaughan," "passion for Violet Dickinson," but the corresponding textual passages are all projections from the most ordinary sort of data. Madge Vaughan was a cousin by marriage whom Virginia knew from the age of seven; at sixteen she adored her still, and once stood in the house paralyzed by rapture, thinking, "Madge is here; at this moment she is actually under this roof"—an emotion, she once said, that she never equaled afterward. Many emotions at sixteen are never equaled afterward. Of Virginia's intense letter-writing to Violet Dickinson—a friend of her dead half-sister—Quentin Bell says: " . . . it is clear to the modern reader, though it was not at all clear to Virginia, that she was in love and that her love was returned." What is even clearer is that it is possible to be too "modern," if that is what enables one to read a sensual character into every exuberant or sympathetic friendship between women. Vita Sackville-West, of course, whom Virginia Woolf knew when both writers were already celebrated, was an established sapphist, and was plainly in pursuit of Virginia. Virginia, she wrote, "dislikes the quality of masculinity," but that was the view of one with a vested interest in believing it. As for Virginia, she "felt," according to her biographer, "as a lover feels—she desponded when she fancied herself neglected, despaired when Vita was away, waited anxiously for letters, needed Vita's company and lived in that strange mixture of elation and despair which lovers—and one would have supposed only lovers—can experience." But all this is Quentin Bell. Virginia herself, reporting a three-day visit from Sackville-West, appears erotically detached: "These Sapphists *love* women; friendship is never untinged with amorosity . . . I like her and being with her and the splendour—she shines in the grocer's shop . . . with a candle lit radiance." She acknowledged what she readily called Vita's "glamour," but the phrase "these Sapphists" is too mocking to be lover's language. And she was quick to criticize Vita (who was married to Harold Nicolson) as a mother: ". . . she is a little cold and off-hand with her boys." Virginia Woolf's biographer nevertheless supposes—he admits all this is conjecture—"some caressing, some bedding together." Still, in the heart of this love, if it was love, was the ultimate withdrawal: "In brain and insight," Virginia remarked in her diary, "she is not as highly organised as I am." Vita was splendid but "not reflective." She wrote "with a pen of brass." And: "I have no enormous opinion of her poetry." Considering all of which, Quentin Bell notes persuasively that "she could not really love without feeling that she was in the presence of a superior intellect." Sackville-West, for her part, insisted that not only did Virginia not like the quality of masculinity, but also the "possessiveness and love of domination in men."

Yet Leonard Woolf dominated Virginia Woolf overwhelmingly—nor did she resist—not so much because his braininess impressed her (his straightforwardly thumping writing style must have claimed her loyalty more than her admiration), but because he possessed her in the manner of —it must be said again—a strong-minded nurse with obsessive jurisdiction over a willful patient. The issue of Virginia Woolf's tentative or potential lesbianism becomes reduced, at this point, to the merest footnote of possibility. Sackville-West called her "inviolable"; and the fact is she was conventionally married, and had conventional expectations of marriage. She wanted children. For a wedding present Violet Dickinson sent her a cradle. "My baby shall sleep in [it]," she said at thirty. But it stood empty, and she felt, all her life, the ache of the irretrievable. "I don't like the physicalness of having children of my own," she wrote at forty-five, recording how "the little creatures"—Vanessa's children—"moved my infinitely sentimental throat." But then, with a lurch of candor: "I can dramatise myself a parent, it is true. And perhaps I have killed the feeling instinctively; or perhaps nature does." Two years after declaring the feeling killed, during a dinner party full of worldly conversation with the Webbs and assorted eminences, she found herself thinking: "L. and myself . . . the pathos, the symbolical quality of the childless couple."

The feeling was not killed; it had a remarkable durability. There is no record of her response to the original decision not to have children. That decision was Leonard's, and it was "medical." He consulted three or four people variously qualified, including Vanessa's doctor and the nurse who ran the home to which Virginia was sent when most dangerously disturbed (and to whom, according to Bell, Leonard ascribed "an unconscious but violent homosexual passion for Virginia"—which would, one imagines, make one wonder about the disinterestedness of her advice). Leonard also requested the opinion of Dr. George Savage, Virginia's regular physician, whom he disliked, and was heartily urged to have babies; soon after we find him no longer in consultation with Dr. Savage. Bell tells us that "in the end Leonard decided and persuaded Virginia to agree that, although they both wanted children, it would be too dangerous for her to have them." The "too dangerous" is left unexplained; we do not even know Leonard's ostensible reason. Did he think she could not withstand pregnancy and delivery? She was neither especially frail nor without energy, and was a zealous walker, eight miles at a time, over both London and countryside; she hefted piles of books and packed them for the Hogarth Press; she had no organic impediments. Did he believe she could not have borne the duties of rearing? But in that class there was no household without its nanny (Vanessa had two), and just as she never had to do a housekeeping chore (she never laid a fire, or made a bed, or washed a sock), she need not have been obliged to take physical care of a child. Did he, then, fear an inherited trait—diseased offspring? Or did he intend to protect the phantom child from distress by preventing its birth into a baleful household? Or did he mean, out of some curious notion of intellectual purity, not to divide the strength of Virginia's available sanity, to preserve her undistracted for her art?

Whatever the reason, and to spare her—or himself—what pains we can only guess at, she was in this second instance released from "normality." Normality is catch-as-catch-can. Leonard, in his deliberateness, in his responsibility, was more serious than that, and surrendered her to a program of omissions. She would be spared the tribulations both of the conjugal bed and of childbed. She need not learn ease in the one; she need not, no, must not, venture into the other. In forbidding Virginia maternity, Leonard abandoned her to an unparalleled and unslakable envy. Her diary again and again records the pangs she felt after visits with Vanessa's little sons—pangs, defenses, justifications: she suffered. Nor was it a social suffering—she did not feel deprived of children because she was expected to. The name

"Virginia Woolf" very soon acquired the same resonance for her contemporaries ("this celebrity business is quite chronic," she wrote) as it has for us—after which she was expected to be only Virginia Woolf. She learned, after a while, to be only that (which did not, however, prevent her from being an adored and delightful aunt), and to mock at Vanessa's mothering, and to call it obsessive and excessive. She suffered the envy of the childless for the fruitful, precisely this, and nothing societally imposed; and she even learned to transmute maternal envy into a more manageable variety—literary begrudging. This was directed at Vanessa's second son, Julian Bell, killed in the Spanish Civil War, toward whose literary ambitions Virginia Woolf was always ungenerous, together with Leonard; a collection of Julian's essays, prepared after his death, Leonard dubbed "Vanessa's necrophily." Vanessa-envy moved on into the second generation. It was at bottom a rivalry of creatureliness, in which Virginia was always the loser. Vanessa was on the side of "normality," the placid mother of three, enjoying all the traditional bourgeois consolations; she was often referred to as a madonna; and at the same time she was a thorough-going bohemian. Virginia was anything but placid, yet lived a sober sensible domestic life in a marriage stable beyond imagining, with no trace of bohemianism. Vanessa the bohemian madonna had the best of both hearth-life and free life. Virginia was barred from both.

Without the authoritative domestic role maternity would have supplied, with no one in the household dependent on her (for years she quarreled with her maid on equal or inferior terms), and finding herself always—as potential patient—in submission, Virginia Woolf was by degrees nudged into a position of severe dependency. It took odd forms: Leonard not only prescribed milk at eleven in the morning, but also topics for conversation in the evening. Lytton Strachey's sister-in-law recalls how among friends Leonard would work up the "backbone" of a subject "and then be happy to let [Virginia] ornament it if she wanted to." And he gave her pocket money every week. Her niece Angelica reports that "Leonard kept Virginia on very short purse-strings," which she exercised through the pleasures of buying "coloured string and sealing-wax, notebooks and pencils." When she came to the end of writing a book, she trembled until Leonard read it and gave his approval. William Plomer remembers how Leonard would grow alarmed if, watching Virginia closely, he saw her laugh a little too convulsively. And once she absent-mindedly began to flick bits of meat off her dinner plate; Leonard hushed the company and led her away.*

—All of which has given Leonard his reputation for saintliness. A saint who successively secures acquiescence to frigidity, childlessness, dependency? Perhaps; probably; of course. These are, after all, conventual vows—celibacy, barrenness, obedience. But Leonard Woolf was a socialist, not an ascetic; he had a practical political intelligence; he was the author of books called *Empire and Commerce in Africa* and *Socialism and Co-operation*; he ran the Hogarth Press like a good businessman; at the same time he edited a monthly periodical, *The International Review*; he was literary editor of *The Nation*. He had exactly the kind of commonsensical temperament that scorns, and is repelled by, religious excess. And of Virginia he made a shrine; of himself, a monk. On the day of her death Virginia walked out of the house down to the river Ouse and drowned herself; not for nothing was that house called Monk's House. The letter she

* Joan Russell Noble, ed., *Recollections of Virginia Woolf by Her Contemporaries* (William Morrow & Company, Inc., 1972).

left for Leonard was like almost every other suicide note, horribly banal, not a writer's letter at all, and rich with guilt—"I feel certain I am going mad again. I feel we can't go through another of those terrible times . . . I can't go on spoiling your life any longer." To Vanessa she wrote, "All I want to say is that Leonard has been so astonishingly good, every day, always; I can't imagine that anyone could have done more for me than he has . . . I feel he has so much to do that he will go on, better without me . . ."

Saints make guilt—especially when they impose monkish values; there is nothing new in that. And it was the monk as well as her madness she was fleeing when she walked into the Ouse, though it was the saint she praised. "I don't think two people could have been happier than we have been," the note to Leonard ended. A tragic happiness—such a thing is possible: cheerful invalids are a commonplace, and occasionally one hears of happy inmates. A saintly monk, a monkish nurse? All can be taken together, and all are true together. But the drive toward monkishness was in Leonard. What was natural for himself he prescribed for Virginia, and to one end only: to prevent her ongoing nervous crises from reaching their extreme state; to keep her sane. And to keep her sane was, ultimately, to keep her writing. It is reasonable to imagine that without Leonard Woolf there would have been very little of that corpus the name Virginia Woolf calls to mind—there would have been no *Mrs. Dalloway*, no *To the Lighthouse*, no *The Waves*, no *Common Reader*. And it may be that even the word Bloomsbury—the redolence, the signal—would not have survived, since she was its center. "She would not have been the symbol" of Bloomsbury, T. S. Eliot said, "if she had not been the maintainer of it." For Bloomsbury as an intellectual "period" to have escaped oblivion, there had to be at least one major literary voice to carry it beyond datedness. That voice was hers.

The effort to keep her sane was mammoth. Why did Leonard think it was worth it? The question, put here for the second time, remains callous but inevitable. Surely it would have been relieving at last (and perhaps to both of them) to let her slide away into those rantings, delusions, hallucinations; she might or might not have returned on her own. It is even possible that the nursing was incidental, and that she recovered each time because she still had the capacity to recover. But often enough Leonard—who knew the early symptoms intimately—was able to prevent her from going under; each pulling-back from that brink of dementia gained her another few months of literary work. Again and again he pulled her back. It required cajolery, cunning, mastery, agility, suspiciousness, patience, spoon-feeding, and an overwhelming sensitiveness to every flicker of her mood. Obviously it drained him; obviously he must have been tempted now and then to let it all go and give up. Almost anyone else would have. Why did he not? Again the answer must be manifold. Because she was his wife; because she was the beloved one to whom he had written during their courtship, "You don't know what a wave of happiness comes over me when I see you smile";* because his conscience obliged him to; because she suffered; because—this before much else—it was in his nature to succor suffering. And also: because of her gift; because of her genius; for the sake of literature; because she was unique. And because she had been a Miss Stephen; because she was Thoby Stephen's sister; because she was a daughter of Leslie Stephen; because

* From an unpublished letter in the Berg Collection. Quoted in *The New York Times*, June 14, 1973.

she was, like Leonard's vision of Cambridge itself, "compounded of . . . the atmosphere of long years of history and great traditions and famous names [and] a profoundly civilized life"; because she was Bloomsbury; because she was England.

For her sake, for art's sake, for his own sake. Perhaps above all for his own sake. In her he had married a kind of escutcheon; she represented the finest grain of the finest stratum in England. What he shored up against disintegration was the life he had gained, a birthright he paid for by spooning porridge between Virginia Woolf's resisting lips.

Proust is right to tell us to go to a writer's books, not to his loyalties. Wherever Leonard Woolf is, there Virginia Woolf is not. The more Leonard recedes or is not present, the more Virginia appears in force. Consequently, Quentin Bells' biography—the subversive strength of which is Leonard—demands an antidote. The antidote is, of course, in the form of a reminder—that Virginia Woolf was a woman of letters as well as a patient; that she did not always succumb but instead could be an original fantasist and fashioner of an unaccustomed way of seeing; that the dependency coincided with a vigorous intellectual autonomy; that together with the natural subordination of the incapacitated she possessed the secret confidence of the innovator.

Seen through Leonard's eyes, she is, in effect, always on the verge of lunacy. "I am quite sure," he tells us in his autobiography, "that Virginia's genius was closely connected with what manifested itself as mental instability and insanity. The creative imagination in her novels, her ability to 'leave the ground' in conversation, and the voluble delusions of the breakdown all came from the same place in her mind—she 'stumbled after her own voice' and followed 'the voices that fly ahead.'" At the same time her refusal to eat was associated with guilt—she talked of her "faults"—and Leonard insists that "she remained all through her illness, even when most insane, terribly sane in three-quarters of her mind. The point is that her insanity was in her premises, in her beliefs. She believed, for instance, that she was not ill . . ."

Seen through the books, she is never "ill," never lunatic. Whether it was mental instability or a clear-sighted program of experiment in the shape of the novel that unhinged her prose from the conventional margins that had gone before is a question not worth speculating over. Leonard said that when mad she heard the birds sing in Greek. The novels are not like that: it is not the data that are altered, but the sequence of things. When Virginia Woolf assaulted the "old" fiction in her famous *Mr. Bennett and Mrs. Brown*, she thought she was recommending getting rid of the habit of data; she thought this was to be her fictive platform. But when she grappled with her own inventions, she introduced as much data as possible and strained to express it all under the pressure of a tremendous simultaneity. What she was getting rid of was consecutiveness; precisely the habit of premises. If clinging to premises was the sanity of her insanity, then the intent of her fiction was not an extension of her madness, as Leonard claimed, but its calculated opposite. The poetry of her prose may have been like the elusive poetry of her dementia, but its steadfast design was not. "The design," she wrote of *Mrs. Dalloway*, "is so queer and so masterful"; elated, she saw ahead. She was an artist; she schemed, and not through random contractions or inflations of madness, but through the usual methods of art: inspired intellection, the breaking down of expectation into luminous segments of shock.

A simpler way of saying all this is that what she achieved as a stylist cannot really be explained through linking it with madness. The diaries give glimpses of rationalized prefigurations; a letter from Vanessa suggests moths, which metamorphosed into *The Moths*, which became *The Waves*. She knew her destination months before she arrived; she was in control of her work, she did what she meant to do. If the novels are too imaginatively astonishing to be persuasive on this point, the essays will convince. They are read too little, and not one of them is conceptually stale, or worn in any other way. In them the birds do not sing in Greek either, but the Greek—the sign of a masterly nineteenth-century literary education—shows like a spine. In the essays the control of brilliant minutiae is total—historical and literary figures, the particulars of biography, society, nationality, geography. She is a courier for the past. In Volume III of the *Collected Essays*, for instance, the range is from Chaucer through Montaigne through some Elizabethans major and minor, through Swift and Sterne and Lord Chesterfield, Fanny Burney and Cowper. She was interested also in the lives of women, especially writers. She studies Sara Coleridge, the poet's daughter; Harriette Wilson, the mistress of the Earl of Craven; Dr. Johnson's Mrs. Thrale; and Dorothy Osborne, a talented letter-writer of the seventeenth century. The language and scope of the essays astound. If they are "impressionistic," they are not self-indulgent; they put history before sensibility. When they are ironic, it is the kind of irony that enlarges the discriminatory faculty and does not serve the cynical temper. They mean to interpret other lives by the annihilation of the crack of time: they are after what the novels are after, a compression of then and now into the simultaneity of a singular recognition and a single comprehension. They mean to make every generation, and every instant, contemporaneous with every other generation and instant. And yet—it does not contradict—they are, taken all together, the English Essay incarnate.

The autonomous authority of the fiction, the more public authority of the essays, are the antidotes to Bell's Woolf, to Leonard's Virginia. But there is a third antidote implicit in the whole of the work, and in the drive behind the work, and that is Virginia Woolf's feminism. It ought to be said at once that it was what can now be called "classical" feminism. The latter-day choice of Virginia Woolf, on the style of Sylvia Plath, as a current women's-movement avatar is inapposite and mistaken. Classical feminism is inimical to certain developing strands of "liberation." Where feminism repudiates the conceit of the "gentler sex," liberation has come to reaffirm it. Where feminism asserts a claim on the larger world, liberation shifts to separatism. Where feminism scoffs at the plaint of "sisters under the skin," and maintains individuality of condition and temperament, liberation reinstates sisterhood and sameness. Where feminism shuns self-preoccupation, liberation experiments with self-examination, both psychic and medical. Classical feminism as represented by Virginia Woolf meant one thing only: access to the great world of thinking, being, and doing. The notion of "male" and "female" states of intellect and feeling, hence of prose, ultimately of culture, would have been the occasion of a satiric turn for Virginia Woolf; so would the idea of a politics of sex. Clive Bell reports that she licked envelopes once or twice for the Adult Suffrage League, but that she "made merciless fun of the flag-waving fanaticism" of the activists. She was not political—or, perhaps, just political enough, as when Chekhov notes that "writers should engage themselves in politics only enough to protect themselves from politics." Though one of her themes was women in history (several of her themes, rather; she took her women one by one, not as a race, species, or nation), presumably she would have mocked at the invention of a "history of women"—what she cared for, as *A Room of One's Own* both lucidly and passionately lays out, was access to a unitary culture. Indeed, *Orlando* is the metaphorical expression of this idea. History as a record of division or exclusion was precisely what she set herself against: the Cambridge of her youth kept women out, and all her life she preserved her resentment by pronouncing herself undereducated. She studied at home, Greek with Janet Case, literature and mathematics with her father, and as a result was left to count on her fingers forever—but for people who grow up counting on their fingers, even a Cambridge education cannot do much. Nevertheless she despised what nowadays is termed "affirmative action," granting places in institutions as a kind of group reparation; she thought it offensive to her own earned prestige, and once took revenge on the notion. In 1935 Forster, a member of the Committee of the London Library, informed her that a debate was under way concerning the admission of women members. No women were admitted. Six years later Virginia Woolf was invited to serve; she said she would not be a "sop"—she ought to have been invited years earlier, on the same terms as Forster, as a writer; not in 1941, when she was already fifty-nine, as a woman.

Nor will she do as martyr. Although Cambridge was closed to her, literary journalism was not; although she complains of being chased off an Oxbridge lawn forbidden to the feet of women, no one ever chased her off a page. Almost immediately she began to write for the *Times Literary Supplement* and for *Cornhill*; she was then twenty-two.

She was, of course, Leslie Stephen's daughter, and it is doubtful whether any other young writer, male or female, could have started off so auspiciously: still, we speak here not of "connections" but of experience. At about the same time she was summoned to teach at Morley, a workers' college for men and women. One of her reports survives, and Quentin Bell includes it as an appendix. "My four women," she writes, "can hear eight lectures on the French Revolution if they wish to continue their historical learning"—and these were working-class women, in 1905. By 1928, women had the vote, and full access to universities, the liberal professions, and the civil service. As for Virginia Woolf, in both instances, as writer and teacher, she was solicited—and this cannot be, after all, only because she was Leslie Stephen's daughter. She could use on the spot only her own gifts, not the rumor of her father's. Once she determined to ignore what Bell calls the "matrimonial market" of upper-class partying, into which for a time her stepbrother George dragooned her, she was freed to her profession. It was not true then, it is not true now, that a sublime and serious pen can be circumscribed.

Virginia Woolf was a practitioner of her profession from an early age; she was not deprived of an education, rather of a particular college; she grew rich and distinguished; she developed her art on her own line, according to her own sensibilities, and was acclaimed for it; though insane, she was never incarcerated. She was an elitist, and must be understood as such. What she suffered from, aside from the abysses of depression which characterized her disease, was not anything like the condition of martyrdom—unless language has become so flaccid that being on occasion patronized begins to equal death for the sake of an ideal. What she suffered from really was only the minor inflammations of the literary temperament. And she was not often patronized: her fame encouraged her to patronize others. She could be unkind, she could be spiteful, she could envy—her friendship with Katherine Mansfield was always unsure, being founded on rivalry. Mansfield and her husband, the journalist John Middleton Murry, "work in my flesh," Virginia Woolf wrote, "after the manner of the jigger insect. It's annoying, indeed degrading, to have these bitternesses." She was bitter also about James Joyce; she thought him, says Bell, guilty of "atrocities." Her diary speaks of "the damned egotistical self; which ruins Joyce," and she saw *Ulysses* as "insistent, raw, striking and ultimately nauseating." But she knew Joyce to be moving in the same direction as herself; it was a race that, despite her certainty of his faults, he might win. By the time of her death she must have understood that he *had* won. Still, to be outrun in fame is no martyrdom. And her own fame was and is in no danger, though, unlike Joyce, she is not taken as a fact of nature. Virginia Woolf's reputation in the fifty and more years since her death deepens; she becomes easier to read, more complex to consider.

To Charlotte Brontë, born sixty-six years before Virginia Woolf, Robert Southey, then Poet Laureate, had written, "Literature cannot be the business of a woman's life, and it ought not to be." No one addressed Virginia Woolf of Bloomsbury in this fashion; she was sought out by disciples, editors, litterateurs; in the end Oxford and Cambridge asked her to lecture before their women's colleges. If the issue of martyrdom is inappropriate (implying as it does that a woman who commits suicide is by definition a martyr), what of heroism? Virginia Woolf's death was or was not heroic, depending on one's view of suicide by drowning. The case for Leonard's heroism is more clear-cut: a saint is noble on behalf of others, a hero on behalf of himself. But if Virginia Woolf is to be seen as a heroine, it must be in those modes outside the manner of her death and even the manner of her life as a patient in the house.

If she is to be seen as a heroine, it must be in the conjuring of yet another of those Bloomsbury photographs—this time one that does not exist. The picture is of a woman sitting in an old chair holding a writing board; the point of her pen touches a half-filled page. To gaze at her bibliography is, in a way, to conjure this picture that does not exist—hour after hour, year after year, a life's accumulation of stupendous visionary toil. A writer's heroism is in the act of writing; not in the finished work, but in the work as it goes.

Vanessa's son gives us no heroine: only this stubborn and sometimes querulous self-starving madwoman, with so stoic, so heroic, a male nurse. And when she runs away from him to swallow the Ouse, the heroism of both of them comes to an end.

Diary-Keeping

AGAIN THESE LYRICAL, allusive, and alluring names!* Lytton, Carrington, Clive, Roger, Vanessa, Duncan, Leonard, Maynard, Gertler, Ka, Kot, Janet, Aldous, Bob, Arnold, Ottoline, Morgan, Logan, Katherine, Desmond, Murry, Nick, Saxon, Alix . . . Miniaturized by the Cyclops eye of hindsight, with the gold dust shaken out of them, one or two have broken out of legend to survive—E. M. Forster solidly and on his own, also the economist Keynes; the rest shakily and in shadow, reduced to "period" names: the polemicist Toynbee rapidly growing quaint, Aldous Huxley's novels long ago turned problematical, Katherine Mansfield fallen even out of the anthologies, Sidney and Beatrice Webb fixed in Fabian caricature. The "men of letters"—Robert Trevelyan, John Middleton Murry, Desmond MacCarthy, Logan Pearsall Smith: how far away and small they now seem! And the painters, Vanessa Bell, Duncan Grant, Mark Gertler, and the art critics, Clive Bell and Roger Fry—lost molecules in the antiquity of modernism.

* *The Diary of Virginia Woolf, Volume One: 1915-1919*, edited by Anne Olivier Bell, Introduction by Quentin Bell, Harcourt Brace Jovanovich, 1977.

And Saxon Sydney-Turner? Less than a molecule; a civil servant in the British Treasury. Lytton Strachey? A minor psychological historian given to phrasing both fustian and trite; he had his little vogue. Leonard Woolf? An ungainly writer and social reformer active in anticolonial causes, an early supporter of the League of Nations—who thinks of him as anything other than Virginia Woolf's husband?

Merited fame, when it outlives its native generation (we may call this genius if we wish), is the real Midas touch. "Bloomsbury" means Virginia Woolf and her satellites. The men and women she breathed on shine with her gold. She did not know she was their sun, they did not know they were her satellites; but it is easy now, scores of years after they all seemed to glitter together, to tell the radiance from the penumbra. Even now—she is still ascending—she is not a genius to everyone; Lionel Trilling dismissed her, probably for her purported "subjectivity," and the women's movement claims but distorts her, for the same reason. Her genius does no one any good, has no social force or perspective, and—like most literature—is not needed: it is the intolerant genius of riddle. But not the sort of riddle-of-the-absurd that is left there, amorphous and mystical on the page. She will not fail to deliver. Her riddles are all concretely and dazzlingly solved by organization into ingenious portraiture. Hers is a beaklike and unifying imagination, impatient (unlike Forster's) with muddle or puzzle; she will seize any loose flying cloth and make it over for a Jolly Roger. Identity discovered in flux is all. So the mystery of her own mother was deciphered through Mrs. Ramsay in *To the Lighthouse*; and so the stippled occasions of daily life are drawn into coherency through the device of a secret diary.

This first volume, covering the years of the Great War,

tells of shortages and moonlit air raids, of strikes and huddling in cellars, of frustrations with servants and in-laws; it is also the period of the founding of the Hogarth Press, the acquisition of Monk's House, and the publication of Virginia Woolf's earliest novels, *The Voyage Out* and *Night and Day*; it is the time when many of the remarkable essays that became *The Common Reader* were beaten out under the guise of journalism written against a deadline. All these matters amaze because they are familiar; we know them from a dozen other sources; we are already in possession of Virginia Woolf, after all—and yet how shocking to peer through her window at last, how astounding to hear her confirm everything in her own voice! A diary is a time machine; it puts us not simply on the doorstep but inside the mind, and yields to curiosity its ultimate consummation.

Yet Virginia Woolf's diary is not (to stumble on that perilous word again) "subjective." There are few psychological surprises. A Freudianly-inclined reader might be interested in the juxtaposition, in a single paragraph, of a memory of a childhood fear of "being shut in"; zoo animals that "grunt and growl"; and a visit to an "invalid" just emerged from a healthy childbirth. But there is no intent to record moods. Learning that Lady Ottoline Morrell keeps a diary, Virginia notes with light contempt that it is "devoted however to her 'inner life'; which made me reflect that I haven't an inner life." By and large, this is an accurate enough description of her own diary-keeping. It eschews "feelings"; it is dense with happenings: visits, party-goings, walks, scenery and season, political meetings, concerts, conversations; the purchase of a wristwatch, a pen (the dipping kind), a glass bottle, new spectacles. It is built not on sensibility but on the *pointillisme* of chronicle.

Chronicle is the foundation, but the structure is all explicit portraiture, and each portrait is fixed, final, locked into its varnish forever. If she begins in murk, with hints and signs, she carries her inquisitiveness into graphic intelligibility.

Of Robert Trevelyan, poet and classicist:

> . . . he manages to be more malevolent than anyone I know, under a cover of extreme good nature. He reminds me of the man with the pointed stick, who picks up scraps of paper. So Bob collects every scrap of gossip within reach.

Of Beatrice Webb:

> She has no welcome for one's individuality . . . Marriage [she said] was necessary as a waste pipe for emotion, as a security in old age . . . & as a help to work. We were entangled at the gates of the level crossing when she remarked, "Yes, I daresay an old family servant would do as well."

Of Sidney Webb:

> . . . one could even commit the impropriety of liking him personally, which one can hardly do in the case of Mrs. Webb.

Of Lytton Strachey's fame:

> How did he do it, how is he so distinct & unmistakable if he lacks originality & the rest? Is there any reputable escape from this impasse in saying that he is a great deal better than his books?

Of the painter Mark Gertler:

> He is a resolute young man; & if good pictures can be made by willing them to be good, he may do wonders. No base motive could have its way with him; & for this reason I haven't great faith in him. Its too moral and intellectual an affair . . . I advised him, for arts sake, to keep sane; to grasp, & not exaggerate, & put sheets of glass between him & his matter . . . But he can think pianola music equal to hand made, since it shows the form, & the touch & the expression are nothing.

Of Lytton's brother James Strachey (whom Freud later analyzed):

> He has all the right books, neatly ranged, but not interesting in the least—not, I mean, all lusty & queer like a writer's books.

They parade by, these portraits, by the dozens, then by the hundreds; they cascade and grow orchestral; the diary, as she acknowledges, begins to comprehend its own meaning. The portraits are extraordinary not only for the power of their penetration, but for language as strong and as flexible and as spontaneous as that of any of the English masters, including Dickens. And they have the gift of seeing through the flummery of their moment: though Lytton Strachey is a more significant friend to the style of Virginia Woolf's imagination than Leonard Woolf (whose comings and goings to reformers' meetings crisscross these pages), though they converse in the bliss of perfect rapport, she judges him with the dispassion of posterity. Nearly all the portraits have this singular contemporary balance—contemporary, that is, with *us*.

But she is also malicious in the way of the class she was born into. She calls the common people "animals," "a tepid mass of flesh scarcely organized into human life." Unlike the majority of her class, she mocked the war; but the celebrations that mark its end she ridicules as "a servants peace." Of famine following massacre: "I laughed to myself over the quantities of Armenians. How can one mind whether they number 4,000 or 4,000,000? The feat is beyond me." She has no piety or patriotism, but retains the Christian bias of the one, and the Imperial bias of the other. "I do not like the Jewish voice; I do not like the Jewish laugh," she writes of Leonard's sister, and the two visiting Ceylonese with whom Leonard is forming committees on colonial oppression she refers to as "persistent darkies." In all these instances there may be the little devil's-tail flick of self-derision; still, the spite stands. Though hospitality is constant, her sister Vanessa is not much on her mind, but she misses no opportunity to disparage Leonard's family; and perhaps, one discovers, even Leonard himself. In an ominous sentence seemingly directed at a speech by the socialist theosophist Annie Besant, but more dangerously at the principled Leonard, she comments, "It seems to me more & more clear that the only honest people are the artists, & that these social reformers & philanthropists get so out of hand, & harbour so many discreditable desires under the guise of loving their kind, that in the end there's more to find fault with in them than in us." In all Leonard's plethora of meeting after meeting, there is no way that "us" can be made to include Virginia Woolf's husband.

Yet, for all that, the social distaste and the portraits—those astonishing projections into the long view—are not what the diary is about, or for. Why does she keep it, and keep it up? How explain the compulsion to write nearly every day, from New Year's Day 1915 until the onset of mental illness in February; then again from August 1917 unceasingly until December 1919? To write through bombings, flu, strikes, Leonard's malaria, changes of residence (the Woolfs voyaged continually between London and the country), house-buying, hand-printing? Above all, to write while writing? It was a discipline she admits to wanting to be only a pleasure, but clearly she needed to do it. The reasons she gives are various: to interpret the thirty-seven-year-old Virginia to the "old Virginia" of fifty; or "my belief that the habit of writing thus for my own eye only is good practice" for writing well; and sometimes one sees how it is a "therapy journal" for writer's depression, in which the terror of self-doubt is ministered to again and again by the furious craving for praise. Now and then a future reader twinkles in these private pages—why else would she meticulously speak of "my father Sir Leslie," and is it for herself she notes that "almost always the afternoon is dry in England"? On occasion the diary serves as a pouch for leakings of unwritten essays—energetic readings of Byron and Milton. And of course it is nice to know that Virginia Woolf, catered to by two servants—how easy it was for her to have crowds of friends for dinner and tea and weekends! —once lost her underpants in the street in the middle of winter. (She lets this pass without comment; the sneer comes two entries later, when women get the vote.)

But all these useful reasons, pretexts, needs—her eye sidelong on us, more directly on her own intelligence—are not to the point, and especially do not explain the explosions of portraiture. "I might in the course of time [she tells herself in a meditation on the "kind of form which a diary might attain to"] learn what it is that one can make of this loose, drifting material of life; finding another use for it than the use I put it to, so much more consciously & scrupulously, in fiction." That was April 1919. Two months earlier, she had already made that find, but failed to recognize it. On February 5, adopting the tone of a governess, she scolds, "What a disgraceful lapse! nothing added to my disquisition, & life allowed to waste like a tap left running. Eleven days unrecorded."

Life allowed to waste, and still she did not see what she meant. The following October 7, during a railway strike that "broke in to our life more than the war did," the riddle begins to unravel: "Is it [the diary] worth going on with? . . . I wonder why I do it. Partly, I think, from my old sense of the race of time 'Time's winged chariot hurrying near'— Does it stay it?"

In the end she knew what she meant, and what keeping the diary was for. It was literally a keeping—not for disclosure, but for "staying," for making life stay, for validating breath. Her diary, though it is a chronicle and a narrative, is all the same not intended solely for a "record." A record is a hound padding after life. But a diary is a shoring-up of the ephemeral, evidence that the writer takes up real space in the world. For Virginia Woolf, as these incandescent streams of language show, the life she lived and the people she knew did not become real until they were written down.

Morgan and Maurice

POSSIBLY THE MOST famous sentence in Forster's fiction is the one that comes out of the blue at the start of Chapter Five of *The Longest Journey*: "Gerald died that afternoon." The sentence is there with no preparation whatever—no novelistic "plant," no hidden tracks laid out in advance. Just before the turning of the page we have seen Gerald resplendent in his sexual prime, "with the figure of a Greek athlete and the face of an English one," a football player of no special distinction but the fact of his glorious aliveness. Then, without warning, he is "broken up."

The suddenness of Gerald's death has been commented on almost too often by Forster seminarians; it is, after all, a slap in the reader's face, and must be accounted for. Asked about it in a 1952 interview (it was then forty-five years since the book had first appeared), Forster would only say, "It had to be passed by." An insulting answer. Forster is a gentleman who never insults unintentionally; he also intends to shock, and he never shocks inadvertently. Shock is the nearest he can come to religious truths. If you are reading a Forster story about a vigorous young man and happen, in the most natural way, to forget for just that moment how Death lies in ambush for all of us, Forster will rub your nose in reminders. How dare you forget that Death is by, how dare you forget Significance? Like those medieval monks who kept a skull on their desks, Forster believes in the instructiveness, the salubriousness, of shock. He believes that what is really important comes to us as a shock. And like nature (or like religion bereft of consolation), he withholds, he is unpredictable, he springs, so as to facilitate the shock.

That is in the fiction. His own life seemed not like that. He endured the mildest of bachelor lives, with, seen from the outside, no cataclysms. He was happiest (as adolescents say today, he "found himself") as a Cambridge undergraduate, he touched tenuously on Bloomsbury, he saw Egypt and India (traveling always, whether he intended it or not, as an agent of Empire), and when his mother died returned to Cambridge to live out his days among the undergraduates of King's. He wrote what is called a "civilized" prose, sometimes too slyly decorous, occasionally fastidiously poetic, often enough as direct as a whip. His essays, mainly the later ones, are especially direct: truth-telling, balanced, "humanist"—kind-hearted in a detached way, like, apparently, his personal cordiality. He had charm: a combination of self-importance (in the sense of knowing himself to be the real thing) and shyness. In tidy rooms at King's (the very same College he had first come up to in 1897), Forster in his seventies and eighties received visitors and courtiers with memorable pleasantness, was generous to writers in need of a push (Lampedusa among them), and judiciously wrote himself off as a pre-1914 fossil. Half a century after his last novel the Queen bestowed on him the Order of Merit. Then one day in the summer of 1970 he went to Coventry on a visit and died quietly at ninety-one, among affectionate friends.

That was the life. That none of this was meant to be trusted, not, certainly, to be taken at face value—least of all the harmonious death—suddenly came clear when the British Museum let it be known it was in possession of an unpublished Forster novel*, written in 1913, between the two masterpieces *Howards End* and *A Passage to India*; and that the novel was about homosexual love. Biographically, the late publication of *Maurice* is the precise equivalent of "Gerald died that afternoon." (Trust the fiction, not the life.) It was to be sprung on us in lieu of a homily, and from the grave itself—another audacious slap in the face.

But literary shock, especially when it is designed to be didactic, has a way of finally trivializing. The suddenness of Gerald's death presses so hard for Significance that Significance itself begins to give way, and wilts off into nothing more impressive than a sneer. Forster, prodding the cosmos to do its job of showing us how puny we are, is left holding his little stick—the cosmos has escaped him, it will not oblige. Gerald's death may surprise, but the teaching fails: death qua death is not enough. We must have grief to feel death, and Forster did not give us enough Gerald to grieve over. We were never allowed to know Gerald well, or even to like him a little; he is an unsympathetic minor character, too minor to stand for the abyss. Shock does not yield wisdom on short acquaintance.

Maurice is meant to convey wisdom on longer acquaintance: here is a full-scale history of a homosexual from earliest awakening to puzzlement to temporary joy to frustration to anguish, and at last to sexual success. In *Maurice* it is society Forster prods, not the cosmos; it is one of Forster's few books in which death does not reverberate in

* *Maurice* by E. M. Forster, W. W. Norton & Co., 1971.

any major way. But like the cosmos in *The Longest Journey*, society in *Maurice* eludes Forster's stick. In *Howards End* it did not: he impaled English mores in the house-renting habits of Mr. Wilcox, and wrote of the money-and-property mentality in such a way as to dishevel it permanently. *Howards End* is, along with *Middlemarch* thirty-odd years before, the prototypical English Wisdom novel—wisdom in the category of the-way-things-really-are, the nest of worms exposed below the surface of decency. *Maurice* is even more ambitious: it appears not merely to attack and discredit society, but to outwit it. How? By spite; by spitting in the eye of conventional respectability; by inventing a triumphant outcome against the grain of reality and (then) possibility. "A happy ending was imperative," Forster explained in a message that accompanies the novel in the manner of a suicide note (and is, in fact, styled by him a "Terminal Note"); like a suicide note it represents defense, forethought, revenge—the culmination of extensive fantasizing. "I shouldn't have bothered to write otherwise. I was determined that in fiction anyway two men should fall in love and remain in it for the ever and ever that fiction allows."

The key words are: in fiction. *Maurice*, in short, is a fairy tale. I don't choose this term for the sake of an easy pun, or to take up the line of ribaldry, and certainly not to mock. I choose it because it is the most exact. *Maurice* is not merely an idyll, not merely a fantasy, not merely a parable. It is a classical (though flawed and failed) fairy tale in which the hero is stuck with an ineradicable disability. In the standard fairy tale he may be the youngest of three, or the weakest, or the poorest and most unlikely—in Maurice's instance he is the oddest, and cannot love women. In the prescribed manner he encounters sinister advice and dissembling friends and gets his profoundest wish at the end, winning—as a reward for the wish itself—the hand of his beloved. The essence of a fairy tale is that wishing *does* make it so: the wish achieves its own fulfillment through its very steadfastness of desire. That is why fairy tales, despite their dark tones and the vicissitudes they contain so abundantly, are so obviously akin to daydreams—daydreaming is a sloughing-off of society, not an analysis of it. To wish is not to explain; to wish is not to reform. In real life wishing, divorced from willing, is sterile and begets nothing. Consequently *Maurice* is a disingenuous book, an infantile book, because, while pretending to be about societal injustice, it is really about make-believe, it is about wishing; so it fails even as a tract. Fairy tales, though, are plainly literature; but *Maurice* fails as literature too. In a fairy or folk tale the hero, even when he is a trickster, is a model of purity and sincerity. What is pure and sincere in him is the force of his wish, so much so that his wish and his nature are one. But Maurice as hero has a flaw at the center of him; he is conceived impurely and insincerely.

This impurity Forster himself appears to concede. "In Maurice," the Terminal Note explains further, "I tried to create a character who was completely unlike myself or what I supposed myself to be: someone handsome, healthy, bodily attractive, mentally torpid, not a bad business man and rather a snob. Into this mixture I dropped an ingredient that puzzles him, wakes him up, torments him and finally saves him." The impurity, then, is the ingredient of homosexuality dropped into a man who is otherwise purely Mr. Wilcox, lifted temperamentally intact out of *Howards End*: a born persecutor whom fear of persecution "saves" from the practice of his trait.

But whatever Forster's hope for Maurice was, this is not the sensibility he has rendered. It is impossible to believe in

Maurice as a businessman or a jock (in Cambridge vocabulary, a "blood"). He is always Ricky of *The Longest Journey* (which means he is always Morgan Forster) got up in a grotesque costume—The Sensitive Hero as Callous Philistine—and wearing a wobbly wig. Whenever Maurice is most himself, the prose gives a lurch: it is Forster remembering, with a mindful shudder, to throw in a liter of mental torpidity here, a kilo of investment shrewdness there. But all that is artifice and sham. Forster loves music; Maurice is ignorant of it; consequently Maurice's self-knowledge occurs partly through Tchaikovsky. Forster at school recoiled from games and fell in love with Hellenism; Maurice has "physical pluck" and is an indifferent scholar (his "Greek was vile"); consequently on Prize Day he delivers a Greek Oration. No matter how Forster sidesteps it, Maurice keeps coming out Forster. After a while the absurdity of the effort to coarsen Maurice—to de-Morgan him, so to speak—fatigues; Forster's pointless toil at this impossibility becomes, for the reader, an impatience and an embarrassment. It is embarrassing to watch a writer cover his tracks in the name of exploring them. Purporting to show a hard man turn soft under the pressure of alienation from the general run of society, Forster instead (and without admitting it) shows a soft man turn softer—so soft he slides off into the teleology of the fairy tale. This falsification is the real impurity of the novel. Its protagonist falls apart at the marrow, like a book left outdoors overnight in the rain. *Maurice* cannot hold because Maurice is made of paper and breaks like dough at the first moist lover's squeeze.

One suspects Forster knew this. How could he not? He had already published three nearly perfect minor novels and one extraordinary major one. He had already created the

Schlegels and the Wilcoxes. Written in his own handwriting across the top of the British Museum's typescript of *Maurice*, and put there possibly as late as 1960, were the Delphic words: "Publishable, but is it worth it?" The ambiguity is typical. Is the reference to the homosexual theme—or to the level of craftsmanship? That Forster was distinctly capable of detecting a falling-off from his own standard we know from his account of *Arctic Summer*, a work he abandoned midway because of "fiction-technicalities." Comparing the texture of his unfinished novel with the "density" of *A Passage to India*, he explained, "There must be something, some major object toward which one is to approach . . . What I had in *Arctic Summer* was thinner, a background and color only." If he was able to sense the thinness of one novel and then let it go, why did he preserve *Maurice*, which he must surely have perceived as at least equally thin? In 1960, the date of the Terminal Note, thirty-three years had already passed since Forster's invention (in *Aspects of the Novel*) of the terms "flat" and "round" to describe the differences between characters in novels. A flat character is always predictable; a round character is not. Maurice is neither flat nor round, but something else—a ghost—and Forster must have known it. How could he not? What made him want to hang on to a protagonist so dismally flawed? The answer may be in the "something, some major object toward which one is to approach." In *Maurice* it is painfully easy to see what that major object is: sex, overt and unfudged. Forster preserved the approach but did not arrive. "There is no pornography," the Terminal Note scrupulously reports. So much the worse for Maurice. He is there—he was put to paper neither flat nor round—only for the sake of the sex scenes; and the sex scenes are hardly there at all. Maurice—neither flat nor round—is the ghost of undepicted, inexplicit coitus, of the missing "pornography."

Except for those absent sex scenes—one feels them struggling to be born, and Forster stamping them regretfully out at their earliest gasp—*Maurice* has no reason to be. It is a novel, if one can say such a thing, without a cause. Or, rather, the only genuine cause for it, the force that got it written, was a fresh and potent interest in all those matters that did *not* get written: the caresses in detail, the embraces, the endearments precisely depicted. Instead we are only handed plot. And to be handed plot is, in the case of *Maurice*, to be handed something worn out almost to risibility. It is not that *Maurice* has no plot; it does, and I suppose I am bound to recount a little of it; but it is a plot that Forster has dealt with at least twice before in the two novels of which *Maurice* is the shadow-novel, and, in fact, in what may have been the very first short story he ever wrote.

In all of these—"Albergo Empedocle," *The Longest Journey, A Room with a View*—a poetic but naïve hero (or heroine) falls in love with a woman (or man) who appears at first to be even more sensitive and poetic, but who betrays by turning out to be unable to love with equal tenderness or sincerity. In *The Longest Journey* Ricky, charmed by the ecloguelike scene he witnesses of the "Greek athlete" Gerald kissing Agnes in the dell, marries Agnes and finds instead that he has surrendered his spirit to coldness and cynicism. In *A Room with a View* Lucy, whose poetic nature is expressed in music, becomes engaged to Cecil; Cecil is brilliant, and therefore seems to be in love with art, Leonardo, and Italy, but is in reality "like a Gothic statue," which "implies celibacy, just as a Greek statue implies fruition." "Albergo Empedocle" describes the breakup of an engagement between Mildred, a young woman intellectually immersed in Hellenism, and Harold, who suddenly feels himself to be the reincarnation of a Greek youth. For the moment Mildred is romantically enraptured at the notion. But she ends up thinking her fiancé mad—whereupon he displays his love for another youth, ancient Greek-style. All these tender lovers, genuinely won to the Greek ideal of the body, are betrayed by a capricious and false Hellenism.

Maurice too finds his hard-earned Hellenism betrayed. In the joyfully liberating atmosphere of Cambridge he is introduced to music, Plato, and Clive Durham, a worshiper of Greece and a lapsed Christian. Like the others, they have their day in the dell and become lovers, though mainly sentimentally (Clive "abstained . . . almost from caresses"). Then Clive goes on a pilgrimage to Greece, and there—in Greece; irony!—"becomes normal." He has "turned to women," and enters the life of conventional county society, marrying coldly and growing more and more worldly and opportunistic. Maurice's outlook darkens. He too tries to "become normal." There follow relatively good, though thin, Forsterian scenes with a doctor (who can only say "Rubbish" to the idea of homosexuality) and a hypnotist (who decides the case is hopeless). Then comes the happy ending. Just as Lucy in *A Room with a View* flees from Cecil to marry the Panlike figure of George Emerson, Maurice flees his family, his work, and society altogether, going off to live tenderly ever after with a rough-mannered but loving gamekeeper.

"There is no pornography." In short, a daydream without pictures. But what *Maurice* lacks, and what is necessary to it because it belongs at the heart of its imagining, *is* the pictures, *is* the "pornography"—or what Forster significantly continued to think of as pornography. What surely was not necessary was the reflex of Forster's ineluctable plot —the same story of compulsive attraction and callous faithlessness that he was driven to manipulate again and again, looking for some acceptable means to tell what he *really* wanted to tell about the importance of the body. It was pointless to write a book like *Maurice* unless the body in its exact—not implied, not poeticized—male lineaments could be truly shown. Forster did not show it truly. It is clear enough that he longed to show it truly—he lingers over those blurry passages in which he might have shown it truly, and instead reaches desperately for the expedient of poetry. "And their love scene drew out . . . Something of exquisite beauty arose in the mind of each at last, something unforgettable and eternal, but built of the humblest scraps of speech and from the simplest emotions." And of the flesh. But it is the flesh that Forster omits.

The reason for this omission, it seems to me, is not that in the England of 1913 Forster still did not dare to put it explicitly in (Gide in France had already launched *Corydon*, but that was France), and not even that Forster still belonged mentally to the England of 1897. No. The reason —unlikely though it may appear at first hearing—is that Forster thought homosexuality wrong: naturally wrong, with the sort of naturalness that he did not expect to date. (The Terminal Note admits that *Maurice* "certainly dates" in other respects, and mentions its "half-sovereign tips, pianola-records, norfolk jackets.") But if *Maurice* is a fairy tale, it is not because two men do not ever, then or now, out of fiction as well as in, live together happily and permanently, but because Forster himself believed that except in fiction and daydream they ought not to. Against his deepest wish he set his still deeper belief. *They ought not to:* despite the fact that he was always openly in favor of the liberalization in England of laws concerning homosexuality, despite the fact that as early as 1928, beginning with the *Well of Loneliness* case, he went to court to testify against the suppression of a homosexual novel, the first of a succession of such books he publicly defended and praised.

Forster's own books are full of veiled* portraits of repressed or hidden or potential homosexuals, from Ansell in *The Longest Journey* to Tibby in *Howards End* (who warms the teapot "almost too deftly," is called "Auntie Tibby" for fun, and is declared not to be "a real boy"). The description of Cecil in *A Room with a View* fits not only what the young Tibby will become, but what Maurice's lover Clive already is: "He is the sort who are all right as long as they keep to things—books, pictures—but kill when they come to people." Many of Forster's clergymen are seen to be embittered ascetics who, had they not suppressed the body, would have loved men. Mr. Borenius, the rector in *Maurice*, jealously accuses the gamekeeper of being "guilty of sensuality." It is because Forster himself is always on the side of sensuality, of "fruition" as against "celibacy," that all his spokesmen-characters, with profound sadness, eventually yield up their final judgment—on moral and natural grounds, and despite Forster's renowned liberalism—against homosexuality. *Maurice*, where the wish for lasting homoerotic bliss is allowed to come true, is no exception to Forster's moral conviction.

* So successfully "veiled," in fact, that Lionel Trilling, who had published a critical volume on Forster's fiction as early as 1943, commented to me in a 1972 letter that "it wasn't until I had finished my book on Forster that I came to the explicit realization that he was homosexual. I'm not sure whether this was because of a particular obtuseness on my part or because . . . homosexuality hadn't yet formulated itself as an issue in the culture. When the realization did come, it at first didn't seem of crucial importance, but that view soon began to change." The two did not meet until after the publication of Trilling's book. In the wake of that "slight personal acquaintance," Trilling explained, his view "changed radically."

It is precisely on this issue of sensuality that Forster's reservations rest. Forster believes, with Christianity, that the opposite of sensuality is sterility. And not sterility in any metaphorical sense—not in the meaning of an empty or unused life. With Christianity, Forster believes that sensuality is designed to beget progeny. The most melancholy passage in *Maurice* occurs at Maurice's most ecstatic moment—when he is at last physically in possession of Clive:

> An immense sadness—he believed himself beyond such irritants—had risen up in his soul. He and the beloved would vanish utterly—would continue neither in Heaven nor on Earth. They had won past the conventions, but Nature still faced them, saying with even voice, "Very well, you are thus; I blame none of my children. But you must go the way of all sterility." The thought that he was sterile weighed on the young man with a sudden shame. His mother or Mrs. Durham might lack mind or heart, but they had done visible work; they had handed on the torch their sons would tread out.

And it is Ansell in *The Longest Journey* who gives the homosexual's view of progeny, which is renunciation. He is strolling in the British Museum talking of "the Spirit of Life" when he is told that Ricky and Agnes are expecting a child. His response: "I forgot that it might be." Then: "He left the Parthenon to pass by the monuments of our more reticent beliefs—the temple of the Ephesian Artemis, the statue of the Cnidian Demeter. Honest, he knew that here were powers he could not cope with, nor, as yet, understand." Artemis the protectress of women, Demeter the goddess of fertility. Thus Ansell. And thus Auden. Somewhere Auden has written that homosexual men do not love their sterility; that homosexuals too would welcome parenthood; but out of decency and selflessness forgo it.

"Be fruitful and multiply." That Forster alone perhaps of all homosexual writers is willing to take seriously the Biblical injunction, and is left feeling desolated by it, is a measure of how attached he remained to Christian morals. In this attachment he was unlike any homosexual in his Cambridge generation, and possibly unlike any English-speaking homosexual in the generations afterward, Auden excepted. The Gay Liberation argument that homosexual activity is a positive good in a world afflicted by over-population would not have won Forster over.

Homosexuality did not begin with Lytton Strachey, but homosexual manners did. All those habits and signals that we now associate with the educated homosexual sensibility can be said to have had their start in Cambridge when Strachey was an undergraduate; and Strachey set the style for them. Sects and persuasions, like nationalities, have their forerunners and traditions: presumably Franciscans still strive to retain the mind-set of Saint Francis, Quakers recall George Fox, the white American South continues to feel itself patrician. Forster himself was influenced in liberal thinking by his ancestors in the Clapham Sect, an abolitionist group. The recollection need not be conscious; we inherit, rather than mimic, style. So with educated homosexual manners. The passion for beauty and distinction, the wit with its double bur of hilarity and malice, the aesthetic frame of mind, even the voice that edges thinly upward and is sometimes mistaken for "effeminacy"—all these are Stracheyisms. Strachey at Cambridge and afterward was so forceful in passing on Stracheyism that he founded a school, active to this day. It had, and has, two chief tenets: one was antiphilistinism expressed as élitism (one cannot imagine Strachey making a hero of a gamekeeper with no grammar, or addressing, as Forster did, a Working Men's College); the other was a recoil from Christianity. In these tenets especially Forster did not acquiesce.

Though Forster knew Strachey well at Cambridge (he even confesses that a Cambridge character in *Maurice* was modeled on Strachey), he remained peripheral to the Strachey set. This astounding group was concentrated in the Cambridge Conversazione Society, better known as the Apostles, which mingled older alumni and undergraduates, never much more than a dozen at a time, and was devoted to intellectual wrangling, high wit, snobbery toward "bloods," and, in an underground sort of way, homosexuality: its brilliant members kept falling in and out of love with one another. At one time Strachey and John Maynard Keynes were both furious rivals for the love of one Duckworth; afterward Keynes, like Clive Durham, "became normal" and married a ballerina. Through all this Forster kept himself apart and remote, "the elusive colt of a dark horse," as Keynes called him. The Apostles churned out barristers, chief justices, governers of outlying parts of the Empire, dons, historians, economists, mathematicians, philosophers, many of them with family attachments to one another: in short, the ruling intellectual class of England more or less reproducing itself. The smaller "aesthetic" section of this privileged and brainy caste withdrew to become Bloomsbury; but from Bloomsbury too Forster held himself in reserve. One reason was his temperamental shyness, his inclination toward an almost secretive privateness. The more compelling reason was that he did not think or feel like the Apostles, or like Bloomsbury. He was more mystical than skeptical. The ideal of freedom from all restraint made him uncomfortable in practice. Unlike Strachey, he did not scoff easily or vilify happily (though it ought to be noted that there is a single radiant "Balls" in *Maurice*), and did not use the word "Christian" as a taunt. To the Apostles —self-declared "immoralists," according to Keynes—and to Bloomsbury he must have seemed a little out of date. He never shared their elation at smashing conventional ideas; though himself an enemy of convention, he saw beyond convention to its roots in nature. Stracheyan Bloomsbury assented to nothing, least of all to God or nature, but Forster knew there were "powers he could not cope with, nor, as yet, understand." Bloomsbury was alienated but not puzzled; Forster was puzzled but not alienated. His homosexuality did not divide him from society, because he saw that society in the largest sense was the agent of nature; and when he came to write *A Passage to India* he envisioned culture and nature as fusing altogether. Homosexuality led him not away from but toward society. He accepted himself as a man with rights—nature made him—but also very plainly as a deviant—nature would not gain by him. It is no accident that babies are important in his books.

The shock of the publication of *Maurice*, then, is not what it appears to be at first sight: Forster as Forerunner of Gay Lib. Quite the opposite. He used his own position as an exemplum, to show what the universe does not intend. If that implies a kind of rational martyrdom, that is what he meant; and this is what shocks. We had not thought of him as martyr. For Forster, "I do not conform" explains what does conform, it does not celebrate nonconformity. He was a sufferer rather than a champion. Now suddenly, with the appearance of *Maurice*, it is clear that Forster's famous humanism is a kind of personal withdrawal rather than a universal testimony, and reverberates with despair. Christopher Lehmann-Haupt in a *New York Times* review remarks that Maurice's homosexuality is "a symbol of human feelings." But Forster would disagree that homosexuality stands for anything beyond what it is in itself, except perhaps the laying-waste of the Cnidian Demeter. Homosexuality to Forster signified sterility; he practiced it like a blasphemer, just as he practiced his humanism like a blasphemer. There is no blasphemy where there is no belief to be betrayed; and Forster believes in the holiness of the goddess of fertility: Demeter, guardian of the social order and marriage. The most dubious social statement Forster ever made is also his most famous one: if I had to choose between betraying my country or my friend, I hope I would have the guts to betray my country. He says "I"; the note is personal, it is not an injunction to the rest of us. *Maurice* instructs us explicitly in what he understands by "friend"; in Maurice's boyhood dream the word "friend" foretells the love of a man for a man. We have encountered that charged word in Forster before. The statement about betrayal cannot be universalized, and Forster did not mean it to be. Declarations about bedmates do not commonly have general application.

Does it devalue the large humanistic statement to know that its sources are narrowly personal? Yes. And for Forster too: he does not ask society to conform to him, because he believes—he says it again and again everywhere in his books, but nowhere more poignantly than in his novel about homosexual love—he believes in the eternal stream. He died among affectionate friends, but not harmoniously; he was not content to go the way of all sterility, to vanish utterly. Books are not progeny, and nature does not read.

I append to my observations about Forster's *Maurice* a reply to a correspondent who charged me with not loving Forster enough.

Forster as Moralist: A Reply to Mrs. A. F.

Lionel Trilling begins his book about Forster with this observation: "E. M. Forster is for me the only living novelist who can be read again and again and who, after each reading, gives me what few writers can give us after our first days of novel-reading, the sensation of having learned something." To this statement another can be added, virtually a corollary: Forster is also one of those very few writers (and since Forster's death, there is none now living) who excite competitive passions—possessive rivalries, in fact—among serious readers, each of whom feels uniquely chosen to perceive the inner life of the novels.

In recent years Forster has grown thinner for me, especially as essayist. Not that I would now deny Forster's powers or his brilliance, or claim that the masterpieces are not masterpieces, still giving out, as Trilling said almost thirty years ago, "the sensation of having learned something." But what we learn from the novels is not what we learn from the essays. The novels do not preach morality and the essays, in their way, do. Or, to put it differently, the novels preach a novelistic morality—in the early ones, the ethics of Spontaneity; in *A Passage to India*, the anti-ethics of a mystical nihilism. But the essays—preëminently "What I Believe," which Mrs. F. cites—tell us how we are to go about living from moment to moment. "Where do I start?" Forster asks. And answers: "With personal relationships." Of this approach Mrs. F. says: "I like it well."

I do not, because it strikes me as incomplete and self-indulgent. Nevertheless I recognize Mrs. F.'s tone—it was once mine, and I think we can spot our erstwhile psychological twins—at the end of her letter, when she concludes that I do "not love [Forster] enough—for what he *did* do." I withdraw from the contest and agree that Mrs. F. is right. She *does* love Forster's ideas and qualities, if not more than I once did, certainly more than I do now.

And the reasons I have, so to speak, fallen out of love with Forster are the very reasons she is still in thrall to him. A novelist, as she says, is both psychologist and metaphysician (and social historian). That is why we become most attached to those novels which give us an adequate account of the way the world seems to us. Novelists interpret us, and when we "choose" a novelist we are really choosing a version of ourselves. The same is true of essayists. What I no longer choose to choose among Forster's ideas is "Only Connect," which signifies, of course, "personal relationships." When I said in my remarks on *Maurice* that it devalued "the large humanistic statement to know that its sources are narrowly personal," I was not referring to Forster's novelistic imagination (of course the women in his novels are women and not disguised male homosexuals), but to his liberalism. We are now unambiguously apprised of Forster's homosexuality, and *Maurice* makes it shudderingly plain that Forster considered homosexuality to be an affliction, the ineradicable mark of a fated few. To use language grown shabby from repetition, he regarded himself as part of an oppressed minority; and, applying Only Connect, he could stand in for and champion other oppressed minorities—Indians under English colonialism, for instance, who suffered from the English public-school mentality precisely as he had suffered from it. But this, after all, is a compromised liberalism. There is nothing admirable in it; it is devalued by the presence of the vested interest. It is no trick, after all, for a Jew to be against antisemitism, or for a homosexual to be against censorship of homosexual novels. The passion behind the commitment may be pure, but the commitment is not so much a philosophy of liberalism as it is of self-preservation. Morality must apply some more accessible standard than personal hurt. In *Howards End* Mr. Wilcox, disapproving of Helen's affair with Leonard Bast, gets his nose rubbed in a reminder of his own affair, long ago, with Mrs. Bast: what's sauce for the goose is sauce for the gander. But suppose the gander has had no sauce? I am not a homosexual; if I had been in England in 1935, should I not have been disturbed by the law that interfered with the untrammeled publication of *Boy*, as Forster was? (See his essay "Liberty in England.") Liberalism, to be the real thing, ought to be disinterested.

But the inadequacy of Only Connect—that it is *not* disinterested—is not the whole of my charge against "personal relationships" as the ultimate moral standard. Deciding your behavior person by person (Forster was apparently the inventor of an early form of situation ethics) seems to me a localized, partial, highly contingent, catch-as-catch-can sort of morality. "This is my friend; I love him; therefore I will not kill him" is, in my view, inferior to saying, once and for all, "Thou shalt not kill." The reason is not simply that the overall Commandment is relatively more efficient than figuring it out one person at a time as you go along, but also that it is more reliable. "This is my friend; I love him" can too easily turn into "This was my friend; now I hate him." And if that is all there is to it, if there is no larger motive than "personal relationships" to govern human behavior, one might as well kill him. It is not only that "Love and loyalty to an individual can run counter to the claims of the State" (though the single example Forster can think of to illustrate this possibility is Brutus and Cassius vis-à-vis Caesar, not exactly the sort of situation that one is likely to encounter on an everyday basis)—it is also, as Forster himself recognizes, that love and loyalty can run counter to themselves; in short, they rot. They are "a matter for the heart, which signs no documents." That is why, taking up —as Forster himself does—the question of reliability, and writing about these matters on stone some four thousand years before Forster, Moses thought that having it down on a document might not be a bad idea. "But reliability," Forster sensibly answers Moses, "is not a matter of contract —that is the main difference between the world of personal relationships and the world of business relationships." It is also one of the differences between personal relationships and universal ethics. To Forster, Moses comes out a businessman with a contract, and in the same essay (we are still in "What I Believe") he says he prefers Montaigne and Erasmus. "My temple stands," he asserts, "not upon Mount Moriah but in that Elysian Field where even the immoral are admitted." It is not a very great distance from an Elysian Field that makes no distinction between innocents and murderers (for we have a right to take the persons Forster calls "immoral" at their most extreme) to the *ou-boum* of the Marabar Caves, which swallows up both good and evil into one of the unknown black holes of the universe, similarly without distinction. The problem with Forster's "personal relationships"—or, to use Mrs. F.'s term, his personal loyalties—is that they tend to slip away at the first intrusion of something spooky or ineffably cosmic—of something, in brief, that suggests his notion of Religion, which is pagan in the sense of fearfulness, imbued with the uncanniness of *lacrimae rerum*, un-human, without relation to the world of men and women. When Mrs. Moore in the cave hears the *ou-boum* of nothingness, she "lost all interest, even in Aziz [who had become her good friend], and the affectionate and sincere words that she had spoken to him seemed no longer hers but the air's."

Mrs. Moore in the Marabar Caves is obviously an extreme example of the dissolution of a friendship. But Forster, as we know, is fond of extremes, so it is not too much to say that Mrs. Moore is also an extreme example of someone who —quoting Mrs. F. quoting Forster—"hate[s] the idea of causes." Her hatred of causes does not strengthen her in friendship. She betrays her friend by losing interest in him, because the universe has shown her that it is impersonal, and that friendship and betrayal and loss are all the same to it. She has no "cause"—no motivation, no ideal contract— that restricts her from betraying her friend. Forster's dedication to personal relationships without contract is doomed to work only very rarely, not only because friendship succeeds only very rarely, but because it is, in a world of friends and non-friends, not enough. "Do not lie about your friend, whom you love" is, in moral distance, a light-year from "Do not tell lies about anyone at all"—or, as it is more commonly formulated, "Do not bear false witness." A contractual, or communal, ethics, when violated, at least leaves the standard intact. A catch-as-catch-can ethics, based on your feelings for your friend, leaves everything in a shambles when it is violated.

A case can of course be made that Forster's ethics of privacy derives through Romanticism with its discovery of the Individual from Nonconformism with its emphasis on regulating personal morality through conscience. Whatever their sources, though, the moral and political positions that emerge from "What I Believe" seem to me to be disturbingly partial. They may do a certain credit to the sensibility of a hurt man who knows enough to be thoughtful about the hurts of others, but they fail of universal application. Forster never comes head-on against the problem of how to get the "bloods" to behave less callously. Or, rather, he dodges the problem by loading it: by giving Mr. Wilcox an old affair to hide, by making Maurice a homosexual. His untroubled men turn out not to be untroubled at all; Forster appears incapable of accepting the *principle* of not hurting without first making a hurt felt. His humanity goes from wound to wound. His politics, his morality, ultimately his liberalism, all signify the humanism of the vulnerable. It is too thin. The thugs escape.

The difficulty, I think, is that Mrs. F. mixes up these specific questions raised by Forster's political and moral positions with a general analysis of the novelistic imagination. Her description of the "miracle" of the fictive imagination is superb and very nearly complete, but I am puzzled about why she has introduced it. My judgment on Forster's humanism does not lead logically to any judgment on his capacity to imagine. If I believe, as I do, that Forster's sense of himself as a kind of martyr taints the candor of his liberalism with a hidden self-interest, how does this relate to Mrs. F.'s notion that I somehow also believe the novels to be homosexual disguises? They are obviously not homosexual disguises. Nothing in what I wrote suggested they might be. That there are in Forster's fiction men with homosexual tendencies has always been clear and is now clearer. A pair of obvious examples: Ricky and Ansell, Aziz and Fielding. Revisited in the aftermath of *Maurice* (I have, for instance, been rereading *A Passage to India*), they have new resonances; so does the passionate "friend" in the essay called "Notes on the English Character" (1920), who is an adumbration of Aziz as Forster himself in that essay is an adumbration of Fielding. As for Forster's use of the word "friend": until some industrious clod of a graduate student gives us the definitive concordance for that word in Forster's *oeuvre*, we shall not know how often he intended it wistfully and how often straightforwardly. But until we get the concordance, we will have to rely on impressions—and my impression is that it is a word Forster most often uses wistfully. I feel certain—it is an impression—that the friend for whom Forster would betray his country is thought of wistfully. When you betray your country, that is treason, a capital offense. Betraying your country for your friend, you die. I quote Mrs. F. quoting Maurice in a passage she herself calls "the epitome of the homosexual 'friend'": "He could die for such a friend . . . they would make any sacrifice for each other, and count the world nothing." Maurice would betray his country for such a friend; Forster is largely indistinguishable from Maurice; and yet Mrs. F. writes, "I don't believe you can imagine him to mean by 'friend' anything different from what you or I or anyone would mean by it." My impression is otherwise.

But all this is about friendship between men. Against the rest—Mrs. F.'s catalogue of "love, courtship, marriage, sisterhood, fatherhood, sonhood"—nothing can be insinuated. Forster believed, as I have said, in Demeter, the most domestic of all the goddesses.

So two cheers for Forster's Friendship. "Two cheers are quite enough," Forster remarked of Democracy, saving his third for "Love the Beloved Republic." If, as Mrs. F. asserts, I do not love Forster enough for what he has done, it is not because I fail to celebrate his novelistic imagination, but rather because I would dislike living in his Republic, where personal relationships govern (one might dare to say seethe) and there are no communal contracts. I save half my third cheer for the Covenant; and the other half, following Forster in all his novels but the last, for Demeter.

Emerging Dreiser

Theodore Dreiser: At the Gates of the City, 1871-1907, the first volume of Richard Lingeman's two-part biography, reaches only seven years beyond the initial publication of *Sister Carrie*, when, in the wake of early neglect, the book was successfully reissued. Its 1907 revival—and victorious arrival—is an appropriate biographical climax. A first novel by the son of a German Catholic immigrant, *Sister Carrie* is also the first recognizably "American" novel—urban American in the way we feel it now. Springing up in a period when the novel's tone was governed chiefly by aristocrats of English-speaking stock—William Dean Howells, Edith Wharton, Henry James—Dreiser's driven prose uncovers the unmistakable idiom of a raw Chicago and the New York of dumbwaiters and flophouses. To find one's way into the streets and flats of Dreiser's two cities is to experience the unfolding of literary history—to see how the English novel, itself an immigrant, finally pocketed its "papers" and became naturalized.

But to enter these cramped flats and teeming streets is to re-experience personal history as well. Dreiser's salesmen and managers, his factory girls and two-dollar-a-week boarders, his images of shirtwaists, sweatshops, horsecars, are the fabric of our grandparents' world; we know it with the kind of intimacy we cannot bring to Hawthorne's Puritans or James's high-caste international visitors. *Sister Carrie* is a turn-of-the-century vat boiling with the hot matter—and cold materialism—of old Broadway, West Side apartment houses newly built, glimmers of restaurants, hotels, and theaters that once were remote names out of newspapers in our own households. Unless you are descended from John Quincy Adams—unless no one in your family ever passed through Castle Garden—*Sister Carrie*, read now and for the first time, is an oddly private voyage home: a time machine into the harrowings of an era not yet dimmed, when jobs meant unbroken drudgery, and when the eight-hour working day, Social Security, and publicly funded relief were futuristic socialist visions. Into just such confusions and predicaments our immigrant relations tumbled.

Richard Lingeman's impressive marshalings build toward the consummation of this landmark work, and if a new life of Dreiser needs any justification at all, then the unremitting veracity and inclusiveness of *Sister Carrie* are reason enough. It is strengthening to Mr. Lingeman's undertaking that he is preceded by an already admirable procession of biographers and critics—among the latter the late Ellen Moers, unsurpassed in robust Dreiserian advocacy. Still, a fresh biography becomes a necessity only if more life is imagined for it, more than there was before. Biography remains, after all, the one form where the chronological empowerment of character, in the way of the nineteenth-century novel, continues to dominate—with the difference, of course, that the life in it is "real." Some biographies require no successors—Leon Edel's *Henry James* springs to mind—because their subjects are permeated with the conviction of sufficiency. It is not that they have been recorded merely; they have "come to life," and break through the page once and for all. In this sense there is still plenty of room, and opportunity, for the psychological illumination of Theodore Dreiser—for a biography with the blood-force of a novel.

Lingeman's representation of Dreiser is scrupulously, massively—devotedly—constructed; everything is in it, including a clear passion for the social issues of the period. And it is immaculately rendered, free of tendentiousness of any kind. But it is an expository library construction, not an elastically breathing imaginative reanimation. The great Dreiserian riddle is not even so much as approached, still less appraised: how is it that a workhorse daily journalist—a needy and febrile Grub Street factotum grinding out newspaper copy at fire-truck speed—could transform himself into a novelist of such encompassing gritty recalcitrant power? Lingeman asserts this miracle without examining it. "Dreiser's greatest strength," he tells us at the halfway mark, "is his empathy with his characters, which reaches its peak [in *Sister Carrie*] in the final scenes about Hurstwood. In the supreme effort to make believable the climactic downfall of this, the most strongly imagined figure in the book, Dreiser *became* Hurstwood, producing his every thought, his every emotion, from inside himself." (That Dreiser would "become Hurstwood" again later on, and far less metaphorically, is a vivid connection with the future Lingeman crucially lets slip.)

Yet Lingeman, from inside *himself*, offers no comparable becoming. His Dreiser is for the most part a product of strong information, not strong imagining. Hence "Theodore," as Lingeman calls his subject—with undelivered intimations of insight—remains just that: a subject, a datum on the surface of the text. Theodore—the living Dreiser—is not exactly *there*. But his evidences are everywhere, and they are rich and dense. A biography of information is not overwhelmingly inferior to a biography of psychological re-creation; and flashy re-creation (such a thing is possible) without the dedicated accumulation of a store of diligent accuracies is a cheat. Lingeman's biography of information is never a cheat. On the contrary. Such patient assimilation of old and new particularity not only earns our homage, but, on its own terms, exhilarates. Once warned that Theodore—i.e., Dreiser as *mind*—is not exactly there, we can marvel at what is.

And what is there, punctiliously there, is a chronicle of emergence—of an especially American kind. Dreiser was an obsessive reader of Balzac, but his own story is tonally different from that of Balzac's young man from the provinces who sets out to seize literary fame in the glorious city. In much of Dreiser's America, city and boondocks were alike in newness and rootlessness; both were more provisional than traditional, more contingent than composed. The Midwest was only just fashioning itself; a family line was often no longer than a single generation. Dreiser's father was himself, to use that striking old immigrant's tag, right off the boat; his English was never unblemished. All ten of his children (Theodore was the ninth) were given combinations of names that would have been more at home in his native Mayen in Alsace-Lorraine than in Terre Haute, Indiana. All the children eventually anglicized their Christian names—Alphons Joachim, for instance, became Al—and the oldest, Johann Paul, Jr., changed Dreiser to Dresser and ended as Paul Dresser, the celebrated songwriter. The mother of this first-generation family came of an earlier German-American migration. A Mennonite, she abandoned the "plain people" strictures of her sect and converted to Catholicism to please her rigidly devout husband.

These shifts of vowels and allegiances, these fresh and strange alliances, would have been unthinkable in any society less bent on mutation. Emerging from the American backwater was not so much a matter of making one's way as it was of finding a way to make oneself up. Dreiser was determined to emerge—he allowed himself no other course—because he was born, so to speak, sunk. His father, a wool worker, rose briefly to mill manager and then, after a head injury, descended into unbalanced religious fanaticism and irreversible joblessness and poverty. The mother moved the children from Hoosier town to Hoosier town, taking in washing and boarders. Dreiser's brother Paul sang in blackface and for a time lived with the madam of a prosperous bordello. Dreiser's sisters went off to be "kept." One gave birth to an out-of-wedlock child. Another, Emma, fled first to Canada and then to New York with a Chicago thief and absconder named Hopkins: the flagrant domestic seed of *Sister Carrie*. In New York, Hopkins, like the fictional Hurstwood, collapsed into indigent apathy. So finally did Dreiser's father. Respectability was no part of Dreiser's family inheritance; he grew up on the underside, among the spurned. At twenty he stole money to buy himself an overcoat. If, in later years, he wrote with a journalist's detachment of the "curious shifts of the poor," it was nevertheless out of bitter familiarity. For Dreiser, being poor was life, not hypothesis.

The instruments of his emergence were two. The first was social gentility: Sara White, nicknamed Jug, the woman he romantically fixed on to marry (he went on dreaming and letter-writing through a drawn-out courtship), belonged to a prominent small-town Missouri family of transplanted Virginia aristocrats. The second instrument was journalism. Dreiser's climb from legman to free lance to full-time reporter to "magazinist" to editor, with pratfalls and loss of footing along the way, is the sovereign thread of Lingeman's narrative. It includes Dreiser's peculiarly dependent friendship—an entrance into psychological twinship—with his fellow journalist Arthur Henry: "If he had been a girl, I would have married him," Dreiser once remarked. Instead, Henry moved in with the newlyweds, Dreiser and Jug, on West 102nd Street, and the pair—Dreiser and Henry—formed a writing partnership, sharing assignments and fees. The summer before, they had shared Henry's house on the idyllic Maumee, in Ohio. Urged on by Henry—with whom he eventually broke—Dreiser began writing his first fiction.

Lingeman's meticulous account of Dreiser's work history—covering Pittsburgh, St. Louis, Chicago, New York, a progression of cities in growth—yields also a masterly impressionist history of American journalism in the preëminent age of newspapers, and in the heyday of a variety of popular periodicals now obsolete: song sheets, song magazines, and even dress-pattern magazines. The sale of song sheets made Paul Dresser rich; his hit, "On the Banks of the Wabash," partly written by Dreiser, quickly acquired the credentials of a folk melody. *Ev'ry Month*, a song magazine for the parlor piano that had been launched by the success of "The Sidewalks of New York," took Dreiser on as editor; he soon transformed it, and even found room for an essay by Arthur Henry entitled "The Philosophy of Hope." This was in 1897; that same year Dreiser was fired. A decade beyond saw him editor of the Butterick pattern periodical, *The Delineator*, which he authoritatively refashioned into a more comprehensive women's magazine. He had risen to become a major editor in New York, quartered in genteelly plush offices. In between, he was successively at the helm of *Smith's* and *Broadway*—"a prototype of *Vanity Fair* and the *New Yorker*"—where his assistant, a young intellectual fresh out of Bryn Mawr, "thought her boss a commercial hack—until she read *Sister Carrie* and became a worshiper."

Sister Carrie had been grudgingly brought out in 1900 against the wishes of its own publisher, Frank Doubleday, who had accepted the novel on the basis of Frank Norris's enthusiasm, and then precipitately changed his mind midway. A libertine according to conventional judgment, Dreiser's heroine not only goes unpunished, but ascends to become a brilliant figure in the world. To Doubleday this was 'indecent," and though both Jug and Arthur Henry worked at softening—bowdlerizing—certain problematical passages, the publisher, fearing scandal, barely fulfilled his contract; the novel was stillborn. Dreiser, however, was counting on William Dean Howells, who had the power of making reputations. No review by Howells appeared. When Dreiser ran into him by chance, Howells told him brusquely: "I didn't like *Sister Carrie*."

With the failure of his novel, Dreiser's morale gradually foundered, and from this moment—a hundred pages or so before the close of this first volume, and the harbinger perhaps of larger resonances in the second—Lingeman increases in psychological force and imaginative presence. His record of Dreiser's extraordinary decline, after a period of pointless wandering—"an aching desire to be forever on the move," Dreiser called it—into the lost life of lodging-house hall bedrooms is a cutting portrait of mental depression and the disintegrations of "neurasthenia." But it is also something more. Dreiser as railway crew member, Dreiser spending the night in a Bowery flophouse—here is the mystery of a vigorous and self-disciplined writer melting into the character and fate of his creation: Dreiser astoundingly turning himself into his own Hurstwood. Lingeman is able to penetrate this eerie and prodigious darkness, I think, because he lets it unfold almost novelistically on its own: he surrenders to its unaccountability.

Earlier, Lingeman had plausibly reminded us of "Dreiser's sense of the economic tragedy at the heart of American life." In a Prologue, he sketches the stringent atmosphere of Dreiser's ripening years—"the mass migration to the cities, the widening fissure between rich and poor, the rise of industry, the centralization of economic (and political) power in the corporations and trusts," and more. It is true that much of this entered Dreiser's fictional domestic scenery. An anonymous reviewer of *Sister Carrie* observed how the downward course of Hurstwood illustrated a rule: that "civilization is at bottom an economic fact," that "if the economic pilings on which . . . lives are built are swept away, they will sink into destitution, loss of self-respect, moral squalor." Lingeman appears to attribute this altogether programmatic position to Dreiser himself. Possibly. (Toward the end of his life Dreiser did become markedly programmatic, to the extent of endorsing Communism and supporting Earl Browder's opposition to the war against Hitler.)

And yet something there is in the enigma of literary dreaming that eludes even the most searching social thesis. Those economic pilings cannot be made to sustain or explain the whole range of the human predicament, and it is hard to believe that Dreiser—as novelist—ever took such a view. Dreiser sinking into the very vision his art foretold—Dreiser becoming Hurstwood—is in a place where socio-economic theory cannot reach. His recovery and return to achievement, followed by the gratifying reissue of *Sister Carrie*, stand poignantly apart from any determinist social analysis. *Sister Carrie*—the story of a woman dreaming her way out of poverty—may powerfully exemplify the migration to the cities and the fissure between rich and poor, and indeed the entire American "economic tragedy" of a century ago; but what Carrie exemplifies hardly accounts for her. And Hurstwood too is governed as much by his own threadbare imagination as by any external collapse of "economic pilings." Carrie is Dreiser's dream of the spirit incandescent, Hurstwood of the snuffed. It is not a contradiction that Dreiser is signally recorded among the realists.

I spoke at the start of the rare chance of encountering *Sister Carrie* now and for the first time. Who, after so many school assignments, will have such good luck? But to come to *Sister Carrie* minus the baggage of unripe exposure and stale critical disparagements—to cut loose from Dreiser's reputation for ponderous eyesore sentences—is to fall into a living heat, the truth of things. The well-accepted abuse of Dreiser's style—how relieving it is that Lingeman steers clear of any of this—seems a calumny. Taken by itself and for itself, Dreiser's novel is life-hard: stubborn, nervy, gaudy and bawdy, full of weather, sex, hope, inertness, toil, sadness, dirt, dream. A work with no lying—toward which Mr. Lingeman's lucid sympathies and resourceful labor form a strong and granite corridor.

William Gaddis and the Scion of Darkness

Carpenter's Gothic is William Gaddis's third work of fiction in thirty years. That sounds like a sparse stream, and misrepresents absolutely. Gaddis is a deluge. *The Recognitions*, his first novel, published in 1955, matches in plain bulk four or five ordinary contemporary novels. His second, *JR*, a burlesquing supplementary footnote appearing two decades later, is easily equivalent to another three or four. Gaddis has not been "prolific" (that spendthrift coin); instead he has been prodigious, gargantuan, exhaustive, subsuming fates and conditions under a hungry logic. His two huge early novels are great vaults or storehouses of crafty encyclopedic scandal—omniscience thrown into the hottest furnaces of metaphor. Gaddis knows almost everything: not only how the world works—the pragmatic cynical business-machine that we call worldliness—but also how myth flies into being out of the primeval clouds of art and death and money.

To call this mammoth reach "ambition" is again to misrepresent. When *The Recognitions* arrived on the scene, it was already too late for those large acts of literary power ambition used to be good for. Joyce had come and gone, leaving footprints both shallow and deep everywhere in Gaddis's ground—the opening dash, for instance, as a substitute for quotation marks: a brilliantly significant smudge that allows no closure and dissolves voices into narrative, turning the clearest verisimilitude into something spectral. Gaddis, imperially equipped for masterliness in range, language, and ironic penetration, born to wrest out a modernist masterpiece but born untimely, nonetheless took a long draught of Joyce's advice and responded with surge after surge of virtuoso cunning. *The Recognitions* is a mocking recognition of the implausibility of originality: a vast fiction about fabrication and forgery, about the thousand faces of the counterfeit, and therefore, ineluctably, about art and religion. In the desert years of long ago, when I was a deluded young would-be writer tangled up in my own crapulous ambition, *The Recognitions* landed on my grim table (and on the grim tables of how many other aspirants to the holy cloak of Art?) and stayed there, month after month, as a last burnished talisman of—well, of Greatness, of a refusal to relinquish the latter-day possibilities of Joyce, Mann, James, Woolf, Proust, the whole sacral crew of those old solar boats. That, I think now, was a misreading of Gaddis's chosen ground. He knew what monuments had gathered behind him, but—seizing Joyce's dialogue-dash as staff—he willingly moved on. He was not imitating a received literature; he was not a facsimile Joyce.

Gaddis was, in fact—and is—new coinage: an American original. To claim this is to fall into Gaddis's own comedy of "enamored parodies weighed down with testimonial ruins." Originality is exactly what Gaddis has made absurd; unrecognizable. Yet if it is obligatory to recapitulate Gaddis's mockery through the impact—the dazzling irruption—of his three-decades-old first novel, it is because *The Recognitions* is always spoken of as the most overlooked important work of the last several literary generations. Tony Tanner: "The critical neglect of this book is really extraordinary." David Madden: "An underground reputation has kept it on the brink of oblivion." Through the famous obscurity of *The Recognitions*, Gaddis has become famous for not being famous enough. *Carpenter's Gothic*—a short novel, but as mazily and mercilessly adroit as the others—should mark a turning: it should disclose Gaddis's terrifying artfulness, once and for all, to those whom tonnage has kept away. *Carpenter's Gothic* may be Gaddis-in-little, but it is Gaddis to the brim.

The title itself, the name of an architectural vogue, is a dangerous joke. It alludes to a style of charm that dissembles—that resplendent carved-wood fakery seductively laid out along the Hudson a century ago, "built to be seen from the outside," its unplanned insides crammed to fit in any which way—"a patchwork of conceits, borrowings, deceptions," according to McCandless, the owner of one of these "grandiose visions . . . foolish inventions . . . towering heights and cupolas." McCandless is a geologist, a novelist, a heavy smoker with a confusing past. He has locked up one room containing his papers, reserving the right to visit it, and rented the house to a young married couple, Paul and Elizabeth Booth. Paul, like the house, has grandiose visions. He works as a public relations man for the Reverend Ude's evangelical operations, which reach as far as Africa; when Ude drowns a boy while baptizing him, Paul in his inventive fecundity—he is a desperately hollow promoter—twists this into a usable miracle. Liz, Paul's wife—wistful, abused, hopeful, humble, herself quietly deceitful—is, along with her ne'er-do-well brother Billy, heir to a mining combine intent on scheming itself back into a business empire's version of African colonialism. Paul, a combat veteran, was formerly bagman for the company under the chairmanship of Liz's father, a suicide; the company is now in the hands of Adolph, the trustee. Adolph keeps Liz, Billy, and Paul on short rations. Obedient to Paul's several scams, Liz goes from doctor to doctor, patiently pursuing an insurance fraud. McCandless reveals himself as the discoverer of the African gold the company is after, and seduces Liz. But there is no gold; McCandless is a lunatic impostor. In the end, brother and sister die of too much imposture.

All this crammed-in conspiring, told bare, is pointless soap-opera recounting. We have run into these fictional scalawags before, rotted-out families, rotted-out corporations, seedy greedy preachers and poachers, either in cahoots with or victims of one another, and sometimes both. They are American staples; but "plot" is Gaddis's prey, and also his play. Triteness is his trap and toy. He has light-fingered all the detritus that pours through the news machines and the storytelling machines—the fake claims, fake Bible schools, fake holy water out of the Pee Dee River spreading typhus, a bought-and-paid-for senator, an armed "Christian survival camp," fake identities (Paul, pretending to be a WASP Southerner, is probably a Jew), the mugger Paul kills. Plot is what Gaddis travesties and teases and two-times and swindles.

Yet these stereotypical illusions, these familiar dumping grounds of chicanery, turn to stony truths under Gaddis's eye—or, rather, his ear. Gaddis is a possessed receiver of voices, a maniacal eavesdropper, a secret prophet and moralizer. His method is pure voice, relentless dialogue, preceded by the serenely poised Joycean dash and melting off into the panning of a camera in the speaker's head. Speech is fragmented, piecemeal, halting and stunted, finally headlong—into telephones continually, out of radio and television. Through all these throats and machines the foul world spills. The radio is a perpetual chorus of mishap and mayhem, pumping out its impassive dooms while the human voice lamenting in the kitchen moans on:

> – Problem Liz you just don't grasp how serious the whole God damn thing is . . . the bottle trembled against the rim of the glass,—after him they're after me they're after all of us . . . He'd slumped back against word of two tractor trailer trucks overturned and on fire at an entrance to the George Washington bridge,—fit the pieces together you see how all the God damn pieces fit together, SEC comes in claims some little irregularity on a Bible school bond issue next thing you've got the IRS in there right behind with misappropriation of church funds for openers, problem's their new computer down there's just geared to their mailing list if they don't build their mailing list there won't be any funds what the whole God damn thing is all about, you get these Bible students they're smart enough digging up Ephusians but they count on their fingers nobody knows where in hell the last nickel went,

and on and on: fire, death, fraud, money, voice voice voice. The voices are humanity seeping out, drop by drop, a gradual bloodletting. It isn't "theme" Gaddis deals in (his themes are plain) so much as a theory of organism and disease. In *Carpenter's Gothic* the world is a poisonous organism, humankind dying of itself.

The process is gargoylish: a vaudeville turn. Paul's scribbled diagram of a promotion scheme, with all its arrows pointing cause-and-consequence, is mistaken for a map of the fourteenth-century Battle of Crécy. The "big ore find on the mission tract," a lie, is designed to lure American military imperialism into Africa. Liz, roused against McCandless, cries out (quoting Paul muddying it up: Ephusians for Ephesians, now Clausnitz for Clausewitz), "Clausnitz was wrong, it's not that war is politics carried on by other means it's the family carried on by other means," and McCandless, sneering at tribe against tribe, nation against nation, replies: "Well good God! They've been doing that for two thousand years haven't they?"

McCandless is Gaddis's strong seer, a philosophical trader in scourging tirades: " . . . talk about a dark continent I'll tell you something, revelation's the last refuge ignorance finds from reason. Revealed truth is the one weapon stupidity's got against intelligence and that's what the whole damned thing is about . . . you've got enough sects slaughtering each other from Londonderry to Chandigarh to wipe out the whole damned thing . . . just try the Children's Crusade for a sideshow, thousands of kids led into slavery and death by a twelve year old with a letter from Jesus. . . .—all four horsemen riding across the hills of Africa with every damned kind of war you could ask for . . . seven hundred languages they've all been at each other's throats since the creation war, famine, pestilence, death, they ask for food and water somebody hands them an AK47 . . ." Paul, meanwhile, is Gaddis's weak seer, discloser of the shoddy morning news: "Draw the line, run a carrier group off Mombasa and a couple of destroyers down the Mozambique channel, bring in the RDF and put the SAC on red alert. They've got what they want."

Is *Carpenter's Gothic* a "political" novel? An "apocalyptic" novel? A novel of original sin without the illusion of salvation? It is tempting to judge Gaddis as Liz finally judges McCandless: "Because you're the one who wants it," she accuses him, "to see them all go up like that smoke in the furnace all the stupid, ignorant, blown up in the clouds and there's nobody there, there's no rapture or anything just to see them wiped away for good it's really you, isn't it. That you're the one who wants Apocalypse, Armageddon all the sun going out and the sea turned to blood you can't wait no, you're the one who can't wait! . . . because you despise their, not their stupidity no, their hopes because you haven't any, because you haven't any left." But not long after this outburst Liz learns from McCandless's wife—who appears out of nowhere like a clarifying messenger—that McCandless was once in a mental hospital. Another clue hints at a frontal lobotomy. A world saturated in wild despair, and only in despair, turns out to be a madman's image.

Even while he is handing over this straw of hope—that the evangelist of darkest calamity is deranged—Gaddis the trickster may be leading us more deeply into hopelessness. If McCandless, the god of the novel and its intellectual sovereign, the owner of that false-front house of disaster, whose pitiless portrait of our soiled planet we can recognize as exactly congruent with truth-telling—if McCandless is not to be trusted, then where are we? Does Gaddis mean us to conclude that whoever sees things-as-they-are in their fullest tragic illumination will never be credible except under the badge of lunacy? Or does he mean McCandless—whose name, after all, suggests he is the scion of darkness—to speak for the devil? And if so, is Gaddis on the devil's side, if only because the devil is the most eloquent moralist of all? And a novelist to boot, whose papers are irredeemably scrambled in that secret messy room he is forever cleaning up, that room "like Dachau," choked with smoke, where the Bible is stored upside down?

The true god of the novel—god of invention, commerce, and cunning—is of course mercurial Gaddis himself. He is a preternatural technician and engineer: whatever turns, turns out to turn again; things recur, allusions multiply, pretexts accrete, duplicities merge, greed proliferates, nuances breed and repeat. The center holds horribly: "you see how all the God damn pieces fit together." No one in *Carpenter's Gothic* is innocent or uninjured or unheard. It is an unholy landmark of a novel; an extra turret, so to speak, added on to the ample, ingenious, audacious Gothic mansion William Gaddis has slowly been building in American letters.

Truman Capote Reconsidered

TIME AT LENGTH becomes justice. A useful if obscure-sounding literary aphorism, just this moment invented. What it signifies is merely this: if a writer lives long enough, he may himself eventually put behind him the work that brought him early fame, and which the world ought to have put aside in the first place.

I remember reading somewhere not long ago a comment by Truman Capote on his first novel: it was written, he said, by somebody else.

Cruel time flashes out this interesting, only seemingly banal, remark: who is this tiny-fingered flaccid man, with molasses eyes and eunuch's voice, looking like an old caricature of Aeolus, the puff-cheeked little god of wind? We see him now and then on television talk shows, wearing a hay-seed hat, curling his fine feet, his tongue on his lip like a soft fly, genially telling dog stories. Or we read about the vast celebrity parties he is master of, to which whole populations of the famous come, in majestic array of might and mind. Or we hear of him in New Orleans some months ago, in the company of Princess Radziwill, observing the

Rolling Stones and their congregations, with what secret thoughts print will soon make plain. Or we catch him out as a cabal-sniffing inquisitor in *Playboy*, confiding in an interview how "other backgrounds" are not being "given a chance" because of the "predominance of the Jewish Mafia" in American letters. Or, back on television again, we learn from him about the psychology of criminals—which inadvertently lets us in a little on the psychology of people who are attracted to the psychology of criminals. Or we discuss, for months, his puzzling coinage "nonfiction novel," as if some new theory of literature had broken on the world —what he means, it turns out on publication, is the spawn of garden-variety interview journalism, only with this out: he is not to be held morally accountable for it.

(He is not even to be held accountable for his first non-nonfiction novel: it was written by Somebody Else.)

Were all these non-qualities implicit in that long-ago Somebody Else—that boy whose portrait on the back cover of *Other Voicess, Other Rooms* became even more celebrated than the prose inside? Who can forget that boy?—languid but sovereign, lolling in the turn of a curved sofa in bow tie and tattersall vest, with tender mouth and such strange elf-cold eyes. Like everyone else whose youth we have memorized and who has had the bad luck to turn up on television afterward, he was bound to fatten up going toward fifty; and like everyone else who has made some money and gained some ease in the world, he was bound to lose that princely look of the furious dreamer.

On the face of it he was bound to become Somebody Else, in short: not only distant physically from the Dorian Gray of the memorable photograph, and not simply psychologically distant according to the chasm between twenty-three and forty-eight, and not merely (though this chiefly) distant from the sort of redolent prose craft that carried *Other Voices, Other Rooms* to its swift reputation. An even more radical distancing appears to intervene.

It's not only ourselves growing old that makes us into Somebody Else: it's the smell of the times too, the invisible but palpable force called *Zeitgeist*, which is something different from growth, and more capricious. Books change because we change, but no internal reasons, however inexorable, are enough to account for a book's turning to dust twenty-four years afterward. *Other Voices, Other Rooms* is now only dust—glass dust, a heap of glitter, but dust all the same.

Robert Gottlieb, former editor-in-chief of Knopf, some time ago in *Publishers Weekly* took shrewd notice of how the life expectancy of books is affected: Solzhenitsyn, he said, can write as he does, and succeed at it, because in Russia they do not yet know that the nineteenth century is dead.

A century, even a quarter of a century, dies around a book; and then the book lies there, a shaming thing because it shows us how much worse we once were to have liked it; and something else too: it demonstrates exactly how the world seems to shake off what it does not need, old books, old notions of aesthetics, old mind-forms, our own included. The world to the eager eye is a tree constantly pruning itself, and writers are the first to be lopped off. All this means something different from saying merely that a book has dated. All sorts of masterpieces are dated, in every imaginable detail, and yet survive with all their powers. *Other Voices, Other Rooms* is of course dated, and in crucial ways: it would be enough to mention that its Southern family has two black retainers, an old man and his granddaughter, and that when he dies the old man is buried under a tree on the family property, the way one would bury a well-loved dog, and that the granddaughter, having gone north for a new life, is gang-raped on the way, and comes back to the white family's kitchen for love and safety . . . In Harlem now, and in Washington, Los Angeles, Detroit, Newark, and New Rochelle, they are dancing on the grave of this poetry. It was intolerable poetry then too, poetry of the proud, noble, but defective primitive, but went not so much unnoticed as disbelieved; and disbelief is no failing in an aesthetic confection. Even then no one thought Jesus Fever, the old man, and Zoo, the kitchen servant, any more real than the figures on a wedding cake; such figures are, however vulgar, useful to signify outright the fundamental nature of the enterprise. Dated matter in a novel (these signals of locale and wont) disposes of itself—gets eaten up, like the little sugar pair, who are not meant to outlive the afternoon. Dated matter in a novel is not meant to outlive the *Zeitgeist*, which can last a long time, often much longer than its actual components, digesting everything at hand.

But *Other Voices, Other Rooms* is not a dead and empty book because Zoo is, in today's understanding, the progenitrix of black militancy, or because the times that appeared to welcome its particular sensibility are now lost. Indeed, the reason "dated matter" has so little effect on *Other Voices, Other Rooms* is that it is a timeless book, as every autonomous act of craft is intended to be. A jug, after all, is a jug, whether bought last week at the five-and-dime or unearthed at Knossos: its meaning is self-contained—it has a shape, handles, a lip to pour. And *Other Voices, Other Rooms* has a meaning that is similarly self-contained: Subjectivity, images aflash on a single mind, a moment fashioned with no reference to society, a thing aside from judgment. One can judge it as well made or not well made; but one cannot judge it as one judges a deed.

And this is why it is not really possible to turn to the *Zeitgeist* to account for *Other Voices, Other Rooms'* present emptiness. In fiction in the last several years there have been two clearly recognizable drives: to shake off the final vestiges of narration as a mechanism to be viewed seriatim, and to achieve an autonomous art—"where characters," William Gass explains in a remark derived from Gnosticism in general and from MacLeish in particular, "unlike ourselves, freed from existence, can shine like essence, and purely Be." The atmosphere of our most recent moments—Gass's sentence is their credo—ought both to repulse and retrieve *Other Voices, Other Rooms*: it begins deep in narrative like Dickens (a boy setting out on his own to find the father he has never seen), but ends in Being, and shines like "essence," which I take to be, like Tao or satori, recognizable when you have it but otherwise undefinable—and not, surely, accessible, like a deed, to judgment.

The literary *Zeitgeist* is, to use the famous phrase, Against Interpretation; and it is into such a philosophy, freed from existence, and above all freed from the notion of the morally accountable Deed, that *Other Voices, Other Rooms* ought almost flawlessly to glide. For just as its outmoded Negroes do not matter—essence transcends history—so also does the impediment of its rusty narrative works vanish in the dazzle of its prose-poem Being. *Other Voices, Other Rooms* is, as we always boringly say, a vision: a vision apart from its components, which include a paralyzed father who signals by dropping red tennis balls, a Panlike twin, a midget, a transvestite cousin, the aforementioned sad-happy darkies, not one but two decaying manses (one of which is called the Cloud Hotel), and the whole apparatus of a boy's *rite de passage* into probable homosexuality. But the vision is not the sum of any combination of its parts, no more than some or all of the churches of the world add up to the idea of a planet redeemed. Joel Knox, the boy who comes to Skully's Landing in search of his father, is nevertheless after a redemption that has nothing to do with the stuff of the story he passes through; and at the close of the novel he *is* redeemed, because the novel itself is his redemption, the novel is a sacrament for both protagonist and novelist.

A less fancy way of saying all this is that *Other Voices, Other Rooms* is the novel of someone who wanted, with a fixed and single-minded and burning will, to write a novel. The vision of *Other Voices, Other Rooms* is the vision of capital-A Art—essence freed from existence. And what is meant by the cant phrase "the novel ought to be about itself" is this: the will to write a novel expresses the novel itself; the will to make art expresses art itself—"expresses" not in the sense that one is equivalent to the other, but that the fulfillment of desire is itself a thing of value, or enough for literature. This is so much taking the imagining to signify the thing itself (which is, after all, *literature*) that quotidian life—acts followed by their consequences—is left behind at the Cloud Hotel. To quote the theoretician Gass again: "Life is not the subject of fiction."* One would be willing to broaden this comment to strike a more percipient grain: life is not the subject of the sort of fiction that is at home in the American *Zeitgeist* at this moment—despite some beginning strands of dissent. The novel that is said to be "about itself," or "about its own language," belongs not to the hard thing we mean when we say "life," but rather to transcendence, incantation, beatification, grotesquerie, epiphany, rhapsody and rapture—all those tongues that lick the self: a self conceived of as sanctified

* It ought to be noted, though, that much of Gass's fiction brilliantly contradicts his theory of fiction.

(whether by muses or devils or gods) and superhuman. When life—the furious web of society, manners, institutions, ideas, tribal histories, and the thicket of history-of-ideas itself—when life is not the subject of fiction, then magic is. Not fable, invention, metaphor, the varied stuff of literature—but *magic*. And magic is a narcissistic exercise, whether the magic is deemed to be contained within language or within psychology: in either case the nub is autonomous inwardness.

The *Zeitgeist* is just now open to all this. Yet *Other Voices, Other Rooms*—a slim, easy, lyrical book—can no longer be read. Dead and empty. And what of 1948, the year of its publication? What was that time like, the time that sped Capote and his novel to a nearly legendary celebrity that has not since diminished?

In 1948, cruising the lunchbag-odorous Commons of Washington Square College, I used to keep an eye out for *Other Voices, Other Rooms*. That place and that time were turbulent with mainly dumb, mainly truculent veterans in their thirties arrived under the open enrollment of the GI Bill, and the handful of young aesthetes, still dewy with high-school Virgil (*O infelix Dido!*), whose doom it was to wander through that poverty-muttering postwar mob in hapless search of Beauty, found one another through Truman Capote. Other voices, other rooms—ah, how we felt it, the tug of somewhere else, inchoate, luminous, the enameled radiance of our eternal and gifted youth. Instead, here were these veterans, responsible clods, jerks, and dopes, with their preposterous eye-wrinkles, their snapshots of preposterous wives and preposterous little children, the idiotic places they lived in, dopey Quonset huts on some dopey North Brother Island, slow-witted all, unable to conjugate, full of angry pragmatic questions, classroom slumberers grinding their joyless days through English and history and language, coming alive only for Marketing and Accounting, sniggering at Sheats and Kelley, hating Thomas Wolfe, with every mean money-grubbing diaper-stinking aging bone hating Poetry and Beauty and Transfiguration . . .

Capote was the banner against this blight. To walk with Capote in your grasp was as distinctive, and as dissenting from the world's values, as a monk's habit. Capote: that is what the pseudonym signified: a concealing cloak, to be worn by enraptured adepts.

If *Other Voices, Other Rooms* was written by Somebody Else, it was, even more so, read by Somebody Else. Who made Capote famous? I, said the fly, with my covetous eye —I and all those others who clung to him and made him our cult, I and my fellow cabalists for whom he embodied Art Incarnate (among them the late Alfred Chester, who, priestlike, claimed to have Capote's unlisted telephone number). He was not much older than we were, and had already attained what we longed for: the eucharist of the jacket biography. So we seized the book, the incongruous moment, the resplendent and ecstasy-stung words:

> . . . the run of reindeer hooves came crisply tinkling down the street, and Mr. Mystery, elegantly villainous in his black cape, appeared in their wake riding a most beautiful boatlike sleigh: it was made of scented wood, a carved red swan graced its front, and silver bells were strung like beads to make a sail: swinging, billowing-out, what shivering melodies it sang as the sleigh, with Joel aboard and warm in the folds of Mr. Mystery's cape, cut over snowdeep fields and down unlikely hills.
>
> . . .

> Whereupon the room commenced to vibrate slightly, then more so, chairs overturned, the curio cabinet spilled its contents, a mirror cracked, the pianola, composing its own doomed jazz, held a haywire jamboree: down went the house, down into the earth, down, down, past Indian tombs, past the deepest root, the coldest stream, down, down, into the furry arms of horned children whose bumblebee eyes withstand forests of flame.

Who could withstand these forests of flaming prose? In the generation of his own youth Capote was the shining maggot in the fiction of the young.

The *Zeitgeist* then had nothing to do with it. The *Zeitgeist* now ought to have everything to do with it, but masses of the young do not now read the early Capote; the new cults generally form around anti-stylists.

Something needs to be explained. It is not that the novel was written, and read, by Somebody Else; after a fistful of years all novels are. It is not that the mood of the era is now against Poetry and Transfiguration; the opposite is true. Above all, it is not that *Other Voices, Other Rooms* is dead and empty only now; it always was.

What needs to be explained is the whole notion of the relation of *Zeitgeist* to fiction. In fact there is none, yet there is no fallacy more universally swallowed. For what must be understood about an era's moods is this: often they are sham or nostalgia or mimicry, and they do not always tell the truth about the human condition; more often than not the *Zeitgeist* is a lie, even about its own data. If, as Gottlieb persuades us, Solzhenitsyn comes to us with all the mechanism of the Tolstoyan novel intact, and yet appears to come to us as a living literary force, it is not because the nineteenth century is not yet dead in the Russian mind, although that may be perfectly true. It is because, whatever its mechanics, the idea of the novel is attached to life, to the life of deeds, which are susceptible of both judgment and interpretation; and the novel of Deed is itself a deed to be judged and interpreted. But the novel that is fragrant with narcissism, that claims essence sans existence, that either will not get its shoes drekky or else elevates drek to cultishness—the novel, in short, of the aesthetic will—*that* novel cannot survive its cult.

Further: one would dare to say that the survival of the novel as a form depends on this distinction between the narcissistic novel and the novel of Deed.

On the surface it would seem that Capote's progress, over a distance of seventeen years, from *Other Voices, Other Rooms* to *In Cold Blood*—from the prose-poetry of transfiguration to the more direct and plain, though still extremely artful, prose of his narrative journalism—is a movement from the narcissistic novel to the novel of Deed; Capote himself never once appears in the pages of his crime story. But there is no forward movement, it is all only a seeming; both the novel and the "nonfiction novel" are purely aesthetic shapes. In *Other Voices, Other Rooms* it is the ecstasy of language that drives the book; in *In Cold Blood* it is something journalists call "objectivity," but it is more immaculate than that. "My files would almost fill a whole small room up to the ceiling," Capote told an interviewer; for years he had intertwined his mind and his days with a pair of murderers—to get, he said, their point of view. He had intertwined his life; he was himself a character who impinged, in visit after visit, on the criminals; and yet, with aesthetic immaculateness, he left himself out. Essence without existence; to achieve the alp of truth without the risk of the footing. But finally and at bottom he must be taken at his word that *In*

Cold Blood has the blood of a novel. He cannot have that *and* the journalist's excuse for leaving himself out of it—in the end the "nonfiction novel" must be called to account like any novel. And no novel has ever appeared, on its face, to be more the novel of Deed than this narrative of two killers—despite which it remains judgment-free, because it exempts itself from its own terms. Chekhov in "Ward No. 6," one of the most intelligent short novels ever written, understood how the man who deals with the fate of the imprisoned begins to partake of the nature of the imprisoned; this is the great moral hint, the profound unholy question, that lurks in *In Cold Blood*. But it is evaded, in the name of objectivity, of journalistic distance, all those things that the novel has no use for. In the end *In Cold Blood* is, like *Other Voices, Other Rooms*, only another design, the pattern of a hot desire to make a form; one more aesthetic manipulation. It cannot go out of itself—one part of it leads only to another part. Like *Other Voices, Other Rooms*, it is well made, but it has excised its chief predicament, the relation of the mind of the observer to the mind of the observed, and therefore it cannot be judged, it escapes interpretation because it flees its own essential deed. Such "objectivity" is as narcissistic as the grossest "subjectivity": it will not expose itself to an accounting.

Despite every appearance, every modification of style, Capote is at the root *not* Somebody Else. The beautiful reclining boy on the jacket of *Other Voices, Other Rooms* and the middle-aged television celebrity who tells dog stories are one, more so than either would imagine; nothing in Capote as writer has changed. If the world has changed, it has not touched Capote's single and persistent tone. Joel Knox in the last sentence of *Other Voices, Other Rooms* looks back "at the boy he had left behind." False prophecy. Nothing has been left behind—only, perhaps, the younger writer's habit of the decorated phrase. What continues in Capote, and continues in force, is the idea that life is style, and that shape and mood are what matter in and out of fiction. That is the famous lie on which aesthetics feeds the centuries. Life is not style, but what we do: Deed. And so is literature. Otherwise Attic jugs would be our only mentors.

What Drives Saul Bellow

A CONCORDANCE, A REPRISE, a summary, all the old themes and obsessions hauled up by a single tough rope—does there come a time when, out of the blue, a writer offers to decode himself? Not simply to divert, or paraphrase, or lead around a corner, or leave clues, or set out decoys (familiar apparatus, art-as-usual), but to kick aside the maze, spill wine all over the figure in the carpet, bury the grand metaphor, and disclose the thing itself? To let loose, in fact, the secret? And at an hour no one could have predicted? And in a modestly unlikely form? The cumulative art concentrated, so to speak, in a vial?

For Saul Bellow, at age sixty-eight, and with his Nobel speech some years behind him, the moment for decoding is now, and the decoding itself turns up unexpectedly in the shape of *Him with His Foot in His Mouth*, a volume of five stories, awesome yet imperfect, at least one of them overtly a fragment, and none malleable enough to achieve a real "ending." Not that these high-pressure stories are inconclusive. With all their brilliant wiliness of predicament and brainy language shocked into originality, they are magisterially the opposite. They tell us, in the clarified tight compass he has not been so at home in since *Seize the Day*, what drives Bellow.

What drives Bellow. The inquiry is seductive, because Bellow is Bellow, one of three living American Nobel laureates (the only one, curiously, whose natural language is English), a writer for whom great fame has become a sort of obscuring nimbus, intruding on the cleanly literary. When *The Dean's December* was published in 1982, it was not so much reviewed as scrutinized like sacred entrails: had this idiosyncratically independent writer turned "conservative"? Had he soured on Augiesque America? Was his hero, Albert Corde, a lightly masked Saul Bellow? Can a writer born into the Jewish condition successfully imagine and inhabit a WASP protagonist? In short, it seemed impossible to rid Bellow's novel of Bellow's presence, to free it as fiction.

In consequence of which, one is obliged to put a riddle: if you found this book of stories at the foot of your bed one morning, with the title page torn away and the author's name concealed, would you know it, after all, to be Bellow? Set aside, for the interim, the ruckus of advertised "models": that Victor Wulpy of "What Kind of Day Did You Have?" has already been identified as the art critic Harold Rosenberg, Bellow's late colleague at the University of Chicago's Committee on Social Thought; that the prodigy-hero of "Zetland: By a Character Witness" is fingered as the double of Isaac Rosenfeld, Bellow's boyhood friend, a writer and Reichian who died at thirty-eight. There are always anti-readers, resenters or recanters of the poetry side of life, mean distrusters of the force and turbulence of the free imagination, who are ready to demote fiction to the one-on-one flatness of photo-journalism. Omitting, then, extraterritorial interests not subject to the tractable laws of fiction—omitting *gossip*—would you recognize Bellow's muscle, his swift and glorious eye?

Yes, absolutely; a thousand times yes. It is Bellow's Chicago, Bellow's portraiture—these faces, these heads!—above all, Bellow's motor. That Bellow himself may acknowledge a handful of biographical sources—"germs," textured shells—does not excite. The life on the page resists the dust of flesh, and is indifferent to external origins. Victor Wulpy is who he is as Bellow's invention; and certainly Zetland. These inventions take us not to Bellow as man, eminence, and friend of eminences (why should I care whom Bellow knows?), but to the private clamor in the writing. And it is this clamor, this sound of a thrashing soul—comic because metaphysical, metaphysical because aware of itself as a farcical combatant on a busy planet—that is unequivocally distinguishable as the pure Bellovian note. "The clever, lucky old Berlin Jew, whose head was like a round sourdough loaf, all uneven and dusted with flour, had asked the right questions"—if this canny sentence came floating to us over the waves, all alone on a dry scrap inside a bottle, who would not instantly identify it as Bellow's voice?

It is a voice demonized by the right (or possibly the right) questions. The characters it engenders are dazed by what may be called the principle of plenitude. Often they appear to take startled credit for the wild ingenuity of the world's abundance, as if they had themselves brought it into being. It isn't that they fiddle with the old freshman philosophy-course conundrum, Why is there everything instead of nothing? They ask rather: What is this everything composed of? What is it preoccupied with? They are knocked out by the volcanic multiplicity of human thought, they want to count up all the ideas that have ever accumulated in at least our part of the universe, they roil, burn, quake with cosmic hunger. This makes them, sometimes, jesters, and sometimes only sublime fools.

"What Kind of Day Did You Have?," the novella that is the centerpiece of this volume, also its masterpiece, gives us a day in the life of "one of the intellectual captains of the modern world"—Victor Wulpy, who, if love in sublime and lovers foolish, qualifies as a reacher both high and absurd. Reaching for the telephone in a Buffalo hotel, Victor calls his lover, Katrina Goliger, in suburban Chicago, and invites—commands—her to fly in zero weather from Chicago to Buffalo solely in order to keep him company on his flight from Buffalo to Chicago. "With Victor refusal was not one of her options," so Trina, sourly divorced, the mother of two unresponsive young daughters, acquiesces. Victor's egotism and self-indulgence, the by-blows of a nearly fatal recent illness and of a powerfully centered arrogance, are as alluring as his fame, his dependency, his brilliance, his stiff game leg "extended like one of Admiral Nelson's cannon under wraps," his size-sixteen shoes that waft out "a human warmth" when Trina tenderly pulls them off. Victor is a cultural lion who exacts, Trina surmises, ten thousand dollars per lecture. In Buffalo his exasperating daughter, a rabbinical school dropout who once advised her decorous mother to read a manual on homosexual foreplay as a means of recapturing Victor's sexual interest, hands him her violin to lug to Chicago for repairs; it is Trina who does the lugging. Victor is headed for Chicago to address the Executives Association, "National Security Council types," but really to be with Trina. Trina suffers from a carping angry sister, a doting hanger-on named Krieggstein, who carries guns and may or may not be a real cop, and the aftermath of a divorce complicated by psychiatric appointments, custody wrangling, greed. She is also wrestling with the perplexities of a children's story she hopes to write, if only she can figure out how to extricate her elephant from his crisis on the top floor of a department store, with no way down or out. At the same time Victor is being pursued, in two cities, by Wrangel, a white-furred Hollywood plot-concocter, celebrated maker of *Star Wars*-style films, a man hot with ideas who is impelled to tell Victor that "ideas are trivial" and Trina that Victor is a "promoter."

Meanwhile, planes rise and land, or don't take off at all; there is a bad-weather detour to Detroit and a chance for serendipitous sex in an airport hotel, and finally a perilous flight in a Cessna, where, seemingly facing death in a storm, Trina asks Victor to say he loves her. He refuses, they touch down safely at O'Hare, the story stops but doesn't exactly end. Wrangel has helped Trina dope out what to do about the trapped elephant, but Trina herself is left tangled in her troubles, submissively energetic and calculating, and with no way up or out.

What emerges from these fluid events, with all their cacophonous espousal of passion, is a mind at the pitch of majesty. The agitated, untamable, yet flagging figure of the dying Victor Wulpy, a giant in the last days of his greatness, seizes us not so much for the skein of shrewd sympathy and small pathos in which he is bound and exposed, as for the claims of these furious moments of insatiable connection: "Katrina had tried to keep track of the subjects covered between Seventy-sixth Street and Washington Square: the politics of modern Germany from the Holy Roman Empire through the Molotov-Ribbentrop Pact; what surrealist communism had *really* been about; Kiesler's architecture; Hans Hofmann's influence; what limits were set by liberal democracy for the development of the arts . . . Various views on the crises in economics, cold war, metaphysics, sexaphysics."

Not that particular "subjects" appear fundamentally to matter to Bellow, though they thrillingly engage him. The young Zetland, discovering *Moby-Dick*, cries out to his wife: "There really is no human life without this poetry. Ah, Lottie, I've been starving on symbolic logic." In fact he has been thriving on it, and on every other kind of knowledge. "What were we here for, of all strange beings and creatures the strangest? Clear colloid eyes to see with, for a while, and see so finely, and a palpitating universe to see, and so many human messages to give and receive. And the bony box for thinking and for the storage of thought, and a cloudy heart for feelings."

It is the hound of heaven living in the bony box of intelligence that dogs Bellow, and has always dogged him. If the soul is the mind at its purest, best, clearest, busiest, profoundest, then Bellow's charge has been to restore the soul to American literature. The five stories in *Him with His Foot in His Mouth* are the distillation of that charge. Bellow's method is to leave nothing unobserved and unremarked, to give way to the unprogrammed pressure of language and intellect, never to retreat while imagination goes off like kites. These innovative sentences, famous for pumping street-smarts into literary blood vessels, are alive and snaky, though hot. And Bellow's quick-witted lives of near-poets, as recklessly confident in the play and intricacy of ideas as those of the grand Russians, are Russian also in the gusts of natural force that sweep through them: unpredictable cadences, instances where the senses fuse ("A hoarse sun rolled up"), single adjectives that stamp whole portraits, portraits that stamp whole lives (hair from which "the kink of high vigor had gone out"), the knowing hand on the ropes of how-things-work, the stunning catalogues of worldliness ("commodity brokers, politicians, personal-injury lawyers, bagmen and fixers, salesmen and promoters"), the boiling presence of Chicago, with its "private recesses for seduction and skulduggery." A light flavoring of Jewish social history dusts through it all: e.g., Victor Wulpy reading the Pentateuch in Hebrew in a cheder on the Lower East Side in 1912; or Zetland's immigrant father, who, in a Chicago neighborhood "largely Polish and Ukrainian, Swedish, Catholic, Orthodox, and Evangelical Lutheran . . . preferred the company of musical people and artists, bohemian garment workers, Tolstoyans, followers of Emma Goldman and of Isadora Duncan, revolutionaries who wore pince-nez, Russian blouses, Lenin or Trotsky beards."

What this profane and holy comedy of dazzling, beating, multiform profusion hints at, paradoxically, is that Bellow is as notable for what isn't in his pages as for what is. No preciousness, of the ventriloquist kind or any other; no carelessness either (formidably the opposite); no romantic aping of archaisms or nostalgias; no restraints born out of theories of form, or faddish tenets of experimentalism or ideological crypticness; no neanderthal flatness in the name of cleanliness of prose; no gods of nihilism; no gods of subjectivity; no philosophy of parody. As a consequence of these and other salubrious omissions and insouciant dismissals, Bellow's detractors have accused him of being "old-fashioned," "conventional," of continuing to write a last-gasp American version of the nineteenth-century European novel; his omnivorous

"Russianness" is held against him, and at the same time he is suspected of expressing the deadly middle class.

The grain of truth in these disparagements takes note, I think, not of regression or lagging behind, but of the condition of local fiction, which has more and more closeted itself monkishly away in worship of its own liturgies—i.e., of its own literariness. Whereas Bellow, seeing American writing in isolation from America itself, remembered Whitman and Whitman's cornucopia: in homage to which he fabricated a new American sentence. All this, of course, has been copiously remarked of Bellow ever since Augie March; but these five stories say something else. What Bellow is up to here is nothing short of a reprise of Western intellectual civilization. His immigrants and children of immigrants, blinking their fetal eyes in the New World, seem to be cracking open the head of Athena to get themselves born, in eager thirst for the milk of Enlightenment. To put it fortissimo: Bellow has brain on the brain, which may cast him as *the* dissident among American writers.

But even this is not the decoding or revelation I spoke of earlier. It has not been enough for Bellow simply to have restored attention to society—the density and entanglements of its urban textures, viz.: "He [Woody Selbst in "A Silver Dish"] maintained the bungalow—this took in roofing, pointing, wiring, insulation, air-conditioning—and he paid for heat and light and food, and dressed them all out of Sears, Roebuck and Wieboldt's, and bought them a TV, which they watched as devoutly as they prayed." Nor has it been enough for Bellow to have restored attention to the overriding bliss of learning: "Scholem and I [of "Cousins"], growing up on neighboring streets, attending the same schools, had traded books, and since Scholem had no trivial interests, it was Kant and Schelling all the way, it was Darwin and Nietzsche, Dostoyevsky and Tolstoy, and in our senior year it was Oswald Spengler. A whole year was invested in *The Decline of the West*."

To this thickness of community and these passions of mind Bellow has added a distinctive ingredient, not new on any landscape, but shamelessly daring just now in American imaginative prose. Let the narrator of "Cousins" reveal it: "We enter the world without prior notice, we are manifested before we can be aware of manifestation. An original self exists, or, if you prefer, an original soul . . . I was invoking my own fundamental perspective, that of a person who takes for granted distortion in the ordinary way of seeing but has never given up the habit of referring all truly important observations to that original self or soul." Bellow, it seems, has risked mentioning—who can admit to this without literary embarrassment?—the Eye of God.

And that is perhaps what his intellectual fevers have always pointed to. "Cousins" speaks of it explicitly: "As a man is, so he sees. As the Eye is formed, such are its powers." Yet "Cousins" is overtly about "the observation of cousins," and moves from cousin Tanky of the rackets to cousin Seckel whose "talent was for picking up strange languages" to cousin Motty, who, "approaching ninety, still latched on to people to tell them funny things." All this reflects a powerfully recognizable Jewish family feeling—call it, in fact, family love, though it is love typically mixed with amazement and disorder. The professor-narrator of "Him with His Foot in His Mouth"—the title story—like cousin Motty is also a funny fellow, the author of a long letter conscientiously recording his compulsion to make jokes that humiliate and destroy:

putdowns recollected in tranquillity. But the inescapable drive to insult through wit is equated with "seizure, rapture, demonic possession, frenzy, *Fatum*, divine madness, or even solar storm," so this lambent set of comic needlings is somehow more than a joke, and may touch on the Eye of Dionysus. "A Silver Dish," with its upside-down echo of the biblical tale of Joseph's silver cup, concerns the companionable trials of Woody Selbst and his rogue father, the two of them inextricably entwined, though the father has abandoned his family; all the rest, mother, sisters, aunt, and ludicrous immigrant reverend uncle, are Jewish converts to evangelicalism. Woody, like Joseph in Egypt, supports them all. The Eye of God gazes through this story too, not in the bathetic converts but in the scampish father, "always, always something up his sleeve." "Pop had made Woody promise to bury him among Jews"—neglected old connections being what's up that raffish sleeve. It is Woody's "clumsy intuition" that "the goal set for this earth was that it should be filled with good, saturated with it." All the same, the commanding image in this narrative is that of a buffalo calf snatched and devoured by a crocodile in the waters of the Nile, in that alien country where Joseph footed the family bills and his father Jacob kept his wish to be buried among Jews up his sleeve almost to the end.

The commanding image of this volume—the concordance, so to speak, to all of Bellow's work—turns up in the reflections of one of the cousins, Ijah Brodsky: "'To long for the best that ever was': this was not an abstract project. I did not learn it over a seminar table. It was a constitutional necessity, physiological, temperamental, based on sympathies which could not be acquired. Human absorption in faces, deeds, bodies, drew me toward metaphysical grounds. I had these peculiar metaphysics as flying creatures have their radar."

This metaphysical radar (suspiciously akin to the Eye of God) "decodes" Saul Bellow; and these five ravishing stories honor and augment his genius.

Literary Blacks and Jews

In 1958, in his celebrated collection *The Magic Barrel*, Malamud published a short story about a Negro and a Jew. It was called "Angel Levine," and it contrived for Manischevitz, a Joblike figure who has "suffered many reverses and indignities," the promise of redemption through a magical black man. Manischevitz has already lost his cleaning establishment through fire, his only son through war, his only daughter through a runaway marriage with a "lout." "Thereafter Manischevitz was victimized by excruciating backaches and found himself unable to work . . . His Fanny, a good wife and mother, who had taken in washing and sewing, began before his eyes to waste away . . . there was little hope."

A black man appears. His idiom is elaborate in Father Divine style: "If I may, insofar as one is able to, identify myself, I bear the name of Alexander Levine." Manischevitz at first doubts that this derby-hatted figure is a Jew, but the Negro says the blessing for bread in "sonorous Hebrew" and declares himself to be a "bona fide angel of God," on probation. Of this Manischevitz is not persuaded. "So if

God sends to me an angel, why a black?"

The angel departs, rebuffed by Manischevitz's distrust. Then "Fanny lay at death's door," and Manischevitz, desperate, goes "without belief" in search of the black angel. In a Harlem synagogue he witnesses a small knot of Negro worshipers in skullcaps bending over the Scroll of the Law, conducting something very like a Baptist theology session: "On de face of de water moved de speerit . . . From de speerit ariz de man." Passing through a lowlife cabaret, Manischevitz is jeered at: "Exit, Yankel, Semitic trash." When at last he finds the black Levine, he is broken enough to burst out with belief: "I think you are an angel from God." Instantly Fanny recovers, and as a reward Levine is admitted to heaven. 'In the flat Fanny wielded a dust mop under the bed . . . 'A wonderful thing, Fanny,' Manischevitz said. 'Believe me, there are Jews everywhere.'"

A distinction must be made. Is it the arrival of a divine messenger we are to marvel at, or is it the notion of a black Jew? If this is a story with a miracle in it, then the only miracle it proposes is that a Jew can be found among the redemptive angels. And if we are meant to be "morally" surprised, it is that—for once—belief in the supernatural is rewarded by a supernatural act of mercy. But the narrative is altogether offhand about the question of the angel's identity: Levine is perfectly matter-of-fact about it, there is nothing at all miraculous in the idea that a black man can also be a Jew. In a tale about the supernatural, this is what emerges as the "natural" element—as natural-feeling as Manischevitz's misfortunes and his poverty. Black misfortune and poverty have a different resonance—Manischevitz's wanderings through Harlem explain the differences—but, like the Jews' lot, the blacks' has an everyday closeness, for Manischevitz the smell of a familiar fate. To him—and to Malamud at the end of the fifties—that black and Jew are one is no miracle.

A little more than a decade later, with the publication of *The Tenants*,* the proposition seems hollow. Again Malamud offers a parable of black and Jew culminating in fantasy, but now the fantasy has Jew slashing with ax, black with saber, destroying each other in a passionate bloodletting. The novel's last paragraph is eerily liturgical—the word "mercy" repeated one hundred and fifteen times, and once in Hebrew. Nevertheless *The Tenants* is a merciless book. Here are the two lines which are its last spoken exchange:

"Bloodsuckin Jew Niggerhater."
"Anti-Semitic Ape."

It took the narrowest blink of time for Malamud, who more than any other American writer seeks to make a noble literature founded on personal compassion, to come from "Believe me, there are Jews everywhere" to this. How was the transmutation from magical brotherhood to ax-murder wrought? Is it merely that society has changed so much since the late 1950s, or is it that the author of "Angel Levine" was, even then, obtuse? If the difference in Malamud's imaginative perception lies only in our own commonplace perception that the social atmosphere has since altered in the extreme—from Selma to Forest Hills—then "Angel Levine," far from being a mythically representative tale about suffering brothers, is now no more than a dated magazine story. One test of the durability of fiction is whether it still tells even a partial truth ten years after

* Farrar, Straus and Giroux, 1971.

publication. The conclusion of *The Tenants* seems "true" now—i.e., it fits the current moment outside fiction. But a change in social atmosphere is not enough to account for the evanescence or lastingness of a piece of fiction. There are other kinds of truth than sociological truth. There is the truth that matches real events in the world—in *The Tenants*, it is the black man and the Jew turning on each other—and there is the truth that accurately describes what can only be called aspiration. Even in the world of aspiration, it is a question whether "Angel Levine" remains true. And on the last page of *The Tenants*, when Jew and black cut sex and brains from each other, Malamud writes: "Each, thought the writer, feels the anguish of the other." This is the truth of invisible faith, and it is a question whether this too can survive.

"The anguish of the other" is a Malamudic assumption, endemic in his fiction. The interior of many of Malamud's fables resounds with the injunction that for the sake of moral aspiration one must *undergo*. Yakov Blok of *The Fixer* is an ordinary man with ordinary failings, born a Jew but not yet an accountable Jew until he has undergone, in his own flesh, the terror of Jewish fate. In *The Assistant* Morris Bober's helper, the Italian Frank Alpine, formerly a hold-up man, becomes a Jew through gradually taking on the obligations of a Jew, ultimately even undergoing painful but "inspiring" circumcision. The idea of the *usefulness* of submitting to a destiny of anguish is not a particularly Jewish notion; suffering as purification is far closer to the Christian ethos. Jewish martyrs are seen to be only martyrs, not messiahs or even saints. Malamud's world often proposes a kind of hard-won, eked-out saintliness: suffering and spiritual goodness are somehow linked. The real world of humanity—which means also the real world of the Jews

—is not like this. "Bad" Jews went up in smoke at Auschwitz too—surely embezzlers as well as babies, not only *tsadikim* but misers too, poets as well as kleptomaniacs. Not one single Jew ever deserved his martyrdom, but not every martyr is a holy man. For Malamud all good men are Job.

Nevertheless there remains a thin strand of connection between Malamud's visionary "Angel Levine" and a commonplace of Jewish temperament, between the messianic insistence on the anguish of the other and the common sense of ordinary, "bad," Jews. The sociological—the "real"—counterpart of Malamud's holy fables is almost always taken for granted by Jews: it is, simply put, that Jews have always known hard times, and are therefore naturally sympathetic to others who are having, or once had, hard times. The "naturally" is what is important. It is a feeling so normal as to be unrelated to spiritual striving, self-purification, moral accountability, prophecy, anything at all theoretical or lofty. This plain observation about particularized suffering requires no special sensitiveness; *naturally* there are Jews everywhere, and some of them are black.

But what has surprised some Jews, perhaps many, is that this Jewish assumption—this quiet tenet, to use a firmer word, that wounds recognize wounds—is not only *not* taken for granted by everyone else, especially by blacks, but is given no credibility whatever. Worse, to articulate the assumption is to earn the accusation of impudence. Nowadays the accusers would include numbers of Jews who point out how thoroughly racism has infiltrated the life of Jewish neighborhoods and institutions; Jews, they say, are as racist as anyone—maybe more so, in view of (the litany begins) those Jewish shopkeepers who have traditionally been the face-to-face exploiters of the black ghetto. For all these accusers, "Angel Levine" must seem not just dated, obsolete, a sentimental excrescence of that remote era when Jews were as concerned with CORE as they were with UJA—but *wrong*. And many young blacks writing today would regard its premise not only as not a moral hope, but as a hurtful lie. Or else would see Manischevitz's salvation as simply another instance of Jewish exploitation, this time of black benevolence.

Black distrust of this heritage of Jewish sympathy is obviously a social predicament, but it is, curiously, a literary one as well. If the distrust has caused a blight on the sympathy, it turns out also that the distrust antedates the withering of that sympathy. The historical weight of "Angel Levine" was this: Negroes are not *goyim*, not in the full oppressive meaning of that word. How could they be? Antisemitism is not properly a Negro appurtenance—it is not historically black, any more than plantation-slave guilt is properly a Jewish burden. Thirteen years later *The Tenants* appears to reply: but no, the black man is a *goy* after all; and perhaps always was. Between these contradictory and irreducible formulations, Jewish astonishment came to fruition. It was as improbable for the Jew to imagine himself in the role of persecutor—or even indifferent bystander—as it was for him to imagine the black man in that same role. Yet by the late sixties Jews and blacks were recognizable, for and by one another, in no other guise. In a 1966 symposium in *Midstream* on the relations between blacks and Jews, the sociologist C. Eric Lincoln wrote: "One could argue the expectation that if the Jews are not especially moved by faith, then they ought to be moved by experience. Perhaps so. But the best way to forget an unpleasant experience is not by becoming implicated in someone else's troubles." If this sounded like a sensible generality, it was nevertheless shocking to Jews because it was so thoroughly contrary to the way Jews had been experiencing their own reality, their own normality.

But 1966 was, it turns out, just about midway in time between the redemptiveness of "Angel Levine" and the murderous conclusion of *The Tenants*—the corrosion of relations had already begun. It began perhaps not so much because of the emergence of black political violence and Jewish fear of that violence, and not even because anti-semitism had again become the socialism of the militant masses, but more fundamentally out of the responsiveness of America itself: the Jews have been lucky in America, the blacks not. Manischevitz's daughter—we can imagine it—moves out of the foul old neighborhood to Long Island; the black Levine, according to Malamud, has no place green to go but heaven.

Jews are nowadays reminded that this difference—America felt simultaneously as Jewish Eden and black inferno—has always been exactly the thing that called into question the authenticity of Jewish sympathy; that this disparity from the beginning made the Jews suspect to resentful blacks, that Jewish commitment to black advancement, much less black assertion, *had* to be undermined by the Jews' pleasure in an America open and sweet to them. The statement "The blacks have not been lucky in America" is used now as a reproof to these luckier Jews for the impudence of their empathy, and to show it up as a lie—an ineluctable time-bomb sort of lie: if Jewish identification with black causes was after all not intended to be traitorous, then it was destined by Jewish success to become so. That most American Jews are themselves less than eighty years distant from their own miseries in the Russian Pale is said to be wiped out by their American good luck, and all at once; Jews who lay claim to historical memory are ridiculed as pretentious or bullying—present security is taken for a mandatory form of amnesia.

But this very formulation—the hell of being black in America—that is today raised against Jews to chide them for the vanity and presumptuousness of assuming historical parallels, is nevertheless not tolerated when Jews themselves proffer it. Either it is taken as still another meaningless white *mea culpa*, or else as a sign of greenhorn uppityness: the Jew putting on airs in the pretense of a *mea culpa* he hasn't been around long enough to earn. Lack of sympathy is an obvious offense; sympathy turns out to be more offensive yet. The point is surprising but unsubtle. If the current wound-licking withdrawal of Jews is now seen as an outrage or an expected betrayal, what of that earlier, poignantly spontaneous Jewish concern? In the very hour of its freest, most impassioned expression, it was judged as a means to take the African-American's humanity away from him—even then. To illustrate this astounding statement one must turn from the social side to the literary.

Sociologists—I hope I am permitted this fractionally unfair jibe—arrive at their preconceptions cautiously and soberly, but it is the smoothness of their preconceptions they are all the while aiming for. Literary minds work rawly and unashamedly through their beliefs, and have the skeptical grace to arrive at no man's land. Both Jew and black in *The Tenants* are literary men. Their war is a war of manhood and of art. The book has no conclusion and stops in the middle of an incoherency. Eight years before the publication of *The Tenants*, five years after the appearance of "Angel Levine," at the absolute height of "Jewish concern" for the condition of being black in America, a Jew and a black, both literary men, acted out an adumbration of the tragic discord (this phrase is not too grandiose) of *The Tenants*. Their war was a war of manhood (what does it mean to be human) and of art (what are a writer's most urgent sources). Their clash led to no tangible conclusion and stopped in the middle of a double questioning: "how it seems to Ellison I cannot really say," Irving Howe wrote at the last, "though I should like very much to know." "You should not feel unhappy about this or think that I regard you either as dishonorable or an enemy. I hope," Ralph Ellison had already written, "you will come to view this exchange as an act of, shall we say, 'antagonistic cooperation'?"

("Each, thought the writer, feels the anguish of the other.")

The exchange is seminal and ought to be republished all in one place for its superb documentary value—a collision rich in felt honesty and therefore somehow strange, hurtful and agonizing, eluding decent summarization. Ellison's side in particular is a remarkably useful notation in the history not so much of black as of Jewish self-understanding. That there is space here only to give the argument with the sort of crude speed one would ordinarily eschew is probably, for purposes of illuminating a single point, all to the good—that single point being the response of one profoundly gifted black writer to "Jewish concern."

It ought to be made instantly clear that nothing in Howe's "Black Boys and Native Sons"—the essay that triggered the debate with Ellison, first published in *Dissent* (Autumn 1963)—was overtly written from the viewpoint of a Jew. The essay was, first of all, a consideration of Baldwin and Wright, and finally of Ellison himself. Baldwin, Howe observed, had at the start of his career backed off from Wright's "nightmare of remembrance," hoping to "'prevent myself from becoming *merely* a Negro; or even, merely a Negro writer.'" And Ellison, Howe noted, was the "Negro writer who has come closest to satisfying Baldwin's program." Appraising Ellison's novel *Invisible Man*, Howe marveled at "the apparent freedom it displays from the ideological and emotional penalties suffered by Negroes in this country," but at the same time admitted he was troubled by "the sudden, unprepared, and implausible assertion of unconditioned freedom with which the novel ends." "To write simply about 'Negro experience' with the esthetic distance urged by the critics of the fifties, is a moral and psychological impossibility," Howe charged, "for plight and protest are inseparable from that experience." And while acknowledging that "the posture of militancy, no matter how great the need for it, exacts a heavy price from the writer," Howe set his final sympathies down on the side of Wright's "clenched militancy" and Baldwin's ultimately developed "rage."

As against Ellison's affirmation of America as a place of "rich diversity and . . . almost magical fluidity and freedom," Howe wrote:

> What, then, was the experience of a man with a black skin, would *could* it be in this country? How could a Negro put pen to paper, how could he so much as think or breathe, without some impulsion to protest, be it harsh or mild, political or private, released or buried? The "sociology" of his existence formed a constant pressure on his literary work, and not merely in the way this might be true for any writer, but with a pain and a ferocity that nothing could remove.

Afterward Ellison was to characterize these phrases as "Howe, appearing suddenly in blackface." The reply to

Howe, an essay of great flexibility and authority, came in the pages of *The New Leader* the following winter, and what Ellison made plain was that he was first of all a writer and a man, and took his emotional priorities from that: "Evidently Howe feels that unrelieved suffering is the only 'real' Negro experience, and that the true Negro writer must be ferocious . . . One unfamiliar with what Howe stands for would get the impression that when he looks at a Negro he sees not a human being but an abstract embodiment of living hell."

In coming out for the autonomy of art, Ellison seemed to leave Howe stuck with all the disabilities, crudenesses, and ingenuousness of the militant Protest Novel. Yet in almost the next breath here is Ellison defending his own militancy as unassailable: "I assure you that no Negroes are beating down my door, putting pressure on me to join the Negro Freedom Movement, for the simple reason that they realize that I am enlisted for the duration . . . Their demands, like that of many whites, are that I publish more novels . . . But then, Irving, they recognize what you have not allowed yourself to see: namely that my reply to your essay is itself a small though necessary action in the Negro struggle for freedom." Here Ellison suddenly seems to be giving Howe a victory. Even in *not* writing the Protest Novel he is protesting; *by virtue of being black* his heart is instantly recognizable—by fellow blacks—as being in the right place, "enlisted."—And had not Howe argued, "But even Ellison cannot help being caught up with the *idea* of the Negro"?

This part of the argument—complex and blazing, essentially the classic quarrel between critic and imaginative artist, and between the artist's own two selves, the "esthetic" and the "engaged"—is also an uncanny fore-echo of one of Malamud's preoccupations in *The Tenants*. There, however, it is the Jew who assumes Ellison's overall position of the free artist committed first of all to the clean fall of his language, and the black man who expresses Howe's implacability. What this reversal portends we shall see in a moment, but first it is necessary to look at Ellison's consideration of Howe as Jew. It comes very suddenly—and I think justly—in his reply, and points to the absence anywhere in Howe's remarks of the admission that he is a Jew. Whether or not Howe himself thought this relevant is not the issue; what is important is that Ellison thought it relevant, and scornfully rounded on Howe for having called himself a "white intellectual."

> . . . in situations such as this [Ellison wrote] many Negroes, like myself, make a positive distinction between "whites" and "Jews." Not to do so could be either offensive, embarrassing, unjust or even dangerous. If I would know who I am and preserve who I am, then I must see others distinctly whether they see me so or no. Thus I feel uncomfortable whenever I discover Jewish intellectuals writing as though *they* were guilty of enslaving my grandparents, or as though the *Jews* were responsible for the system of segregation. Not only do they have enough troubles of their own, as the saying goes, but Negroes know this only too well.
>
> The real guilt of such Jewish intellectuals lies in their facile, perhaps unconscious, but certainly unrealistic, identification with what is called the "power structure." Negroes call that "passing for white." . . . I consider the United States freer politically and richer culturally because there are Jewish Americans to bring it the benefit of their special forms of dissent, their

humor and their gift for ideas which are based upon the uniqueness of their experience.

The statement reads admirably. But if Ellison wants to "see others distinctly," including Howe's distinctiveness as a Jewish rather than a "white" intellectual, he must not object to Howe's seeing *him* distinctly, as a man participating in a certain social predicament—i.e., getting born black in America. Defining an individual's social predicament does not automatically lead to stripping him of his personal tastes and talents, as Ellison assumes earlier in his essay, when he speaks of "prefabricated Negroes . . . sketched on sheets of paper and superimposed upon the Negro community." Jews also have their predicament, or call it their destiny, as Jews; but destiny is something profoundly different from a stereotype.

The second part of Ellison's remarks, ringing though they are, is where the real difficulty lies. If Ellison thought Howe obtuse because he visualized the black as a man in perpetual pain, if Ellison thought Howe was distorting his own more open perception of the effect on blacks of their civil inequities ("matters," Ellison wrote, "about which I could do nothing except walk, read, hunt, dance, sculpt, cultivate ideas")—what could a Jew think of Ellison's Jewish projections? What could be "special" about forms of Jewish dissent that do not include dissent on behalf of others?* What else, in the eye of history, could "special forms of dissent" *mean* if not the propensity to be enlisted in

* Howe has written elsewhere that he became a socialist through realization of what poverty was. And it was the poverty of the rural South that brought it home to him, though at the very moment he was reading about it he was himself an impoverished youth living wretchedly in a Bronx tenement in the middle of the Depression. (That the connection was made through *reading* is perhaps also to the point.)

social causes not intimately one's own? What could be the purpose of ideas based upon the uniqueness of Jewish experience if that uniqueness did not signify at least in part a perennial victimization, and if that experience did not expend itself beyond compassion into identification? How then does it happen that Ellison, in attributing so many useful and distinctive things to Jews, has it all add up to nothing less ugly than "passing for white"?

The trouble, I think, is a simple one. At bottom it is Ellison, not Howe, who fails to nail down the drift of distinctive experience, who imagines the Jew as naturally identifying with the white "power structure." Ellison has some of the psychology right, to be sure—it *was* a case of "perhaps unconscious" identification, but in a way Ellison was curiously unable to conceive of, except for the instant it took for him to ridicule the idea: "Howe, appearing suddenly in blackface." But Howe's call for the "impulsion to protest" was not a matter of burnt cork—he was not coming on as a make-believe Negro (and certainly not as a make-believe member of the "power structure"), but rather as a Jew responding implicitly and naturally—i.e., vicariously—to an urgent moment in history, applying to that moment the "benefit of [his] special form of dissent." That the "identification" was authentic, the vicariousness pragmatic, the dissent genuinely felt, untouched by manipulativeness or cynicism, the next several years in America rapidly made clear, the proof being the rise of black programs of "ferocity," both political and literary—which, interestingly enough, a Jewish critic was able to foretell through the exercise of his own familial sensibility.

In this interpretive retelling, I have perhaps made Howe out to be too much the prototypical Jew. This may be unfair to him. I do not know his personal views or whether he would welcome this characterization. But the exchange with Ellison, at this distance and after so many reversals in the putative black-Jewish alliance (how long ago that now seems, how unreal the very phrase), has taken on the power, and some of the dread, of a tragic parable. Ellison's inability to credit the Jew with a plausible commitment was, as it turned out, representative not only of what was to come, but of what had long been. From the Ellisonian point of view, "Angel Levine" never *was* true: impossible for black man and Jew to share the same skin and the same pair of eyes out of which to assess reality. Ellison's side of the argument, it seems to me, utterly undermines the "sociological" premises of "Angel Levine"—black and Jew are not, will never be seen to be, mutually salvational. But it is not only the nonfictive referents of the tale that are undermined. Little by little even the moral truthfulness begins to seep out of the vision itself—what was radiant, if illusioned, hope at the time "Angel Levine" was conceived has disintegrated into a kind of surrealism, an arbitrary act of art, set apart from any sources of life. Literature (even in the form of fantasy) cannot survive on illusion.

This is perhaps why Malamud went forward from the failed dream of "Angel Levine" to the warlike actualities of *The Tenants*. Ellison, meanwhile, is revealed by the passage of time to be not simply representative but prophetic. Society becomes for the black, if not yet magically fluid, then not nearly so much of a shut box as it is for Malamud's Jew in the claustrophobic world of *The Tenants*, or for the Jew in an America now seen to be inhabited by black as well as white *goyim*, with few temperamental allies. Black political fluidity has increased immeasurably since Ellison wrote, expressing itself in a kind of overall ascendancy of purpose, while Jewish political self-consciousness is static, confined to a handful of Congressional constituencies. But even then, while acknowledging the chasm between himself and the power structure, Ellison made it plain that he was at home in America in the most comfortable sense of country-culture. In the very same essay addressed to Howe there is an account of quail hunting in snowy Ohio fields, and a note of gratitude to Hemingway for having written so well on wing shooting "that I could keep myself and my brother alive during the 1937 Recession by following his descriptions." Few Jews, even of the third or fourth generation, will recognize in themselves this sort of at-homeness with the land, whereas even urban Poles and Italians have land-memory to draw upon. What emerges from the encounter with Howe is that Ellison has a Gentile ease in America—an easier scorn, even, for its blemishes—that Howe and Malamud, with their bookish moral passion, have not. "I could do nothing except walk, read, hunt, dance, sculpt, cultivate ideas." It is almost as if the Jew can do nothing but cultivate ideas.

What happened between Ellison and Howe (behind the back, as it were, of literature) was bound to be seized on by the larger metaphor of the novel. In my own case I have not found it possible to think about *The Tenants* without first turning Howe-Ellison round and round; together they make a bemusing artifact in a reverse archaeology. Dig them up and discover, in genteel form, the savage future.

I came to rehearse their exchange because, in my first reading of *The Tenants*, I was, like many readers, rabidly discontent with Malamud's conception of his black character, Willie Spearmint, later called Spear. Willie Spear is a black writer who has the flavor of an Eldridge Cleaver rather than an Ellison; and this seemed to matter. Malamud, it appeared, had deliberately chosen—for novelistic bite and drama—an unruly spear-carrier, when he might have chosen a poised aristocrat of prose. And up against Spear he set the Jewish writer Harry Lesser, a man almost too fastidious in his craft. The balance was unequal, the antagonists unfairly matched, the Jew too hesitant and disciplined, the black too spontaneous and unschooled.

That the antagonists *have* to be a match for each other at first strikes one as important, because *The Tenants* is partly, despite its directness of language and gesture, a theater piece designed as stately discourse. Though I admit the comparison is inflated, nevertheless one is put in mind of the eye-to-eye feud of Elizabeth and Mary, Queen of Scots, in Schiller's *Maria Stuart*; or of Shaw's Joan at her trial, another example of an elevated contest of societal interpretation. *The Tenants* is obviously barer and coarser than these—airless and arid, a flat plain pitting philosopher-king against philosopher-king. Except for these two figures—the Jew and the black—the book is, by and large, unpeopled. The two writers meet in an almost empty tenement about to be torn down. Lesser still lives in his old apartment, refusing to move out until his novel is finished. Already ten years of his life have gone into trying to finish it. Willie is a squatter—hauls in a typewriter, rustles up an old table and chair, and begins.

The friendship that springs up between them is not really a writers' friendship. In a literary sense it is the relation of higher and lower. Lesser is always the pro, the polisher, authority, patron of opinion; he has published before, one book is moderately famous. Willie, out of the ghetto, is the rough-hewn disciple. Lesser is the cultivated representative of Society-at-Large, and when he speaks as writer he speaks not as a Jew but as a clear-cut descendant of the American literary tradition from Hawthorne to James—

that very James, in fact, who, visiting the Lower East Side in 1904, worried about the effect of Yiddish-influenced impurities on his clean ancestral English. Lesser too feels himself superior: a natural inheritor, like James, of the language, while Willie is only a crude aspirant, likely to damage his material by clumsiness. Lesser observes:

> He has not yet mastered his craft . . . What can I say to a man who's suffered so much personal pain, so much injustice, who clearly finds in his writing his hope and salvation, who defines himself through it? He comes in the end, as in the old slave narratives, to freedom, through his sense of writing as power—it flies up and carries him with it—but mainly in his belief that he can, in writing, help his people overthrow racism and economic inequality. That his freedom will help earn theirs. The Life he writes, whatever he calls it, moves, pains, inspires, even though it's been written before, and better, by Richard Wright, Claude Brown, Malcolm X, and in his way, Eldridge Cleaver. Their self discoveries have helped Willie's. Many black men live the same appalling American adventure, but it takes a unique writer to tell it uniquely, as literature. To make black more than color or culture, and outrage larger than protest or ideology . . . Lesser sees irrelevancy, repetition, underdeveloped material; there are mistakes of arrangement and proportion, ultimately of focus.

Reading this, it is easy to think: Ah, but this is unjustly conceived. Willie is a straw man. Why not a black writer who is not only fully literate, but *accomplished*? Suppose Malamud had given us Ellison instead of Willie—then what? Lesser, like Ellison, believes first of all in the primacy, the loveliness, of the sentence; for him literature is the personal courage by which the language is seized. Beyond that lies propaganda. Granted that two-literary-intellectuals-talking-to-each-other does not make a novel (Mann and the Russians excepted), or, at least, would not make *this* novel, Malamud seems to be asking for the sort of resentment that would soon come to surround his formulation: Jewish Intellectual versus Tough Black Militant. Unequal warfare in the Republic of Letters. Could it not—for fairness—somehow have been contrived as Jewish Intellectual versus Black Intellectual?

There were, of course, good novelistic reasons why it could not. For instance, the conflict that eventually interposes itself between Lesser and Willie is not intellectual but rawly sexual. Willie has a Jewish girl friend, Irene, whom Lesser covets and ultimately wins. Irene is unfortunately a fiction-device and lives only intermittently. Her narrative task is to convert the two writers into enemies through sexual jealousy. Lesser's importuning landlord, Levenspiel, is also a fiction-device—he is there to give us the novel's pivotal "problem," to put time pressure on a stubborn Lesser—but Levenspiel, by contrast, manages to live vividly: "Have a little mercy, Lesser, move out so I can break up this rotten house that weighs like a hunch on my back . . . Hab rachmones, Lesser, I have my own ambition to realize." All this is beside the point. Levenspiel and Irene and Willie's black friends who slide in and out from the wings are all interruptions in the dialogue between Lesser and Willie; they are pretexts for necessary "action," for novelistic progress. They are not what the book fundamentally intends.

If *The Tenants* progresses, it is not through plot but

through revelation. The revelation is one-sided: it happens inside Lesser. We do not really know what happens inside Willie. And what happens inside Lesser is this: the clear realization that the black writer who shares his quarters and also his literary hopes is, more than he is writer, more than he is lover, more even than he is fleshly human being, a ferocious, a mythic, anti-Semite.

It is a revelation to Lesser because, at the start of their closeness, it did not "show." When Willie is angry at Lesser he says "white," he says "ofay," he does not yet see distinctly into his rage at the Jew. Lesser, himself a failing writer, views Willie as a possibly ascending one. All that is in Willie's way is technique. He tells Willie, "Not that you don't work hard but there has to be more emphasis on technique, form . . ." They discuss form:

> Lesser asks Willie to grant him good will. "I know how you feel, I put myself in your place."
>
> In cold and haughty anger the black replies. "No ofay mother-fucker can put himself in *my* place. This is a *black* book we talkin about that you don't understand at all. White fiction ain't the same as *black*. It *can't* be."
>
> "You can't turn black experience into literature just by writing it down."
>
> "Black ain't white and never can be. It is once and for only black. It ain't universal if that's what you are hintin up to. What I feel you feel different. You can't write about black because you don't have the least idea what we are or how we feel. Our feelin chemistry is different than yours. Dig that? It *has* to be so. I'm writin the soul writin of black people cryin out we are still slaves in this fuckn country and we ain't gonna stay slaves any longer. How can you understand it, Lesser, if your brain is white?"

"So is your brain white. But if the experience is about being human and moves me then you've made it my experience. You created it for me. You can deny universality, Willie, but you can't abolish it."

"Bein human is shit. It don't give you any privileges, it never gave us any."

"If we're talking about art, form demands its rights, or there's no order and maybe no meaning. What else there isn't I think you know."

"Art can kiss my juicy ass. You want to know what's really art? *I* am art. Willie Spearmint, *black man*. My form is *myself*."

Up to the moment of Willie's conclusion—"*I* am art"—this exchange is only another chapter of Howe-Ellison, with Willie as Howe, speaking in behalf of "being caught up with the *idea* of the Negro," and Lesser as Ellison, speaking in behalf of the universal values of art and humanity. But the two positions, Ellison's and Willie's, intermingle somewhat. Willie, like Ellison, does not trust his antagonist to "know how you feel, . . . [to] put myself in your place." Addressing Howe, Ellison simultaneously denies and affirms universality: as a black man he considers himself first of all a man, one who despite external disabilities is pleased to walk, read, hunt, etc., like all men; but again as a black he denies that anyone not black can creditably take into himself the day-to-dayness of the black predicament. Willie accepts only the denial: only a black can know what it is to be black, no one else. As for "being human," not only does Willie reject the term "universal," but he sees himself as almost physiologically different ("Our feelin chemistry is different than yours"), and he goes further yet—he freezes himself into the image of a totem, a "*black man*." The statement "My form is *myself*" is beyond humanity, beyond even art. It stands for something more abstract than either: a political position taken at its most absolute. For a totem *is* an absolute politics: an object, an artifact, a *form* representing an entire people, together with its interests, its cult, its power, its history and fate. The totem has no fluidity, its being is its meaning. Willie has turned the politics of a group into an object—himself, *black man*. In Willie Art is Politics, Politics is Art.

This is why it would not have served Malamud's deepest intention if he had chosen not Willie, but a more "realistic," pragmatic, literate, humane, relatively apolitical, less symbolic black for the novel. In *not* choosing an Ellison, of course, Malamud took on himself both a risk and a certainty. The certainty was the charge of "stereotype" and "blacklash," to which *The Tenants* has already been preëminently subject. The risk—a "stereotype" having indeed been chosen—was the failure of the novel as art. To a degree this *has* happened—to the very degree that Willie's stereotyped expectations lead to banalities masking as passions. Something was necessary to stimulate Willie's active vengeance, so we are given a plot-fulcrum, Willie's girl Irene. In return for Lesser's stealing his girl, Willie destroys Lesser's work of ten years; the war is on. Irene exists to accommodate neither Willie nor Lesser, but the exigencies of a made fiction. All this is too obviously and distractingly schematic—even the lineaments of "parable" cannot contain it—and if I seem to be bringing it up again now, it is only to contrast it with the novel's authentic passions. These are in the mimicry of Willie's writing. I will come to them in a moment.

Suppose, though, Malamud *had* chosen an Ellisonlike character to confront his Lesser. The first advantage would have been safety in the world external to the novel: with equal contenders, fewer readers might have cried bigot. And internally, also, there would have been an advantage: the contenders might have met and if necessary separated on the *cultural* issues, as Howe and Ellison did, not on the extraneous ones of purloined women and violated manuscripts. ("But," Malamud might counter, "purloined women and violated literature are the stuff of Willie's culture.") It might even be argued that, if novelistic conflict was what was wanted, if dramatic misunderstanding and distrust were what was wanted, a fictionalized Howe-Ellison clash could have provided them as surely as Lesser-Willie, and with the black man's "humanity" intact, all stereotypes avoided and averted. Inside the air of Malamud's novel, Ellison—or, rather, "Ellison"—would still have found Jewish literary empathy suspect, as the actual Ellison did in the more open world of nonfictional debate; and there would not have occurred, between two civilized beings, the perilous contrast between the "civilized" Jew Lesser and the "savage" Willie. (As the book now stands, though, there is nothing to choose at the end between Willie's and Lesser's savagery.) And not only this: with "Ellison" instead of Willie to do battle with Lesser, the novel would have been intellectually richer, thicker, clearer, the parable more perfect, the fright more frightening because in seemingly safer hands.

With so much to lose from Willie, with so much to gain from "Ellison," why did Malamud opt for what is so plainly a grossness, a caricature, above all a stereotype?

Here is Willie at his grossest:

> " . . . You tryin to kill off my natural writin by pretendin you are interested in the fuckn form of it

> though the truth of it is you afraid of what I am goin to write in my book, which is that the blacks have to murder you white MF's for cripplin our lives." He then cried out, "Oh, what a hypocrite shitass I am to ask a Jew ofay for advice how to express *my* soul work. Just in readin it you spoil what it says. I ought to be hung on a hook till some kind brother cuts off my white balls."

Ellison had complained to Howe (implying Howe was guilty of it too) that nonblack writers tend to create "prefabricated Negroes . . . sketched on sheets of paper and superimposed upon the Negro community." Surely this quotation from Willie fits Ellison's imputations; Willie is unabashedly "prefabricated."

But the real question is: who cast this die, who prefabricated Willie? Not Malamud. The source of a stereotype is everything. When, in the late 1890s, William Dean Howells praised the black poet Paul Dunbar's dialect verse for having "the charming accents of the Negro's own version of our [*sic*] English," chiefly because it exploited "the limited range of the race," which was "the range between appetite and emotion," the stereotype imposed on Dunbar by a white critic killed the poet and the man; he died in bitterness at thirty-four, wretched over the neglect of what he regarded as his real work—"But ah, the world, it turned to praise / A jingle in a broken tongue." In the sixty or so years since Dunbar's death, the "jingle in a broken tongue" has entered the precincts of "soul," and the notion of "our English," when espoused by blacks, receives serious pedagogical and linguistic consideration as a legitimate alternative, a separate language with a distinctive grammar. The stereotype, emerging from Howells, was an insult and a misappropriation; emerging from black pride, it begins to gather the honors of honest coinage.

Malamud did not make Willie. He borrowed him—he mimicked him—from the literature and the politics of the black movement. Willie is the black dream that is current in our world. Blacks made him. Few blacks disavow him. The black middle class, which is ambivalent about Willie, nevertheless does not disavow him—not simply out of loyalty to the underclass (the loyalty is what is in doubt), but out of covert gratitude.* Almost no black writer has disavowed Willie. Ellison is the exception: " . . . what an easy con-game for ambitious, publicity-hungry Negroes this stance of 'militancy' has become!" he exclaimed to Howe, but that was some years ago, and since then, though Willie has grown louder and published amply (he is famous as Amiri Baraka, for instance), Ellison has had nothing to say about him. Surely Baldwin does not disavow Willie; he has become him.

In short, Willie is what he intends himself to be (which is also what he is intended to be by those blacks who do not deny him): a totem, emblem of a community unified in and through Willie's spirit, what he calls his "form"—not man, as Ellison would have it, but *black man*.

What is the meaning of Willie in his self-declared "form"? Willie's form takes up not freedom and fluidity, but unmovable hatred and slavish vengeance. His vengeance is "literary" in two ways: the burning of Lesser's

* Orde Coombs wrote some years back in *Harper's* (January 1972), "The thirty-to-forty-year-old black who holds down a good job in the North must know that his present success is a direct result of past tumult. All his talent, all his effort would not have otherwise given him a toehold in television, in consulting firms, in brokerage firms, in advertising, and in publishing . . . Many of these black men know they owe their livelihoods to their poorer, more militant brethren . . . *In fact, only one group has really benefited from the turbulence; and that is the middle class.*" (Coombs's emphasis.)

book, and the creation of his own—but "his own'" ends as a travesty and spoliation of all humane literary values. Only through the destruction of Jewish culture, says Willie's form, can black culture arise. Lesser finds Willie's notes: "I have got to write better. Better and better. Black but better. Nothing but black. Now or never." And whereas earlier—before the pivotal jealousy episode—writing "black" for Willie had for the most part meant telling the poignant and honest story of his ruined, scarred, and panicked childhood in the ghetto,* now, writing black for vengeance, Willie dreams pogroms. For him literature serves politics—not as propaganda consciously does, as an "arm" or partner or extension or tool of politics—but intrinsically, below the level of rational motivation. Willie's only politics is coextensive with nearly the whole of his literary imagination; it is the politics and the imagination of anti-Semitism.

Lesser finds another of Willie's notes:

> It isn't that I hate the Jews. But if I do any, it's not because I invented it myself but I was born in the good old U. S. of A. and there's a lot of that going on that gets under your skin. And it's also from knowing the Jews, which I do. The way to black freedom is against them.

Now that Willie has stopped seeing Lesser as a more experienced writer and can think of him only as a Jew, Lesser too alters. He is rewriting his lost manuscript in fear and anguish, but the vision slips from him, he is in terror of

* Malamud has mastered the idiom typical of this fiction. For anyone doubtful about Malamud's ear—or, rather, literary eye—an anthology called *What We Must Be: Young Black Storytellers* (Dodd, Mead, 1971) is instructive.

Willie. "I treated you like any other man," he tells Willie. Willie replies, "No Jew can treat me like a man," and Lesser, afraid for his life, turns as savage as Willie, with this difference: " . . . it sickened him deeply"; he remains self-conscious. Nevertheless he gets an ax and chops up Willie's typewriter. On that typewriter Willie had written pages of antisemitic (some of it "anti-Zionist") poetry and prose, fantasizing the murder of Jews. The work of the two writers is contrasted. Lesser's destroyed book is about a writer's struggle to love. The writer is named Lazar Cohen; he is much like Malamud's Fidelman, an artist with a Jewish name who conceives of himself only as artist, almost never as Jew. Willie's stories are about blacks torturing Jews. In one of them, "a Jew slumlord in a fur-collar coat, come to collect his blood-money rents," is stabbed and killed by three blacks, who strip his corpse naked and propose to eat it, but change their minds. "He tastes Jewtaste, that don't taste like nothin good." The story, as Lesser finds it in Willie's notes, ends:

> Then they [the murderers] go to a synagogue late at night, put on yarmulkas and make Yid noises, praying.
>
> In an alternate ending the synagogue is taken over and turned into a mosque. The blacks dance hasidically.

With the apparition once again of a black synagogue, with the word "hasidically," Malamud suddenly and astonishingly blows in a whiff of "Angel Levine"—are his blacks becoming Jews again? Lesser has a fantasy: in a mythical Africa there is a double tribal wedding. A rabbi presides. The chief's son, who turns out to be Willie, is marrying a Jewish girl, who is Irene. Lesser is marrying a black woman. The rabbi exhorts the couples, "Someday God will bring together Ishmael and Israel to live as one people. It won't be the first miracle." Inside his dream Lesser says critically of it, "It's something I imagined, like an act of love, the end of my book, if I dared."

But Malamud himself does not dare. "Angel Levine" is not merely out of date, it is illusion; at the close of *The Tenants* Malamud explicitly acknowledges that it is illusion. Lesser's ax—it is the final vision of the novel—sinks into Willie "as the groaning black's razor-sharp saber, in a single boiling stabbing slash, cut[s] the white's balls from the rest of him." It is curious, horrible, and terrifying to take in what Malamud in *The Tenants* openly posits: that the Jew in America, beginning as Howe did with a cry of identification with black suffering, is self-astonished to find himself responding now in the almost forgotten mood of *zelbshuts*—the *shtetl*'s term for weaponry stored against the fear of pogroms. Lesser, a hesitant intellectual, is driven to hauling an ax. But *The Tenants* insists on more than this. Like much of Malamud's work, and specifically like *The Assistant* and *The Fixer*, it offers the metaphoric incarnation of a Malamudic text: whoever wants to kill the Jew has already killed the human being in himself.

It is not only no failing, it is the best achievement of the novel that Willie, its black militant, is a stereotype devoid of any easy humanity. The clichés appropriate for a political strategy are unsuitable for describing the soul of a living person. Given the extraliterary truth that black militancy, in and out of print, has now come to define itself if not largely then centrally through classical antisemitism, to bestow on a fictional Willie a life beyond his bloody fantasies would have been a savagery akin to Willie's own.

To put it another way: to have ascribed to Willie the full and continuing aspects of a decent breathing human being *but for his hatred of Jews* would have been to subvert the meaning of human.

The Tenants is a claustrophobic fable: its theme is pogrom. It remarks the minutiae of a single-handed pogrom so closely that the outer world is shut out. There is almost no city beyond Lesser's tenement, and there are no white Gentiles in the novel, no faint indication of that identification with the Gentile power structure Ellison claimed Jewish intellectuals were seeking. In *The Tenants* the Jew has no allies. Jew and black fight alone in an indifferent world.

There is no means, at this juncture, of determining whether its current worldly truths will one day seep out of *The Tenants* as the moral radiance of "Angel Levine" had ultimately, through subversion by history, to ebb into falsehood. But—for the moment—Malamud has abandoned the hopefulness of "Angel Levine" and drawn a parable of political anxiety. "Each, thought the writer, feels the anguish of the other" is the last flicker of that hopefulness but does not convince. Willie is Lesser's doom—Lesser, dreaming of love, rigorously apolitical, isolated in his aesthetics, becomes the inescapable victim of an artist whose art is inseparable from butchery.

Yevtushenko, declaiming at the Felt Forum that bombs and balalaikas are in essence always separate,* nevertheless speaks not for Lesser but for Willie. Yevtushenko's

* Yevgeny Yevtushenko, the Soviet poet, gave a reading in New York City the day after a New York group had bombed the offices of Sol Hurok, the agent responsible for booking Soviet cultural events in the United States. A young Jewish woman, a secretary in Hurok's office, was killed. Yevtushenko overnight wrote a poem of commemoration; it compared the girl's death to the gassing of Jews in Auschwitz, and declared that art and politics must be kept separate. The poem noticeably subverted its own thesis.

poem condemning the bombing of Hurok's office, and the death of a secretary there, moved everyone, who could disagree? But the poem is a cheat. To be horrified at the bombing is not automatically to assent to the purity of art. Mozart was played at Auschwitz, and it is a ruse to pretend that any natural "separation" of art keeps it unblemished by political use. Malamud, in plucking Willie out of the black writing that made him, has not invented the politicization of fiction. And in inventing *The Tenants*, Malamud ironically follows Willie—he has written a tragic fiction soaked in the still mainly unshed blood of the urban body politic.

I. B. Singer's Book of Creation

SOME TIME AGO, when Isaac Bashevis Singer first mounted the public platform to speak in English, he was asked whether he really believed in *sheydim*—in imps and demons, ghosts and spirits. The response, partly a skip and partly a glint, followed considerable playful pondering and ended in a long shrug: "Yes and no." The rebuke of an imp guarding secrets, one might judge—but surely a lesser imp, capable mainly of smaller mischiefs: the knotting of elflocks in the audience's hair, perhaps.

Years pass; the astonishing stories accumulate; the great Nobel is almost upon Singer, and the question reliably recurs. Now the answer is direct and speedy: "Yes, I believe there are unknown forces." This is no longer the voice of a teasing imp. Never mind that its tone clearly belongs to an accustomed celebrity who can negotiate a Question Period with a certain shameless readiness; it is also a deliberate leaning into the wind of some powerful dark wing, fearsomely descried.

Whether the majesty of the Nobel Prize for Literature afterward altered Singer's manipulation of this essential question, I do not know. Nevertheless the question remains central, though not quite so guileless as it appears. Should we believe that Singer believes in the uncanny and the preternatural? Is there ever a trustworthy moment when a storymonger is not making things up, especially about his own substance and sources? Doesn't an antic fancy devoted to cataloguing folly always trifle with earnest expectation? And what are we to think of the goblin cunning of a man who has taken his mother's given name—Bashevis (i.e., Bathsheba)—to mark out the middle of his own? Singer's readers in Yiddish call him, simply, "Bashevis." A sentimental nom de plume? His is anything but a nostalgic imagination. Does the taking-on of "Bashevis" imply a man wishing to be a woman? Or does it mean that a woman is hiding inside a man? Or does Singer hope somehow to entangle his own passions in one of literature's lewdest and nastiest plots: King David's crafty devisings concerning the original Bathsheba? Or does he dream of attracting to himself the engendering powers of his mother's soul through the assumption of her name? Given the witness of the tales themselves, we are obliged to suspect any or all of these notions, as well as others we have not the wit or fantasy to conjure up.

Accordingly, nearly every one of the forty-seven stories in *The Collected Stories of Isaac Bashevis Singer** is a snail-whorl narrative grown out of similar schemings, impersonations, contrivances, devices, and transmutations. The story of David and Bathsheba is, without fail, one that Singer's plot-fecundity might have churned up, though it would likely be a demon that dispatches Uriah the Hittite. The story of a woman taking on the semblance of a man, Singer has in fact already invented, in "Yentl the Yeshiva

* Farrar, Straus & Giroux, 1981

Boy," a remarkable fable about a girl who lusts after scholarship. In "The Dead Fiddler," coarse Getsel, in the form of a dybbuk, hides inside a woman, causing the delicate Liebe Yentle to swig and swear. As for the acquisition of names that confer eccentric or arrogant ambitions, there is Zeidel Cohen, a descendant of the exegete Rashi, who prepares to become Zeidlus the First, Pope of Rome; and Alchonon the teacher's helper, a plain fellow who succeeds in passing himself off, in "Taibele and Her Demon," as the lecherous Hurmizah, step-nephew of Asmodeus, King of the Demons.

On one flank Singer is a trickster, a prankster, a Loki, a Puck. His themes are lust, greed, pride, obsession, misfortune, unreason, the oceanic surprises of the mind's underside, the fiery cauldron of the self, the assaults of time and place. His stories offer no "epiphanies" and no pious resolutions; no linguistic circumscriptions or Hemingwayesque self-deprivations. Their plenitudes chiefly serve undefended curiosity, the gossip's lure of what-comes-next. Singer's stories have plots that unravel not because they are "old-fashioned"—they are mostly originals and have few recognizable modes other than their own—but because they contain the whole human world of affliction, error, quagmire, pain, calamity, catastrophe, woe: things happen; life is an ambush, a snare; one's fate can never be predicted. His driven, mercurial processions of predicaments and transmogrifications are limitless, often stupendous. There are whole fistfuls of masterpieces in this one volume: a cornucopia of invention.

Because he cracks open decorum to find lust, because he peers past convention into the pit of fear, Singer has in the past been condemned by other Yiddish writers outraged by his seemingly pagan matter, his superstitious villagers, his daring leaps into gnostic furies. The moral grain of Jewish feeling that irradiates the mainstream aspirations of Yiddish literature has always been a kind of organic extension of Talmudic ethical ideals: family devotion, community probity, *derekh erets*—self-respect and respect for others—the stringent expectations of high public civility and indefatigable integrity, the dream of messianic betterment. In Singer, much of this seems absent or overlooked or simply mocked; it is as if he has willed the crashing-down of traditional Jewish sanity and sensibility. As a result, in Yiddish literary circles he is sometimes viewed as—it is the title of one of these stories—"The Betrayer of Israel."

In fact, he betrays nothing and no one, least of all Jewish idealism. That is the meaning of his imps and demons: that human character, left to itself, is drawn to cleanliness of heart; that human motivation, on its own, is attracted to clarity and valor. Here is Singer's other flank, and it is the broader one. The goblin cunning leads straight to this: Singer is a moralist. He tells us that it is natural to be good, and unholy to go astray. It is only when Lilith creeps in, or Samael, or Ketev Mriri, or the sons of Asmodeus, that evil and impurity are kindled. It is the inhuman, the antihuman, forces that are to blame for harms and sorrows. Surely these imps must be believed in; they may have the telltale feet of geese—like Satan, their sire—but their difficult, shaming, lubricious urges are terrestrially familiar. Yet however lamentably known they are, Singer's demons are intruders, invaders, no true or welcome part of ourselves. They are "psychology"; and history; and terror; above all, obsessive will. If he believes in them, so, unwillingly but genuinely, do we.

And to understand Singer's imps is to correct another misapprehension: that he is the recorder of a lost world, the preserver of a vanished sociology. Singer is an artist and transcendent inventor, not a curator. His tales—though dense with the dailiness of a God-covenanted culture, its folkways, its rounded sufficiency, especially the rich intensities of the yeshiva and its bottomless studies—are in no way documents. The Jewish townlets that truly were are only seeds for his febrile conflagrations: where, outside of peevish imagination, can one come on the protagonist of "Henne Fire," a living firebrand, a spitfire burning up with spite, who ultimately, through the spontaneous combustion of pure fury, collapses into "one piece of coal"? Though every doorstep might be described, and every feature of a head catalogued (and Singer's portraits are brilliantly particularized), parables and fables are no more tied to real places and faces than Aesop's beasts are beasts.

This is not to say that Singer's stories do not mourn those murdered Jewish townlets of Poland, every single one of which, with nearly every inhabitant, was destroyed by the lords and drones of the Nazi Gehenna. This volume includes a masterly memorial to that destruction, the broken-hearted testimony of "The Last Demon," which begins emphatically with a judgment on Europe: "I, a demon, bear witness that there are no more demons left. Why demons, when man himself is a demon?" And sums up:

> I've seen it all . . . the destruction of Poland. There are no more Jews, no more demons. The women don't pour out water any longer on the night of the winter solstice. They don't avoid giving things in even numbers. They no longer knock at dawn at the antechamber of the synagogue. They don't warn us before emptying the slops. The rabbi was martyred on a Friday in the month of Nissan. The community was

> slaughtered, the holy books burned, the cemetery desecrated. *The Book of Creation* has been returned to the Creator . . . No more sins, no more temptations! . . . Messiah did not come for the Jews, so the Jews went to Messiah. There is no further need for demons.

This tenderness for ordinary folk, their superstitions, their folly, their plainness, their lapses, is a classical thread of Yiddish fiction, as well as the tree trunk of Singer's own hasidic legacy—love and reverence for the down-to-earth. "The Little Shoemakers" bountifully celebrates the Fifth Commandment with leather and awl; the hero of "Gimpel the Fool," a humble baker, is endlessly duped and stubbornly drenched in permanent grace; the beautiful story "Short Friday" ennobles a childless old couple who, despite privation and barrenness, turn their unscholarly piety into comeliness and virtue. Shmuel-Leibele's immaculate happiness in prayer, Shoshe's meticulous Sabbath meal, shine with saintliness; Singer recounts the menu, "chicken soup with noodles and tiny circlets of fat . . . like golden ducats," as if even soup can enter holiness. Through a freakish accident—snow covers their little house and they are asphyxiated—the loving pair ascend in death together to paradise. When the demons are stilled, human yearning aspires toward goodness and joy. (Singer fails to note, however, whether God or Samael sent the pure but deadly snow.)

In Singer the demons are rarely stilled, and the luminous serenity of "Short Friday" is an anomaly. Otherwise pride furiously rules, and wild-hearted imps dispose of human destiny. In "The Unseen," a prosperous and decent husband runs off with a lusty maidservant at the urging of a demon; he ends in destitution, a hidden beggar tended by his remarried wife. "The Gentleman from Cracow" corrupts a whole town with gold; he turns out to be Ketev Mriri himself. In "The Destruction of Kreshev," a scholar who is a secret Sabbatian and devil-worshiper induces his wife to commit adultery with a Panlike coachman. Elsewhere, excessive intellectual passion destroys genius. An accomplished young woman is instructed by a demon to go to the priest, convert, and abandon her community; the demon assumes the voice of the girl's grandmother, herself the child of a Sabbatian. A rabbi is "plagued by something new and terrifying: wrath against the Creator," and struggles to fashion himself into an atheist. Character and motive are turned inside out at the bidding of imps who shove, snarl, seduce, bribe, cajole. Allure ends in rot; lure becomes punishment.

This phantasmagorical universe of ordeal and mutation and shock is, finally, as intimately persuasive as logic itself. There is no fantasy in it. It is the true world we know, where we have come to expect anguish as the consequence of our own inspirations, where we crash up against the very circumstance from which we had always imagined we were exempt. In this true world suffering is endemic and few are forgiven. Yet it may be that for Singer the concrete presence of the unholy attests the hovering redemptive holy, whose incandescence can scatter demons. *Yes, I believe in unknown forces.*

Not all the stories in this collection emerge from the true world, however. The eerie authority of "The Cabbalist of East Broadway" is a gripping exception, but in general the narratives set in the American environment are, by contrast, too thin. Even when intentionally spare—as in the marvelous "Vanvild Kava," with its glorious opening: "If a Nobel Prize existed for writing little, Vanvild Kava would have gotten it" — the European settings have a way of turning luxuriantly, thickly coherent. Presumably some of these American locales were undertaken in a period when the fertile seed of the townlets had begun to be exhausted; or else it is the fault of America itself, lacking the centrifugal density and identity of a yeshiva society, the idea of community as an emanation of God's gaze. Or perhaps it is because many of these American stories center on Singer as writer and celebrity, or on someone like him. It is as if the predicaments that fly into his hands nowadays arrive because he is himself the centrifugal force, the controlling imp. And an imp, to have efficacy, as Singer's genius has shown, must be a kind of dybbuk, moving in powerfully from outside; whereas the American narratives are mainly inside jobs, about the unusual "encounters" a famous writer meets up with.

The Collected Stories is supplied with a sparse Author's Note (misleadingly called an Introduction on the book jacket), but it is unsatisfyingly patched, imbalanced, cursory; anyone trusting imps will fail to trust the Note. Apparently Singer thinks fiction is currently under a threat from "the zeal for messages." I wish it were possible to list every translator's name, from Saul Bellow, Isaac Rosenfeld, Dorothea Strauss, Mirra Ginsburg, and Joseph Singer to the less renowned Ruth Schachner Finkel, Evelyn Torton Beck, Herbert Lottman, Rosanna Gerber, Elizabeth Schub, and all the rest. It is interesting that there are so many, and that there are always new ones. Singer has not yet found his Lowe-Porter or Scott Moncrieff. Still, the voice is steady and consistent, as if there were only one voice; undoubtedly it is the imposition of Singer's own. After all these years, the scandalous rumors about Singer's relation to his changing translators do not abate: how they are half-collaborators, half-serfs, how they start out sunk in homage, accept paltry fees, and end disgruntled or bemused, yet transformed, having looked on Singer plain. One wishes Singer would write their frenzied tale, set it in Zamość, and call it "Rabbi Bashevis's Helpers." In any event, his helpers cannot reach the deep mine and wine of Singer's mother tongue, thronged (so it was once explained to me by a Tel Aviv poet accomplished in Hebrew, Yiddish, and English) with that unrenderable Hebrew erudition and burnished complexity of which we readers in English have not an inkling, and are permanently deprived. Deprived? Perhaps. *The Collected Stories*, when all is said and done, is an American master's Book of Creation.

The Fourth Sparrow: The Magisterial Reach of Gershom Scholem

GERSHOM SCHOLEM IS a historian who has remade the world. He has remade it the way Freud is said to have remade it—by breaking open the shell of the rational to uncover the spiraling demons inside. But Freud, in fencing himself off from tradition, was hobbled by the need to invent everything on his own, through case history, trial and error, drug research, venturesome ingenuity, hunch and speculation above all. The little gods he collected, and the vocabulary he borrowed, took him partially and intuitively to Greek and primitive sources. All the same, in purposefully excluding himself from Hebrew origins—in turning Moses into an Egyptian, for instance—Freud inevitably struck loose from an encompassing history of ideas, ending in sensation and in a thesis of individuality suitable to the ardent physician he was; his new formulations stuck close to biology and family drama.

If Freud is regarded as an engine of thought and a sorcerer of fresh comprehension—as one of the century's originals, in short—there are nevertheless those who, without necessarily reducing Freud's stature, think the oceanic work of

Gershom Scholem envelops Freud's discoveries as the sea includes even its most heroic whitecaps. Or, to alter the image: Freud is a peephole into a dark chamber—a camera obscura; but Scholem is a radiotelescope monitoring the universe, with its myriads of dark chambers. This is because Scholem's voyage brought him past those boundaries Freud willfully imposed on himself. Freud dared only a little way past the margins of psychology; whereas Scholem, whose medium was history, touched on the very ground of human imagination. Freud claimed Hannibal as his hero, but Scholem delved beyond the Greek and Roman roots of the classical European education common to them both. Scholem went in pursuit of the cosmos—and that took him straight to the perplexities of Genesis and the Hebrew language. Freud shrugged off religion as "illusion," and ended his grasp of it with that word. Where Freud thought it fit to end, Scholem begins.

In his restrained little memoir, *From Berlin to Jerusalem: Memories of My Youth*, Scholem recounts how even in boyhood he was drawn by mysterious magnets to the remote heritage his parents had deliberately denied him. The elder Scholem was a Jew who, like many Jews in the Germany of his generation and afterward, longed for a kind of social invisibility. The proprietor of a print shop, he thought of himself as a properly bourgeois German; he intended his four sons to distinguish themselves by growing up indistinguishable—he required them to be turned out as educated Germans with no recognizable Jewish quirks of intellect or passion. The two older boys obliged him; the two younger, Werner and Gerhard, were infected by a powerfully Jewish desire to repair a morally flawed world. Werner became a Communist, and, to his father's outrage and shame, was court-martialed for treason, having taken part in an anti-World War I demonstration while wearing a German military uniform. Gerhard Hebraized his identity fully, called himself Gershom, sought out the Yiddish-speaking East European Jewish intellectuals he was expected to scorn, and became a Zionist. In the father's eyes the activities of both sons were "anti-German." The Marxist was unreachable in jail. The Zionist the father threw out of the house. The Marxist died in Buchenwald. The Zionist chose Jerusalem, and emerged as the monumental scholar of Jewish mysticism whose huge researches and daring insights have infiltrated and significantly enlarged the religious imagination of our age.

Scholar, yes—but also rediscoverer. When Scholem began his investigations, the antirational elements in Judaism had long been deliberately suppressed, both by tradition itself and by the historians. Though there are mystical moods in the vastnesses of Talmud, they are almost by-the-by: what dominates is the rabbis' ethical and juridical genius, in the intellectual and rationalist sense. Scholem set out to rescue from distaste and neglect, indeed from ill-repute and shame, those wellsprings of metaphoric vitality that lay in Kabbalah, a proliferating system of symbolic descriptions of creation and revelation deemed capable of seizing the quality of holiness itself. These ancient ideas, some of them bordering on a kind of Jewish Gnosticism, were hidden away in numbers of texts, some forgotten, some misunderstood, some condemned, some—like the Zohar—ringed round with traditional strictures. Scholem cut through disdain and rejection to begin, single-handedly, his life's task of reconstructing the story of Jewish mysticism.

Kabbalah—grounded in a belief in divine disclosure and

the irrepressible hope of redemption—was historically both an inward movement and an outward one. When joined to messianic currents, it exploded the confines of esoteric reflection and burst into real event. The most startling event occurred in the seventeenth century, just after the massive Chmielnitzki persecutions of Polish Jews, when a popularly acclaimed redeemer, Sabbatai Ṣevi, and his prophet and theologian, Nathan of Gaza, set their generation on fire with the promise of an imminent return to Zion and an instantaneous end to exile and its oppressions. Scholem's inexhaustible masterwork on this subject, *Sabbatai Ṣevi: The Mystical Messiah*, divulges with philological, historical, and psychological force the amazing tale of that Sabbatian adventure: how it broke out spectacularly among the Jewish masses, and how it launched reverberations that penetrated into the next two centuries. The would-be deliverer, broken by threats of execution by the Turks—who held the Holy Land—saved his life and abandoned his followers by converting to Islam, bringing a furiously spreading cataclysm of redemptive fever to a tragic and bewildering anticlimax.

Sabbatai Ṣevi is a titanic investigation into the substance and effect of illusion. It explores the rise, in the years 1665 and 1666, of a messianic movement among a profoundly subjugated people, only just recovering from the Inquisition and the Iberian expulsion, thrown into yet another devastation—the catastrophic massacres of the Jews of Poland that began in 1648 and continued until 1655. But the Sabbatian movement was not merely the response of hope to cataclysm. Sabbatai Ṣevi, born in Smyrna, Turkey, did not declare himself the true messiah of the Jews only to abolish their dispersion and restore to them their historic territory;

the idea he represented was a cosmic redemption, the cleansing and renewal of all things, the retrieval of the sparks of holiness from the husks of evil which, according to Kabbalistic thought, bind them fast.

In the wake of Sabbatai Şevi's annunciation came an incalculable penitential wave. The messiah's work could not be completed until the world was cleared of sin, and everywhere—over the whole face of Europe, in Turkey, Morocco, Palestine, Egypt, wherever Jews lived—sanctification made vivid claims in the form of an astonishing spiritual roiling characterized by penitential exercises and charitable works. While the Gentiles around them gaped, Jews stopped in their daily tracks, gave up their livings, sold their possessions—the city of Leghorn, which had a large Jewish merchant class, nearly came to a halt—and prepared to journey to Jerusalem. Though there were doubters, no community of Jews went untouched by the messianic fervor. Legendary reports of the redeemer spread from land to land—a pandemic of ecstatic expectation.

The personality of the messiah himself is remarkably well-documented. He was plump, young, attractive. He had a beautiful singing voice, which he liked to show off in the synagogue, chanting psalms. An undistinguished writer, he was poetic in act rather than word. He was not intellectually notable, although the study of Kabbalah, which formed his character, demands unusual conceptual gifts: Kabbalah is a kind of Einsteinian mysticism—the brilliance of its inventions is precisely the brilliance of an original physics. It is no easy, amoral occultism, rather the vision of a universal moral restitution willed so acutely that only an alteration in the perception of the cosmos can account for it. Without the Kabbalah, Scholem explains, there could have been no Sabbatai Şevi to inaugurate the messianic dream, and no messianic dream to inaugurate the career of Sabbatai Şevi.

But he was, above all, a man of afflictions, subject to periods of "darkness," which then gave way to phases of "illumination." In short, a classic manic-depressive; and, worn and perplexed by his suffering during the cycle of bleakness, he traveled from Jerusalem, where he was tolerated as peculiar though harmless, to Gaza, to receive a healing penance from a twenty-year-old Kabbalist named Nathan. Nathan was a young man of genius—a natural theologian, given to bending Kabbalah with the craft of a chess master plying new openings. Sabbatai Şevi confessed that now and then, in moments of exaltation, he conceived himself to be the messiah—and Nathan, all at once irradiated, confirmed him as exactly that, conferred on him his mission, and theologized his madness.

The madness expressed itself in what was termed "strange acts." When the mania came on him, the messiah's face grew rosy and glowing, and, lifted up by glory, he would compel his followers to engage in unprecedented and bizarre performances. He made changes in the liturgy, pronounced the unutterable Tetragrammaton, called women to the Ark, married himself to the Scrolls of the Law, turned fasts into feasts; once he crammed three holidays into a single week; another time he declared that Monday was the real Sabbath. The glad tidings of the messianic age began to supersede the Law by eroding its strict practice—prayerbooks were amended to include the new messiah—and meanwhile the awakening to redemption burgeoned among all classes of Jews. One widespread group was especially receptive—those refugees called Marranos, who had survived the Inquisition in the guise of professing Christians, all the while secretly maintaining themselves as Jews. Their Catholic inheritance had inclined them toward worship of a Redeemer, and their public apostasy prepared them for the strangest of Sabbatai's strange acts: his conversion to Islam.

The political meaning of the ingathering of the exiles into Turkish-held Palestine was not lost on the sultan and his viziers, who smelled, in so much penitence and prayer, a nuance of insurrection. Sabbatai Şevi was arrested in Smyrna, where he had come home under the triumphant name of King Messiah, Savior and Redeemer. He was offered one or the other: execution or apostasy. He chose to save his life, and with that one signal tossed thousands of his shocked and disillusioned followers back into the ordinary fact of exile, to be swallowed up once again by unmediated, unmiraculous history. But masses of others, the "believers," continued to nurture their faith: for them the messiah's act was a sacred mystery shielding an arcane purpose. An underground literature and liturgy sprang up; Nathan promulgated a new theology of paradox to account for the apostasy, wherein the inward reality of belief was held to be more forceful than the outer reality of happening. The "true" truth is always the concealed truth. The holiness-at-the-core is the real revelation even when it is clothed in seeming evil. The sacred and the profane change places. The Sabbatians came at length to an astounding prayer: "Blessed art Thou, Lord of the Universe, who permittest that which is forbidden."

The crisis of theology brought on by the messiah's apostasy led the believers to abandonment of traditional rabbinic Judaism, and from there with astonishing directness to Reform Judaism, anarchism, Enlightenment, revolutionary utopianism, nihilism, antinomianism, orgiastic excess—all the stupendously complex, often contradictory, strands of ideology that are implicit in the imagination released from the yoke of Commandment. All this was the effect of illusion. We are not finished with Sabbatianism yet, nor with the bafflements it suggests about the mentality of its heirs (Justice Brandeis was descended from a Sabbatian family), or the antiquity of the impulse nowadays called Zionism, or the psychological atmosphere surrounding the development of Christianity in its earliest years, or the whole history of Christianity over the centuries. The career of Sabbatai Ṣevi hints that every messiah contains in himself, hence is responsible for, all the fruits of his being: so that, for instance, one may wonder whether the seeds of the Inquisition somehow lie even in the Sermon on the Mount.

Scholem's interpretations of these extraordinary matters were in themselves shockwaves for those who depended on the conventional histories. Instead of being merely a false messiah and mystagogue who inflamed a desperate people with his maniacal delusions, Sabbatai Ṣevi was now seen as a forerunner of the impassioned idealist Zionism of the nineteenth century; and Nathan of Gaza's formulations, instead of being mere popular nonsense, were revealed as the heir to a deep poetical tradition, dense with luxuriant imaginings and an inspired fecundity of moral feeling: the Kabbalists' yearning was to release the encapsulated divine sparks that would cleanse the world of evil. And beyond all that, Scholem maintained that the disintegration of orthodoxy through the development of Sabbatian mysticism led indirectly to circumstances that favored eighteenth-century Enlightenment and nineteenth-century Reform Judaism. This last—rational stirrings growing out of the heart of an intensely nonrational movement—is only one of Scholem's innumerable contributions to fresh seeing. Scholem's magisterial historical intuition, his capacity to enter and overwhelm several philosophical traditions at once, above all his reclamation of Kabbalah, empowered intellectual-rationalist Judaism to reharness the steeds of myth and mysticism, and to refresh the religious imagination at many wells and springs along the way.

These immense ideas, spilling over from Scholem's histories into literature and even into literary criticism, have made Scholem into one of the great modern masters: a knower who, through the scrupulous use of knowledge, refashions and dominates the way we look at ourselves and our notions of the world.

But even these perplexities are not all. The major wonder is about mysticism itself, about human imagination itself, and how it runs free in religion. Scholem and Deuteronomy do not agree; for Scholem, mysticism is endemic in the sacral orchestration of the human mind, and should not be set aside. But Deuteronomy's agnostic wisdom (29:28) concerning the effort to penetrate the nature and purposes of God is antithetical: "The secret things belong to the Lord"—which is to say, they are not for us.

About the paradoxical personality of Gershom Scholem himself, I once speculated in a story:

> The draw of the irrational has its own deep question: how much is research, how much search? Is the scientist, the intelligent physician, the skeptical philosopher who is attracted to the irrational himself a rational being? How explain the attraction? I think of that majestic scholar of Jerusalem sitting in his university study composing, with bookish distance and

objectivity, volume after volume on the history of Jewish mysticism—is there an objective "scientific interest" or is all interest a snare? Is the hidden cauldron not an enticement and a seduction to its investigator? —Or, to say it even more terribly: it may be that the quarry is all the time in the pursuer.

Accordingly, when I set out to see Scholem,* I went with his memoir under my arm, impatient to put a single question—that notorious conundrum all readers who are fascinated by his explorations surrender to: does the scholar of Kabbalah possess a hidden self (as Kabbalah speaks of a hidden "true" God)? Is there some secret sharer within, an unrevealed soul? Is there, in brief, a shadow-Scholem?

Scholem is quick to answer: "The scholar is never the whole man." Then he does a thing that seems ordinary at the moment, but will turn out to be as tantalizingly wily as a reply from the Delphic oracle—he crosses to his wide scholar's table and hands me a piece of paper, a newspaper review. It concerns Scholem's relations with his great friend, Walter Benjamin. Who Benjamin was, and what he was to Scholem, can be surmised from the dedication prefixed to Scholem's seminal volume, *Major Trends in Jewish Mysticism:* "To the memory of the friend of a lifetime whose genius united the insight of the Metaphysician, the interpretive power of the Critic and the erudition of the Scholar." Benjamin, a breathtaking essayist, a literary thinker drawn to Marxism, unable to share Scholem's Zionist convictions all the way, remained in Europe until it was too late. To avoid being murdered as a Jew he took his own life in 1940, at the age of forty-eight. (Scholem, a Zionist since his teens, arrived in then Palestine in the 1920s.) The

* Gershom Scholem died in 1982.

two brilliant polymaths pursued their mutually enriching exchanges for years; when they were separated, the talk went on copiously, in stunning essaylike letters. The German edition of their correspondence was reviewed in the London *Times Literary Supplement* by George Steiner. "Perhaps you will find the shadow-Scholem *here*," Scholem says; it is Steiner's review he has put in my hands. Among other stringently mournful speculations, I am astonished to read: "Scholem cannot forgive." I am astonished to read it because it has been delivered over to me as a kind of confession. Or perhaps not. The allusion, in any case, is to the Jews of Germany who deceived themselves into believing Germany would accept and absorb them. Presumably Benjamin was among them.

And it is these Jews—this pitiable phenomenon of a passionately loyal citizenry longing only to be good and peaceable Germans—who comprise the furious hidden text of *From Berlin to Jerusalem*. Writing of the bloodthirsty days of Nazi-dominated Munich, Scholem comments: "I had long since made my decision to leave Germany. But it was frightening to encounter the blindness of the Jews who refused to see and acknowledge all that. This greatly encumbered my relations with Munich Jews, for they became extremely jumpy and angry when someone broached that subject." In Frankfurt, Scholem broke off his friendship with Franz Rosenzweig, the remarkable author of *The Star of Redemption*, a vigorously original meditation on Judaism; in spite of his "intense Jewish orientation," Rosenzweig still hoped for "a Jewish community that considered itself German." "Thus I had," Scholem concludes, "one of the stormiest and more irreparable arguments of my youth." And again: "In view of the task of radical renewal of Judaism and Jewish society, Germany was a vacuum in which we would choke."

It is more than an irony, it is an ongoing wound, that *From Berlin to Jerusalem*, incontestably a Zionist book, continues the fraternal drama in its dedication to the Marxist brother who chose Communist "Humanity" over Jewish fate. But if Werner is not yet absolved, neither is Benjamin. "He paid dearly for his flirtation with Marxism," Scholem tells me. Not far from where we sit in the dining room, a long row of books commands an endless shelf: they are all by Walter Benjamin.

We are having this conversation over lunch in Scholem's house in Jerusalem, on green and flowering Abarbanel Street. The books climb and spread over all the walls of every room. Scholem is famous for loving chocolates, so I have brought some, but warily: he is famous also for knowing which chocolates will do and which won't. "Why am I being bribed?" cries Scholem—a very lofty elf with bold elfin ears and an antic elfin glee advertising tricks and enigmas—and I am relieved that my offering has passed muster. The pilgrimages to this house have been many. The critic Leslie Fiedler has been here. The historian Lucy Dawidowicz has been here. The scholar Yosef Yerushalmi has been here. The novelists Mark Mirsky and Norma Rosen have been here. Jorge Luis Borges has been here, in homage, but Scholem disclaims it: "Borges wrote all his work beforehand, before he read me." Patrick White, the Australian Nobel Prize winner, acknowledges Scholem's influence, particularly in the novel *The Riders of the Chariot*. Yale professor Harold Bloom's startling schematic borrowings, in *Kabbalah and Criticism* and elsewhere, prompt Scholem to quip: "It's a free country."

He seems pleased by these varied manifestations of his authority. What he does object to is the questionable uses his prestige is sometimes put to. "I was naïve," he explains. "I believed that if scholarship came, it would drive out charlatanism. Instead, the charlatans go on as before —only now they use me as a footnote." (The charlatans are presumably occult faddists who have appropriated Kabbalah.) He tells how his work is now frequently subject to a kind of veiled plagiarism: "One man wrote a book on Kabbalah and referred to Scholem in a few footnotes. But all the rest of the book was also Scholem!"

Lunch is cold spinach soup, ambrosial in the perpetually patient sunheat of a Jerusalem afternoon; roast veal in a pastry crust; and, for dessert, Mrs. Scholem's homemade pink ices, concocted of fresh strawberries. The meal is elegant, in an atmosphere new to me—is it the way the light laps over these Biblical hills like some heavy celestial ray, is it a redolence of 1912 Berlin? Mrs. Scholem has been thinking about my question—the question about the shadow-Scholem. She shakes her head; she looks grave, but in a riddling way. "I know what the shadow is. And I found out only three years ago. I know it only three years." It has nothing to do with Benjamin; it has nothing to do with any of that. Will she tell? "No, I won't tell." It is a joke and it is not a joke. Later, when I plead with her to tell after all: "Maybe when I am one hundred years old. Until then I won't tell." Scholem, elfin, enjoying this: "What is 'information'? Nothing at all. Use your judgment. Use your imagination." It is as if he does not mind being invented. We begin to speak of the "theater of the self." "I call myself a metaphysical clown," Scholem says; "a clown hides himself in theater." I ask whether Walter Benjamin ever hid himself that way. "Benjamin never played theater." How much of Professor Scholem is theater? Scholem: "Ask Mrs. Scholem." Mrs Scholem: "One hundred percent."

We turn over the pages of Scholem's memoir and study the photographs. There is one of Scholem and his three brothers, all of them under the age of fourteen. "His mother called them the four sparrows," Mrs. Scholem supplies. In the picture Gerhard, the smallest, is only six. I am suddenly emboldened to speculate—though not out loud—about the flight of the last sparrow; it seems to me I know by now what the shadow-Scholem must be. It is the shadow cast by the sparrow's wings on the way from Gerhard to Gershom. It is the capacity to make one's life a surprise, even to oneself—to create the content of one's own mind, to turn out to be something entirely unexpected. Nothing in the narrow Berlin of Gershom Scholem's youth prepared him for where he stands now. When, I inquire, did he begin to sense what his destiny would be? He reflects; he resists. And then: "About the age of twenty. You get the feeling of going in a straight line." And how would he account for this realization of a special intellectual calling? The rejoinder is so plain, and yet so obscure, that it shocks, like the throwing of three ordinary stones. "I wanted to learn about Judaism. I wanted to learn Hebrew. I wanted to learn as much as I could." Mrs. Scholem: "He went to the bottom of the question. Curiosity." Scholem: "Yes, curiosity."

But that cannot satisfy. And, in fact, the particulars of Gershom Scholem's journey, as he describes them in *From Berlin to Jerusalem*, do not quite satisfy either, although they are meant to yield the story of "going in a straight line"—they leave out the mystery of self-surprise. Everything strange remains strange. The eccentricity of an education against all likelihood, begun in parental contempt, seized in contradiction of everything influential—society, the times, the drift and pulse of contemporary scholarship, Germany itself—is not unraveled. The secret of how that miraculous rupture and awakening came about, leading to Scholem's rise as one of the whirlwind masters, teachers, wideners and imaginers of our age, is not revealed. The closest Scholem comes to it is in a single sentence. Alluding to his attraction to Kabbalah, he remarks, "Perhaps I was endowed with an affinity for this area from the 'root of my soul,' as the kabbalists would have put it, or maybe my desire to understand the enigma of Jewish history was also involved—and the existence of the Jews over the millennia *is* an enigma, no matter what the numerous 'explanations' may say."

Yet Scholem will go no further in self-disclosure, or even self-conjecture, than he has already gone; perhaps he cannot. "There will be no second volume of memoirs," he warns. This book, another on Walter Benjamin that follows it, and the volume of correspondence with Benjamin—a trinity of biography, autobiography, and portraiture—are all we are to have in the way of personal history.

What the memoir delivers—and it is, after all, a shining little book—is a pageant of characterizations, rife and roiling, in spots diaphanous, elsewhere speedy, skeletal, and spare. It is all a slender chain of shimmering beads on a string: quicksilver sketches of a hundred brilliant encounters—Rubashov, who became Shazar, Israel's third President, living next door to Scholem in a boarding house packed with brainy but impoverished young Russian Jews; the philosophers Martin Buber and Hermann Cohen; Agnon, the Nobel-winning genius whose stories Scholem was the first to translate and to teach; Simmel, the prototypical self-estranged Jewish intellectual (to whom Buber "sometimes pointed out . . . that a man like himself ought to be interested in seeing to it that men of his type did not disappear"); Franz Rosenzweig; numbers of intellectual young women, German, Jewish, and half-Jewish; and glimpses of Benjamin himself. There is plenty of comedy, some of it melancholy, such as Hermann Cohen's comment to Franz Rosenzweig, reproaching the Zionists, "Those fellows want to be happy!"—"the most profound statement," Scholem writes, "that an opponent of Zionism ever made."

Still, everything flashes by with the quirky velocity of picture cards—people (Scholem is sensitive to looks), ideas, influential books (Kafka especially), Talmud study ("the dialogue of the generations"), extraordinary observations. Though crowded with radiant susceptibilities—for learning, for ideals, for intellectual friendships—yet these anecdotal portraits all run by too quickly. What we want from a memoir, I suppose, is something like the sensation of watching Hans Castorp's thoughts open into new depths before our eyes; or the actual texture of a mind in struggle that John Stuart Mill's *Autobiography* chillingly renders. One aches for a Thomas Mann to make a fat *Bildungsroman* of Scholem's early life—to unfold, for instance, the falling-away of mathematical ambition in the young scholar (who began as a powerful mathematician). What a marvel it would be for those paternal and fraternal crises to play themselves out in dramatic scenes; for the late nights of boarding-house cake-nibbling and philosophy to shout themselves across the page; for the playful and gifted mother who took such twinkling pleasure in writing Scholem's school compositions to draw nearer to us—for every unforeseeable and perplexing wave in Scholem's life to break into novelistic plenitude! But no, the enigma with its aura of conjecture still glimmers —it is there for us to pluck at or reinvent. The shadow persists. The plenitude, and the revelations, are in the work.

S. Y. Agnon and the First Religion

SHMUEL YOSEF AGNON, the 1966 Nobel winner for literature, was born one hundred years ago, in Galicia, Poland, and died in Jerusalem in 1970. Not long after his death, I wrote a story about Agnon, a kind of parable that meant to toy with the overweening scramble of writers for reputation and the halo of renown. It was called "Usurpation" and never mentioned Agnon by name. Instead, I pretended he was still alive, not yet a laureate: "It happens that there lives in Jerusalem a writer who one day will win the most immense literary prize on the planet." I referred to this writer as "the old man," or else as "the old writer of Jerusalem"—but all the while it was Agnon I not so secretly had in mind; and I even included in my story, as a solid and unmistakable clue, one of his shorter fables: about why the Messiah tarries.

To tell the truth, this midrashic brevity (God knows where I came upon it) was the only work of Agnon's I had ever read. Nothing could have tempted me to look more extensively into Agnon, not even the invention of a story about him: enchanted by the dazzlements his great name gave off, my story was nevertheless substantially blind to the illuminations of his pen. I could scarcely blame myself for this. For decades, Agnon scholars (and Agnon is a literary industry) have insisted that it is no use trying to get at Agnon in any language other than the original. The idea of Agnon in translation has been repeatedly disparaged; he has been declared inaccessible to the uninitiated even beyond the usual truisms concerning the practical difficulties of translation. His scriptural and Talmudic resonances and nuances, his historical and textual layers, his allusive and elusive echoings and patternings, are so marvelously multiform, dense, and imbricated that he is daunting even to the most sophisticated Hebrew readers. What, then, can a poor non-Hebraist possibly make of an Agnonic masterwork, when, willy-nilly, it is stripped of a quarter or a half of its texture and its substance, when the brilliant leaves are shaken off the spare, bare, naked-toed trunk? A writer in monolingual America, confined to writing and reading wholly in English, will clearly have no Agnon other than the Agnon who has been Englished. If the prodigal Agnon can be present only in Hebrew, to read him in any other tongue is to be condemned to paucity. The Hebrew prince is an English-language pauper.

So, drawn almost exclusively to the lustiness of literary blue blood, unwilling to see it ransacked and pauperized, it is no wonder that I have kept my distance from the translated Agnon.

But Agnon himself has a different idea of translation and its possibilities. The story that illustrates Agnon's position is both extremely famous and consummately sly—a sort of play, or paradigm, or Oscar Wildean joke. Saul Bellow tells the joke on himself in his Introduction to *Great Jewish Short Stories*, a popular paperback anthology he edited in 1963, some years before either writer had captured the Nobel Prize.

> In Jerusalem several years ago, I had an amusing and enlightening conversation with the dean of Hebrew writers, S. Y. Agnon. This spare old man, whose face has a remarkably youthful color, received me in his house, not far from the barbed wire entanglements that divide the city, and while we were drinking tea, he asked me if any of my books had been translated into Hebrew. If they had not been, I had better see to it immediately, because, he said, they would survive only in the Holy Tongue. His advice I assume was only half serious. This was his witty way of calling my attention to a curious situation. I cited Heinrich Heine as an example of a poet who had done rather well in German. "Ah," said Mr. Agnon, "we have him beautifully translated into Hebrew. He is safe."

Now the "curious situation" Bellow alludes to is the fact (as he comments a moment later) that "Jews have been writing in languages other than Hebrew for two thousand years." No one could have been more aware of this variety of language experience than Agnon—which is why Bellow understood Agnon's remark to be "only half serious." But there are two entirely serious elements to take note of in Agnon's response. The first is his apparent confidence in the power of "beautiful translation." A case can be made that Heine, too, with all *his* strata of sources, from medieval ballads to chivalric romances to French satire, will not readily yield to successful translation—perhaps even less so than Agnon, because a poet is always more resistant to translation than a writer of prose, however complex the prose.

And yet Agnon does not doubt that "we have him," that Heine can be genuinely Heine even in a language as distant from German, and as alien to European literary styles, as Hebrew. All the same, it is not the translator's skill, much as Agnon seems willing to trust in it, that preserves Heine for Agnon. It is Heine's "return," so to speak, as a Jewish poet, to the sacred precincts of the Land of Israel—his return via the Holy Tongue. For Agnon it may be that Heine in German is less fully Heine than he is in Hebrew: to be "safe" is to have entered into the influences of holiness; redemption is signified by the reversal of exile. Whatever happens outside the Land of Israel, whatever ensues in the other languages of the earth, is, to be sure, saturated in its own belongingness, and may indeed be alluring, and without question "counts" in the world of phenomena; but counts differently, because it is outside the historic circle of redemption that only the Land possesses. The world beyond the Land, however gratifying or seductive, is flavored with the flavor of exile.

At first glance Agnon's witticism "He is safe" appears to be in praise of translation as a relatively easy triumph of possibility—but only, it seems, if the text in question is drawn from the tongues of exile into the redemptiveness of Hebrew. Presumably translation *out* of Hebrew would be considered not so much a linguistic as a metaphysical lessening. Or else, since the original continues to stand, Agnon Englished would strike Agnon as irrelevant. The calculated remark "He is safe" is a joke that recognizes, after all, the chanciness of translation, that will in fact *not* guarantee that all translation "saves"; and it is this contradiction that makes the joke, since the redemptiveness of translation can work in one direction only. A flawed rendering of Heine into Hebrew may nevertheless partake of redemption; a brilliant rendering of Agnon into English backslides into the perilous flavors of exile.

And that is the second serious point. When you reverse the direction—when translation becomes *yeridah* (descent from the heights of Jerusalem; desertion) rather than *aliyah* (ascent to the sublime; return)—the witticism collapses, a different tone takes hold, and a chink opens into dread, into the regions of the unsafe, of the irrational, into the dark places of alien myth, of luring mermaid and moon-dazed mountain nymph, of Pan and unbridled Eros. The Lorelei will chant her deadly strains out of the bosom of the Rhine, but never out of Lake Kinneret (the Hebrew name for the Sea of Galilee). And Saul Bellow's domesticized metaphysical anecdote—Agnon drinking tea and speculating about Heine's salvation—becomes a parable that, when set to run in reverse, can turn into a tale of baleful exilic potency. Imagine, for instance, that it is not the Land of Israel that is the magnet, but all the lands beyond. Imagine that the longing of heroic temperaments is for exile rather than for redemption. Imagine everything seen upside down and inside out: a yearning for abroad instead of for Jerusalem; a pilgrimage in search of holy talismans that leads away from the Land toward half-pagan scenes. Imagine a sacred tongue that is not Hebrew. Imagine an Exodus undertaken for the sake of returning to the wilderness. Imagine trading the majestic hymns of Scripture for wild incantations and magical ululations. Imagine the Land of Israel as a site of drought and dearth and death and crumbling parapets and squatters and muteness, while faraway countries flow with rivers and songs and color and grace and beauty and joy.

All these ominous reversals of "He is safe," Agnon has already made; he has made them in a work of fiction. If the Land of Israel assures immortality for Jewish poets, the corollary must be that exile can shore up only the short term, the brief lease, until the final slide into oblivion. But what of the opposite proposition? The proposition that the old, old myths, the legends that precede Sinai by a millennium and more, the fables that continue to girdle and enthrall the world, will outlive all? The proposition that compared to the loud song of the Lorelei, out of whose strong throat beat the hypnotic wing-whirrs of a hundred birds, the biblical Hannah's murmured prayer—unaesthetic, humble, almost not there—falls into insignificance?

Such a proposition may be an unlikely meditation for the pen of the "old writer of Jerusalem," "the dean of Hebrew writers," who in 1950, when he delivered up the tale called *Edo and Enam*, had reached the lively age of sixty-two; sixteen years later we see him flying to Sweden, exultant in a yarmulke. Does the pious yarmulke contradict the tale? The tale may be said to hang on the case of the translation into Hebrew of a pair of newly discovered ancient languages; and yet no redemption will come of it. Heine's "Die Lorelei," a song about death through allurement, is transmuted into a Hebrew ballad, and is thereby deemed "safe." But the Enamite Hymns carry, and carry out, the real power of death by allurement: they are all peril. Transported to the Land of Israel they have the capacity to kill, though they too are "beautifully translated" into the Holy Tongue.

Their devoted translator is Dr. Ginath, a scholar without a yarmulke, a wholly secularized scientific philologist and ethnographer, who will go to any length to get hold of lost languages: once, for example, he posed as a mystical holy man from Jerusalem, "Hacham Gideon," in order to pry out the secret tongue of the living vestige of the tribe of Gad. "These days," remarks the narrator of *Edo and Enam*, "it is as if the earth had opened up and brought forth all that the first ages of man stored away. Has not Ginath discovered things that were concealed for thousands of years, the Edo language and the Enamite Hymns?" Dr. Ginath is the author of "Ninety-nine Words of the Edo Language," and also of an Edo grammar; but

> the Enamite Hymns were more: they were not only a new-found link in a chain that bound the beginnings of recorded history to the ages before, but—in themselves—splendid and incisive poetry. Not for nothing, then, did the greatest scholars come to grips with them, and those who at first had doubted that they were authentic Enamite texts began to compose commentaries on them. One thing, however, surprised . . . All these scholars affirmed that the gods of Enam and their priests were male; how was it that they did not catch in the hymns the cadence of a woman's song?

"I could hear," continues the narrator, "a kind of echo from my very depths . . . ; ever since the day I had first read the Enamite Hymns that echo had resounded. It was a reverberation of a primal song passed on from the first hour of history through endless generations."

That "cadence of a woman's song" belongs to the autochthonous enchantresses, among them the Lorelei; it is the voice of the intoxicated sibyls who speak for what we may call the First Religion, which is the poetry of Eros and nature, of dryad and nymph and oread, of the sacred maidens whose insubstantial temples are the sea, the rivers, the forests, the meadows and the hills. In *Edo and Enam*, Agnon experiments with importing the hymns of this First Religion into the Land of Israel, into the marrow of Jerusalem itself, where such hymns cannot flourish, where they will grow lethal; and he also imports the singer of the hymns, the enchantress Gemulah, who, when she sang in her native realm, "stirred the heart like . . . the bird Grofith, whose song is sweeter than that of any creature on earth."

Gemulah is from a distant mountainous region, though her people originally lived among springs. According to their tradition, they derive from Gad, which once received a biblical blessing for "enlargement." As warriors, they "advanced into the lands of the Gentiles, for they misconceived the text" of the blessing—"they did not know that the blessing refers only to the time when they lived in the Land of Israel, not to their exile in the lands of other peoples." But it is exile itself they have misconceived; they take it for eternity, and have succumbed to the First Religion. While at least formally they maintain their ancestral hope for the return to Jerusalem, and while Gemulah's father, a learned elder of the tribe, is still able to read to the people from the Midrash and the Jerusalem Targum, "which they have in its complete text, and which he translated into their language," the Gadites are by now profoundly separated. Their speech is unlike any other. In fulfillment of their name, Gad, or Luck, they depend on the stars and deal in charms and talismans and magical texts. Though they continue to circumcise their sons, their alien funeral rites are observed "with songs and dances full of dread and wonder." Gemulah herself is "accomplished in all their songs, those that they had once sung . . . by the springs and also those of the mountains." Gemulah's father hands on to her a "secret knowledge laid up by his ancestors," as well as an arcane private language, an antic invention that separates them even from Gad itself; they are a pair of oracles and sorcerers. In order to "learn from the eagles how they renew their youth," Gemulah's father ascends into the mountains, where he is attacked and devoured by an eagle. Following a long mourning, Gemulah is taken by her bridegroom to the Land of Israel, to the city of Jerusalem, where she sickens and falls mute. The First Religion, woven out of filaments of purest nature poetry, is silenced in the domain of monotheism.

A dumbstruck Lorelei, a somnambulist who "walks wherever the moon leads her," like a mermaid drawn by the tides, Gemulah at last becomes equal to the letters of her name when their positions are set free to recombine: a female golem. And indeed at the tale's opening we are privy to some banter about just such a creature—"Wasn't it you who said Dr. Ginath had created a girl for himself?"—and we hear Ibn Gabirol invoked, the Hebrew poet of medieval Spain who is said to have carpentered a woman out of wood.

Gemulah's bridegroom is Gavriel Gamzu, a man in a yarmulke, a dealer in rare books and manuscripts. He began as an ordinary yeshiva student, but discovered himself in thrall to "intrinsic beauty," hence to poetry. In youth once, intending to purchase a copy of the *Shulkhan Arukh*, a compendium of laws, he emptied his pockets for the sake of an exotic *divan* of pure verse. "Because he was so fastened to poetry, he came unfastened at the yeshiva," and was driven to wander the world in search of the ravishments of anonymous hymns. The lure of primeval song has brought him to Gemulah's country. A sandstorm in that region, however, leaves him blind in one eye, perhaps as a divine judgment for preferring intrinsic beauty to the discipline of the codes of conduct. From now on his vision is halved, strangely narrowed. Wearing his yarmulke, he lectures against "read[ing] the Law beyond the text," and keeps a stern eye out for "those Bible critics who turn the words of the living God upside down"; but the next instant this one and only eye abandons piety and fixes on the holiness of poets, whose "hallowed hands" have the power to save from the demons of hell. It appears that intrinsic beauty and the Law cannot rest together in peace within the range of a single eye, and may not wed and live together under a roof in Jerusalem. The bewitchment-seeking spirit of Gavriel Gamzu is for the moment more at home away from home, in the lands of exile. Only there do enchantments thrive unrestrained.

Consequently Gamzu's pursuit of rapture can be fulfilled only outside the Land of Israel, in separated communities compromised by long periods of exile. If the uncanniness of Gemulah's song electrifies him into seizing her as his bride, it is not Gadite poetry alone that stirs Gamzu. In his incessant travels he has happened on other deposits of wondrous lyricism—for instance, exilic Jews whose forefathers were young men driven from Jerusalem by Nebuchadnezzar. Riding on millstones, they were carried aloft to their rescue in the isolation of a mysterious new settlement, where "they saw maidens coming up from the sea," and married them; and not long afterward they "forgot Jerusalem." When Ezra summons them to be restored to the Land of Israel, they hang back. Like the Gadites, they mistake exile for permanence. This lost society, the children of mermaids, develops rites and songs over the generations that deviate signally from the practices of Israel. The close presence of women in their synagogue and the singing of unfamiliar hymns of startling sweetness derive, no doubt, from the habits of their ancestresses the sea-maidens.

In delineating these legendary distant tribes sunk in attrition and dilution, can Agnon have had in mind the real precedent of the Jews of Elephantine? A community founded on an island in the Nile by Jewish mercenaries under Persian governance, even after Ezra's return to Jerusalem in the fifth century B.C.E. they defied the ban on multiple temples and insisted on erecting a separate and rival edifice. The Elephantine Papyri testify to the strong position of women among them: bridegrooms had to provide dowries, for example. But the statuary that crept into their temple architecture, and the customs that invaded their practice, including the outright worship of goddesses, severely divided the Elephantinians from the mainstream, and they disappeared into the belly of exile, leaving behind a mere archaeological vapor. In *Edo and Enam*, Agnon condenses the vapor of wayward paganized Jews into the honeyed elixir of Gamzu's hymns—but when the hymns are introduced into the place where the Temple once stood, havoc rules, and Jerusalem begins to unbuild.

Consider the condition of Jerusalem when Gamzu brings into the city his wife, Gemulah, and her father's talismans—mystical leaves, at first sight colorful, then drained of color, on which certain charms are inscribed. These leaves, long buried in a jar in a cave beneath a mountain crag in Gemulah's country, were given to Gamzu by Gemulah's father; they have the power to retrieve her when she escapes to sleepwalk under a full moon, a malady that occurs chiefly when she is away from her native surroundings. When the charms, in the company of the now-ailing Gemulah, settle into Jerusalem, their influence sets off a rash of departures, a rush back down into exile, an explosion of *yeridah*, signifying a descent from lawful holiness. The narrator's wife and children have left Jerusalem for another town; we are not told why. Gerda and Gerhard Greifenbach, who rent part of their house to the scholarly Dr. Ginath, are yearning for foreign lands, and are about to go on a tour. They are described as "dark and distracted," restless and discontent; it is likely that they suffer from the exilic emanations of the two mystical leaves in their possession, gifts from the itinerant Dr. Ginath—perhaps Ginath found them in a bundle of manuscripts purchased from Gamzu; or perhaps he obtained them in Gemulah's country while impersonating Gideon, the Jerusalem Hacham. The Greifenbachs' house is itself tainted by exilic flaws. It was once inhabited by a quarrelsome sectarian from Germany, who ended by abandoning Jerusalem; and again by a couple named Gnadenbrod: the wife refused to live in Jerusalem, and they re-entered exile in Glasgow—immediately after which an earthquake undermined the house and permanently weakened the roof.

Gemulah's presence insinuates exile into the everyday life of Jerusalem, if exile is understood to mean deterioration, peril, and loss. The water supply dries up in tanks, pipes and taps. Angry Arabs appear out of nowhere to stab young lovers. The city is overrun with housebreakers and squatters. In the general homelessness, newlyweds find it impossible to live together under one roof. All this happens when Gemulah is loosed from her sickbed into Jerusalem, somnambulant, released from muteness only to sing her magical song, *yiddal, yiddal, yiddal, vah, pah, mah*. The body of the city is there, but only as a shell: the spirit of peace is gone from it. Jerusalem itself becomes a kind of golem—which may account for the prevalence of the letter *g—gimel*—in all the names of the tale, Gemulah's among them, since *gimel* too is an anagram for golem. In the last scenes we see Gamzu himself turned into a golem at the sound of Gemulah's private language, the language belonging only to herself and her sorcerer father. Reminiscent of the mystical leaves that initially show brilliant colors and then grow brown as earth, "suddenly the colors began to change in Gamzu's face, until at last all color left it, and there remained only a pale cast that gradually darkened, leaving his features like formless clay." Yet when Gamzu first hears Gemulah's voice, on a mountaintop in her own country, he is entranced: Gemulah stands before him as "one of the twelve constellations of the Zodiac, and none other than the constellation Virgo." She is an oracle, one of the minor divinities of the First Religion, an enchantress, an alien nymph displaced.

And it is displacement that governs the imaginings of *Edo and Enam*. Displacement—the grim principle of exile—is what distinguishes Agnon's fictive commentary on the First Religion from, say, the visionary work of the Sicilian Giuseppe di Lampedusa or the Swedish Pär Lagerkvist, each of whom has written a remarkable modernist novella on the subject of the primal enchantress—or, perhaps, on the theme of ecstatic beauty. The First Religion knows nothing of exile; all the world is home to all the divinities, who flower in forest or sea. Lampedusa's enchantress in "The Professor and the Mermaid" is Lighea, "daughter of Calliope," a mermaid or siren who appears to a student of ancient Greek and couples with him, hoping to lure him to oblivion. Like her mother the muse of poetry, in the name of rapture she urges the erasure of all distinctions: "ignorant of all culture, unaware of all wisdom, contemptuous of any moral inhibitions, she belonged, even so, to the fountainhead of all culture, of all wisdom, of all ethics, and could express this primigenial superiority of hers in terms of rugged beauty. 'I am everything [she chants] because I am simply the current of life, with its detail eliminated.'" Lagerkvist's parable, *The Sibyl*, has a Christian lining, and offers a darker view of the ecstatic: all the same, the oracle's power of annihilation (and self-annihilation) is unmistakable, and her utterances in the pit at the temple of Delhi are, like Gemulah's, in a recondite tongue never before heard by mortal ears: "I began to hiss forth dreadful, anguished sounds, utterly strange to me, and my lips moved without my will; it was not I who was doing this. And I heard shrieks, loud shrieks; I didn't understand them, they were quite unintelligible, yet it was I who uttered them. They issued from my gaping mouth . . . Not long afterward it happened that I was carried out of the oracle pit unconscious, violated by [the] god . . . my ecstasy, my frenzy, was measureless . . . I smelled a sour stench of goat; and the god in the shape of the black goat, his sacred beast in the cave of the oracle, threw itself upon me and assuaged itself and me in a love act in which pain, evil, and voluptuousness were mingled."

The siren and the sibyl, potent representatives of the First Religion, swallow up all things—every achievement, every desire, every idea—into the poetry of ecstatic obliteration, Eros joined with degradation and death. Gemulah's bewitchment of Gamzu is no different, though Agnon's voice, like Gemulah's, is airier:

> Because songs are conjoined, they are linked up with one another, the songs of the springs with the songs of high mountains, and those of high mountains with the songs of the birds of the air. And among these birds there is one whose name is Grofith; when its hour comes to leave the world, it looks up to the clouds and raises its voice in song; and when its song is ended, it departs from the world. All these songs are linked together in the language of Gemulah. Had she uttered

that song of Grofith, her soul would have departed from her, and she would have died.

Yet finally Gamzu opposes Gemulah's sorcery in a way imagination will never dream of opposing the siren's song or the oracle's cry: he puts his hand over Gemulah's mouth to save her from singing the notes of Grofith, the poetry of ecstatic frenzy, which can kill. It is the hand of anti-myth. Who, in the gossamer realms of the First Religion, dares to stop the mouths of Delphic sibyls or glittering mermaids?

And still Gemulah dies. She dies for magic, for voluptuous longing, for ecstasy; she dies singing the song of the bird Grofith after all, bidden to do so by Dr. Ginath, whom she takes to be the Jerusalem Hacham, the magus who once sojourned in her country. As an act of science, the philologist Ginath transcribes the strange syllables of her mysterious language; but Gemulah has no science; she is the antithesis of science. Spellbound under the moon, she walks on the roof of Ginath's part of the Greifenbachs' house—the very roof weakened long ago by an earthquake that came as a judgment upon those who abandon Jerusalem to run after exile. Ginath pursues her, and together they fall to their deaths.

Scanning the obituary notices in the newspaper, the narrator happens on a curious misprint: the announcement of the death of a Dr. Gilath. The letter *l* has been substituted for the letter *n*. Agnon's Hebrew readers can readily guess the reason. "Ginath" (which means "garden") suggests the garden of esoteric knowledge, the fatal *pardes* ("paradise") into which, according to legend, four scholars, all prodigious and original, ventured; only one of them, Rabbi Akiva, came out alive—perhaps because he more than the others revered the Law. And "Gilath"? Omitting the vowels, the root consonants spell out the letters of *galuth*: Hebrew for exile, displacement.

Gemulah is in exile from her country of charms and talismans and conjury and divination and necromantic hymn; Jerusalem, the city of the Law, is inimical to all of these. In her native land, Gemulah blooms unharnessed, under the mild rule of poetry and play and random rapture. But in Jerusalem wizards and their hymns weaken and perish; so Gemulah sickens, and takes to her bed spiritless and speechless; it is well known that a golem lacks the capacity of speech. When the moon calls her, she rises up to meander through Jerusalem, infiltrating her omens and influences through the city, and then Jerusalem too sickens with the sickness of exilic ailments: dread and dryness and departure.

But as soon as Gemulah is destroyed, disordered and disconsolate Jerusalem comes to healthy life again: the water begins to flow freely in the pipes, the exiles stream home, *yeridah* gives way to *aliyah*—the narrator's family returns, the Greifenbachs hurry back from abroad, nothing more is heard of housebreakers, squatters, marauders, or separated couples. The First Religion is routed, and Jerusalem is restored.

How is it, though, that Gemulah's husband, Gamzu, escapes death? Like Ginath, who is punished for flying after the enticements of the languages of exile, Gamzu has been an enamored soul possessed by the music of the First Religion; and yet Gamzu lives. Like Akiva, he survives the penetration into *pardes*. Gamzu is safe—ultimately he can keep his eye, his only eye, on Jerusalem's principle of Law; he wears his yarmulke, and has the power to stop up Gemulah's mouth, so that she will not lose herself in the song of the deadly bird of beauty. Only in the regions beyond Jerusalem is he powerless before savage beauty.

The principle of Jerusalem versus the principle of exile; *aliyah* versus *yeridah*; redemption versus illusion; seeking to be "safe" versus finding oneself swallowed up by the forces of obliteration. A fugue of antagonisms. Nevertheless one cannot be sure of Agnon's definitive passion, whether he is finally on the side of lyrical sorcery or of Torah. Near the close of *Edo and Enam*, the narrator learns that Dr. Ginath has burned all his papers, among them the record of Gemulah's inchoate utterances. Jerusalem, it would seem, has won over the wilderness. But in the very last sentences of the tale, the Enamite Hymns are lauded for their "grace and beauty," and Dr. Ginath is celebrated for saving them for the world: is this jubilant praise rendered in the narrator's voice or in Agnon's own? And in the end how do we know whether Jerusalem itself is really safe, even after the destruction of the enchantress Gemulah? Heine's Lorelei, after all, now sings in the Holy Tongue, the better to sabotage the citizens of Jerusalem.

Out of the Flames: The Recovery of Gertrud Kolmar

NOTE

Gertrud Kolmar, a reclusive German Jewish poet whose lonely and rigorous intensities have been compared to the crystal severities of Paul Celan and Nellie Sachs, was born in Berlin in 1894. The critic Walter Benjamin was her cousin. In 1940, having written in German all her life, she began to teach herself Hebrew; and by 1941, when she was seized for forced labor by the Nazis, she was already experimenting with poetry in Hebrew. She was murdered in Auschwitz in 1943, at age forty-eight.

> Thus saith the Lord God: Come from the four winds, O breath, and breathe upon these slain, that they may live . . . and the breath came into them, and they lived, and stood up upon their feet, an exceeding great army. Then he said: . . . these bones are the whole house of Israel . . . Behold, O my people, I will open your graves, and cause you to come up out of your graves . . . into the house of Israel.
>
> EZEKIEL 37:9-12

A DREAM OF REVERSAL, of reconstruction: who has not, in the fifty years since the European devastation, swum off into this dream? As if the reel of history—and who does not see history as tragic cinema?—could be run backward: these mounds of ash, shoes, teeth, bones, all lifted up, healed, flown speck after speck toward connection, toward flowering, grain on grain, bone on bone, every skull blooming into the quickness of a human face, every twisted shoe renewed on a vivid foot, every dry bone given again to greening life. Ezekiel's vision in the valley of bones.

An imagining with the immensity of "an exceeding great army." Who rises up, what? Populations; a people; a civilization. And everything unmade, undone, unwritten, unread. The children did not live to do their sums, the carpenters did not live to cut the doors to fit the houses that the architects and engineers left in midair, in mid-mind. Unwritten alphabets clog the breath of this dream like so many black hosts of random grit—letters still inchoate, not yet armied into poems, novels, philosophies. Torrents of black letters fill the sky of this imagining like a lost smoke. And singular voices, lost.

Every now and then, though, the dream becomes enfleshed: a voice comes up out of its grave, the living mind resumes its dialogue with history. Anne Frank, most famously; Emanuel Ringelblum's Warsaw Ghetto diaries; Yitzhak Rudashevski's Vilna Ghetto diaries, begun when he was fifteen. But these recovered voices yield direct records of the harrowings. Ezekiel's vision wonders something else: how would the historian Ringelblum have written that history had that history not riven him? What would the mature Anne Frank's novels—she *would* have become a novelist—have turned out to be?

The marvelous recovery of Gertrud Kolmar's poetry signifies the redemption of just such a ripened art.

Gertrud Kolmar died in Auschwitz at age forty-eight; she was given time to become herself, though no time for her name to grow; until this moment, she must be considered unknown. She was published and reviewed barely eight weeks before *Kristallnacht*, that infamous countrywide pogrom called the Night of the Breaking Glass—after which her external precincts narrowed and narrowed toward death. Not so the open cage of her spirit: she felt herself "free in the midst of . . . subjugation." A forced laborer in a Berlin factory, she continued to make poetry and fiction. Ghettoized in a tenement, she began to study Hebrew, and her last—lost—poems were written, most remarkably, defiantly, and symbolically, in the language of the house of Israel.

What has been recovered is not the record of the harrowings—though there is this besides—but the whole blazing body of her poetry, unconsumed. The American poet she is most likely to remind us of is Emily Dickinson—and not so much for her stoic singleness, the heroism of a loneliness teeming with phantasmagorical seeing, as for the daring pressure she puts on language in order to force a crack in the side of the planet, letting out strange figures and fires: she is a mythologist. To fathom this, one must turn finally to the Blake of the *Four Zoas*, or perhaps merely to German folklore: Kolmar too invents fables and their terrible new creatures, intent on tearing out of the earth of the Dark Continent of Europe its controlling demons.

How the devils cry, oh how the deserts cry!

On and on the furnaces of destruction burn; nothing can make them go out, as long as there are you and I to remember who lit them, and why. But now and then a congeries of letters plunges up out of the sparks to give us back a child; a man who meditates on Spinoza in the slave-factory (it was to him Gertrud Kolmar talked of freedom in subjugation); a woman who fabricated original powers in a life beaten out of isolation, sans event until the last cataclysm—and who flies up alive from the cataclysm on the sinewy flanks of these poems.

As if the ash were to speak:

Amazed, I clothe myself.

Primo Levi's Suicide Note

PRIMO LEVI, an Italian Jewish chemist from Turin, was liberated from Auschwitz by a Soviet military unit in January of 1945, when he was twenty-five, and from that moment of reprieve (*Moments of Reprieve* was one of his titles) until shortly before his death in April of 1987, he went on recalling, examining, reasoning, recording—telling the ghastly tale—in book after book. That he saw himself as a possessed scribe of the German hell, we know from the epigraph to his final volume, *The Drowned and the Saved*—familiar lines taken from "The Rime of the Ancient Mariner" and newly startling to a merely literary reader, for whom the words of Coleridge's poem have never before rung out with such an anti-metaphorical contemporary demand, or seemed so cruel:

> Since then, at an uncertain hour,
> That agony returns,
> And till my ghastly tale is told
> This heart within me burns.

Seized by the survivor's heart, this stanza no longer answers to the status of Lyrical Ballad, and still less to the English Department's quintessential Romantic text redolent of the supernatural; it is all deadly self-portrait. In the haven of an Italian spring—forty years after setting down the somber narrative called in Italian "If This Be a Man" and published in English as *Survival in Auschwitz*—Primo Levi hurled himself into the well of a spiral staircase four stories deep, just outside the door of the flat he was born in, where he had been living with his wife and aged ailing mother. Suicide. The composition of the last Lager manuscript was complete, the heart burned out; there was no more to tell.

There was no more to tell. That, of course, is an assumption nobody can justify, and nobody perhaps ought to dare to make. Suicide is one of the mysteries of the human will, with or without a farewell note to explain it. And it remains to be seen whether *The Drowned and the Saved* is, after all, a sort of suicide note.

Levi, to be sure, is not the first writer of high distinction to survive hell and to suggest, by a self-willed death, that hell in fact did not end when the chimneys closed down, but was simply freshening for a second run—Auschwitz being the first hell, and post-Auschwitz the second; and if "survival" is the thing in question, then it isn't the "survivor" whose powers of continuation are worth marveling at, but hell itself. The victim who has escaped being murdered will sometimes contrive to finish the job, not because he is attached to death—never this—but because death is under the governance of hell, and it is in the nature of hell to go on and on: inescapability is its rule, No Exit its sign. "The injury cannot be healed," Primo Levi writes in *The Drowned and the Saved*; "it extends through time, and the Furies, in whose existence we are forced to believe . . . perpetuate the tormentor's work by denying peace to the tormented."

Tadeusz Borowski, for instance, author of *This Way for the Gas, Ladies and Gentlemen*, eluded the gas at both Auschwitz and Dachau from 1943 to 1945; in Warsaw, in 1951, not yet thirty, three days before the birth of his daughter, he turned on the household gas. Suicide. The poet Paul Celan: a suicide. The Austrian-born philosopher Hans Mayer—another suicide—who later became Jean Améry by scrambling his name into a French anagram, was in Auschwitz together with Primo Levi, though the two never chanced on one another. Before his capture and deportation, Améry had been in the Belgian resistance and was subjected to Gestapo torture. After the war, Améry and Levi corresponded about their experiences. Levi esteemed Améry, appeared to understand him, but evidently could not like him—because, he says, Améry was a man who "traded blows." "A gigantic Polish criminal," Levi recounts, "punches [Améry] in the face over some trifle; he, not because of an animallike reaction but because of a reasoned revolt against the perverted world of the Lager, returns the blow as best he can." "'Hurting all over from the blows, I was satisfied with myself,'" Levi quotes Améry; but for himself, Levi asserts,

> "trading punches" is an experience I do not have, as far back as I can go in memory; nor can I say I regret not having it . . . go[ing] down onto the battlefield . . . was and is beyond my reach. I admire it, but I must point out that this choice, protracted throughout his post-Auschwitz existence, led [Améry] to such severity and intransigence as to make him incapable of finding joy in life, indeed of living. Those who "trade

> blows" with the entire world achieve dignity but pay a very high price for it because they are sure to be defeated.

Remarkably, Levi concludes: "Améry's suicide, which took place in Salzburg in 1978 [i.e., nine years before Levi's leap into the stairwell], like other suicides allows for a nebula of explanations, but, in hindsight, that episode of defying the Pole offers one interpretation of it."

This observation—that the rage of resentment is somehow linked to self-destruction—is, in the perplexing shadow of Levi's own suicide, enigmatic enough, and bears returning to. For the moment it may be useful to consider that Primo Levi's reputation—rather, the grave and noble voice that sounds and summons through his pages—has been consummately free of rage, resentment, violent feeling, or any overt drive to "trade blows." The voice has been one of pristine sanity and discernment. Levi has been unwilling to serve either as preacher or as elegist. He has avoided polemics; he has shrunk from being counted as one of those message-bearers "whom I view with distrust: the prophet, the bard, the soothsayer. That I am not." Instead, he has offered himself as a singular witness—singular because he was "privileged" to survive as a laboratory slave, meaning that German convenience, at least temporarily, was met more through the exploitation of his training as a chemist than it would have been through his immediate annihilation as a Jew; and, from our own point of view, because of his clarity and selflessness as a writer. It is selfless to eschew freely running emotion, sermonizing, the catharsis of anger, when these so plainly plead their case before an unprecedentedly loathsome record of criminals and their crimes. Levi has kept his distance from blaming, scolding, insisting, vilifying, lamenting, crying out. His method has been to descibe—meticulously, analytically, clarifyingly. He has been a Darwin of the death camps: not the Virgil of the German hell but its scientific investigator.

Levi himself recognizes that he has been particularly attended to for this quality of detachment. "From my trade," he affirms in *The Drowned and the Saved*,

> I contracted a habit that can be variously judged and defined at will as human or inhuman—the habit of never remaining indifferent to the individuals that chance brings before me. They are human beings but also "samples," specimens in a sealed envelope to be identified, analyzed, and weighed. Now, the sample book that Auschwitz had placed before me was rich, varied, and strange, made up of friends, neutrals, and enemies, yet in any case food for my curiosity, which some people, then and later, have judged to be detached . . . I know that this "naturalistic" attitude does not derive only or necessarily from chemistry, but in my case it did come from chemistry.

Whatever its source—chemistry, or, as others have believed, a lucent and humane restraint—this "naturalistic" approach has astonished and inspired readers and critics. Irving Howe speaks of Levi's "unruffled dignity" and "purity of spirit," James Atlas of his "magisterial equanimity." Rita Levi-Montalcini, a recipient of the 1986 Nobel Prize in medicine and a fellow Turinese, devotes an epilogue in her memoir, *In Praise of Imperfection*, to Levi's "detachment and absence of hatred." You, she addresses Levi, have "come out of the most atrocious of all experiences with an upright forehead and a spirit pure."

A temperament so transparent, so untainted, so unpolemical (indeed, so anti-polemical)—so like clear water—has, however, also provided a kind of relief, or respite, for those who hope finally to evade the gravamen of Levi's chronicle. The novelist Johanna Kaplan sets it out for us: "*Oh, that? Oh, that again?* . . . Because by now, after all the powerful, anguished novels . . . , after all the simple, heartrending documentary accounts, the stringent, haunting historians' texts, the pained and arduous movies—that shocking newsreel footage . . . after all the necessary, nightmare lists of involuntary martyrology, by now our response to the singular horrific barbarity of our time is—just the tiniest bit dutiful." This desire to recoil may describe all of us; and yet we—some of us—drag through these foul swamps, the documents, the films, the photos, the talks, the tales, the conferences, year after year, taking it in and taking it in: perhaps because we are dutiful, perhaps because the fury of outrage owns us, more likely because we are the children of mercy and will not allow the suffering to recede into mere past-ness, a time not ours, for which we are not responsible. We press on with the heartsick job of assimilating the imagination of savagery because in some seizure of helplessly belated justice we want to become responsible for the murdered. In short, guilt: in one form or another we are wounded by conscience. Either, as Jews, we were not there with the others who stood in for us as victims, or, as Christians, we were too much there, represented by the familiar upbringing of the criminals, with whose religious inheritance we have so much in common. Guilt in our absence, guilt in our presence. Jewish guilt; Christian guilt; English, French, Italian, Croatian, Ukrainian, American guilt. Guilt of the Germans whose patriotism gave birth to the criminals. Guilt of the Irish and the Swedes who hid behind neutrality. Guilt over zeal, guilt over apathy.

All of this Levi as naturalist skirts. He appears to have nothing to do with any of it. He is not in favor of a generalized anguish. His aim has been to erect a principled barrier against any show of self-appointed fanaticism, from any direction. Book after book has shied away from the emotive accusatory issues. Above all, Levi is careful not to blur victim and victimizer. He is wary of the sentimentalizers, preeners, hypothesizers: "I do not know," he writes, "and it does not much interest me to know, whether in my depths there lurks a murderer, but I do know that I was a guiltless victim and not a murderer . . . to confuse [the murderers] with their victims is a moral disease or an aesthetic affectation or a sinister sign of complicity." He is a stringent taxonomist, on the side of precision: the crimes and the criminals have an identifiable habitation and name. This may be one reason—it is not the only one—it has been possible to read Levi with soul's pain (how could this be otherwise?), but without guilt. It is not that Levi absolves; rather, he mutes the question of absolution—a question always in the forefront for messengers as radically different from each other as, say, Elie Wiesel and Raul Hilberg. Hilberg's investigations in particular, coolly data-obsessed as they are, have erased the notion of "bystander" status in Nazi Germany. Levi has devoted himself less to social history and psychological motivation than to the microscope, with its exactingly circumscribed field of vision. Society-as-organism is not the area under his scrutiny, as it is for Hilberg; neither is suffering as metaphor, as with Wiesel's emblematic mourning madmen.

The advantage, for many of Levi's readers, has been—dare one say this?—a curious peacefulness: the consequence of the famous "detachment." Levi is far from being a peaceful witness, but because he has not harassed or harangued or dramatized or poetized or shaken a fist or shrieked or politicized (a little of the last, but only a little), because he has restricted himself to observation, notation, and restraint, it becomes alarmingly easy to force him into a false position. If it was futile for him to plead, as he once did, "I beg the reader not to go looking for messages," it is nevertheless disconcerting that of all the various "lessons" that might have been drawn from Levi's penetrations, the one most prevalent is also the coarsest and the most misleading: uplift. Rarely will you come on a publisher's jacket blare as shallow as the one accompanying *The Drowned and the Saved*: "a wondrous celebration of life . . . a testament to the indomitability of the human spirit and humanity's capacity to defeat death through meaningful work, morality and art." Contemptible puffery, undermining every paragraph of the text it ostensibly promotes; and if it is designed to counter "*Oh, that? Oh, that again?*" then it is even more contemptible. Celebration of life? Defeat of death? *Meaningful* work? Morality? Art? What callousness, what cravenness, before the subject at hand! In the Lager world, Levi tells us again and again, "work" was pointless, and deliberately so, in order to intensify torment; morality was reduced to staying alive as long as possible, and by any means; and art was non-existent. Applied to a place where murder claimed daily dominion, "celebration of life" can only be a mockery, or—if that phrase is meant to describe Levi's intent as witness—a double mockery: his intent is to let us see for ourselves the nature, extent, and depth of the German crime.

Yet "celebration of life," that falsifying balm, is hardly untypical of the illusory—or self-deluding—glow of good feeling (or, at best, absence of bad feeling) that generally attaches to Levi's name. Of the scribes of the Holocaust, Levi appears to be the one who least troubles, least wounds, least implicates, the reader. A scientific or objective attitude will inform, certainly, but declines any show of agitation. What we have had from Levi, accordingly, is the portrait of a psychological oxymoron: the well-mannered cicerone of hell, mortal horror in a decorous voice. "Améry called me 'the forgiver,'" Levi notes. "I consider this neither insult nor praise but imprecision. I am not inclined to forgive, I never forgave our enemies of that time . . . because I know no human act that can erase a crime; I demand justice, but I am not able, personally"—here again is this insistent declaration of refusal—"to trade punches or return blows." All the same (untenable as he might consider it), Levi is widely regarded, if not quite as "the forgiver," then as the survivor whose books are, given their subject matter, easiest to take; one gets the impression (and from Levi's own pages) that he has been read in Germany far more willingly than have some others. He writes, as his countrywoman remarked, in the "absence of hatred."

And so it has seemed until this moment. *The Drowned and the Saved* reveals something else. It is a detonation, all the more volcanic because so unexpected. Yet "detonation" is surely, at least from Levi's point of view, the wrong word: concussion is an all-of-a-sudden thing. In *The Drowned and the Saved*, the change of tone is at first muted, faint. Gradually, cumulatively, rumble by rumble, it leads to disclosure, exposure—one can follow the sizzle flying along the fuse; by the last chapter the pressure is so powerful, the rage so immense, that "detachment" has long given way to convulsion. What was withheld before is now imploded in these pages. *The Drowned and the Saved* is the record of a man returning blows with all the might of human fury, in full knowledge that the pen is mightier than the fist. The convulsions of rage have altered the nature of the prose, and—if we can judge by Levi's suicide—the man as well. Almost no one, interestingly, has been disposed to say of Levi's final testimony that it is saturated in deadly anger—as if it would be too cruel to tear from him the veil of the spirit pure. It may be cruel; but it is Levi's own hand that tears away the veil and sets the fuse.

The fuse is ignited almost instantly, in the Preface. "No one will ever be able to establish with precision how many, in the Nazi apparatus, could *not not know* about the frightful atrocities being committed, how many knew something but were in a position to pretend they did not know, and, further, how many had the possibility of knowing everything but chose the more prudent path of keeping their eyes and ears (and above all their mouths) well shut." Here is the heralding of the indictment that will emerge: it is the German people whom Levi subjects to judgment, which may account for his rarely shrinking from the use of "German," where, nowadays, "Nazi" is usually the polite, because narrower, term. In the Preface also may be found the single most terrible sentence ever offered on the issue of what is variously called, "restitution," "changed attitudes," "the new generation," and all the rest: "The crematoria ovens themselves were designed, built, assembled, and tested by a German company, Topf of Wiesbaden (it was still in operation in 1975, building crematoria for civilian use, and had not considered the advisability of changing its name)." *Had not considered the advisability of changing its name*: this applies equally to Krupp, notorious for slave labor, and, in its most celebrated incarnation, to Hitler's "people's car," the ubiquitous Volkswagen, driven unselfconsciously by half the world. (An unselfconscious irony, by the way, that Levi, or his admirable translator, should fall into the phrase "civilian use," meaning, one supposes, the opposite of official governmental policy—i.e., ordinary funerals employing cremation. But who else other than "civilians" were annihilated in the Lager?)

When Levi comes to speak of shame, it is nevertheless not the absence of shame among Germans he invokes, though he condemns the "complicity and connivance" of the "majority of Germans" just before and during the Hitler years; rather, it is the loss of shame in the victims of the Lager, dispossessed of any civilizing vestige, reduced to the animal. The Lager "*anus mundi*," dominated "from dawn to dusk by hunger, fatigue, cold, and fear," "ultimate drainage site of the German universe," was a condition without reciprocity, where you sought to succor and relieve only yourself, to take care of yourself alone. Shame returned with the return of freedom, retrospectively. In the "gray zone" of Lager oppression, contaminated victims collaborated with contaminating persecutors. Arrival at Auschwitz meant "kicks and punches right away, often in the face; an orgy of orders screamed with true or simulated rage; complete nakedness after being stripped; the shaving off of all one's hair; the outfitting in rags," and some of these depredations were conducted by fellow victims appointed as functionaries. Again and again Levi emphasizes the diminishment of every human trait, the violated modesty, the public evacuation, the satanically inventive brutality, the disorientation and desperation. He describes the absolute rule of "small satraps"—the common criminals who became Kapos; the wretched *Bettnachzieher*, whose sole job was to measure the orderliness of straw pillows with a maniacal string and who had the power to punish "publicly and savagely"; the overseers of the "work that was purely persecutory"; the "Special Squads" that operated the crematoria for the sake of a few weeks more of life, only to be replaced and thrown into the fire in turn. These squads, Levi explains, "were made up largely of Jews. In a certain sense this is not surprising, since the Lager's main purpose was to destroy Jews, and, beginning in 1943, the Auschwitz population was 90-95 percent Jews." (Here I interrupt to remind the reader of William Styron's choice in *Sophie's Choice*, wherein we are given, as the central genocidal emblem of Lager policy in those years, a victim who is not a Jew.*) "From another point of view," Levi continues, "one is stunned by this paroxysm of perfidy and hatred: it must be the Jews who put the Jews into the ovens; it must be shown that the Jews, the subrace, the submen, bow to any and all humiliation, even to destroying themselves." Levi admits that merely by virtue of his having stayed alive, he never "fathomed [the Lager] to the bottom." The others, the "drowned," he maintains, those who went down to the lees of suffering and annihilation, were the only true fathomers of that perfidy and hatred.

Levi's reflections appear to be fathomings enough. *The Drowned and the Saved* is much less a book of narrative and incident than it is of siftings of the most sordid deposits of

* Let no one misconstrue this remark. The point is not that Jews suffered more than anyone else in the camps, or even that they suffered in greater numbers; concerning suffering there can be no competition or hierarchy. To suggest otherwise would be monstrous. Those who suffered at Auschwitz suffered with an absolute equality, and the suffering of no one victimized group or individual weighs more in human anguish than that of any other victimized group or individual. But note: Catholic Poland, for instance (language, culture, land), continues, while European Jewish civilization (language, culture, institutions) was wiped out utterly – and that, for Jewish history, is the different and still more terrible central meaning of Auschwitz. It is, in fact, what defines the Holocaust, and distinguishes it from the multiple other large-scale victimizations of the Nazi period.

the criminal imagination—the inescapable struggle of a civilized mind to bore through to the essence and consequence of degradation and atrocity. Levi is not the first to observe that "where violence is inflicted on man it is also inflicted on language," though he may be among the first to inform us of the life-or-death role of language in the Lager. Simply, not to understand German was to go under at once: "the rubber truncheon was called *der Dolmetscher*, the interpreter: the one who made himself understood to everybody." Levi had studied some German at the university to prepare himself as a chemist. He learned more in Auschwitz—grotesquely distorted barbarisms which he deliberately held on to years later, "for the same reason I have never had the tattoo removed from my left arm." As for the tattoo itself—"an autochthonous Auschwitzian invention," "gratuitous, an end in itself, pure offense," "a return to barbarism"—Levi, a secular Jew, is careful to note that Leviticus 19:28 forbids tattooing "precisely in order to distinguish Jews from the barbarians." Even newborn babies, he reports, were tattooed on arrival in Auschwitz.

All this, and considerably more, Levi gathers up under the chilling heading of "Useless Violence," which he defines as "a deliberate creation of pain that was an end in itself." What else was the purpose of the vindictive halt of a boxcar of Jews at an Austrian railroad station, where, while the guards laughed, "the German passengers openly expressed their disgust" at "men and women squatting wherever they could, on the platforms and in the middle of the tracks"? What else was the purpose of emptying out nursing homes filled with elderly sick people already near death and hauling them off to Auschwitz to be gassed? Or forcing grown men to lap up soup like dogs by depriving them of spoons (of which there were tens of thousands at

Auschwitz)? Or using human ash from the crematoria to make "gravel" paths for the SS village that ruled the camp? Or selling human hair to the German textile industry for mattress ticking? Or locking human beings into decompression chambers "to establish at what altitude human blood begins to boil: a datum that can be obtained in any laboratory at minimum expense and without victims, or even can be deduced from common tables"?

A sparse sampling from Levi's meditation on the German abominations, some familiar, some not. Cardinal John O'Connor's theologizing not long ago—which led him to identify the torments of Auschwitz as a Jewish gift to the world—is no doubt indisputably valid Roman Catholic doctrine concerning the redemptive nature of suffering; but, much as the observation was intended to confer grace on the victims, it strikes me as impossible, even for a committed Christian, even for an angel of God, to speak of redemption and Auschwitz in the same breath. What we learn overwhelmingly from Levi is this: if there is redemption in it, it cannot be Auschwitz; and if it is Auschwitz, it is nothing if not unholy. Let no one mistake Primo Levi. If an upright forehead and a spirit pure mean forgoing outrage for the sake of one lofty idea or another—including the renunciation of hatred for the designers of the crematoria—then Primo Levi is as sullied as anybody else who declines to be morally neutered in the name of superior views.

He is in fact not morally neutered, and never was. He is not a "forgiver" (only someone with a clouded conscience would presume to claim that right on behalf of the murdered), and he is not dedicated, as so many believe, to an absence of rancor toward the strategists of atrocity and their followers. He is, as he asserts, a scientist and a logician: nowhere in Levi's pages will you find anything even remotely akin to the notion of "hate the sin, not the sinner." He is not an absurdist or a surrealist; nowhere does he engage in such a severance. On the contrary, his preëminent theme is responsibility: "The true crime, the collective, general crime of almost all Germans of that time, was that of lacking the courage to speak." One thinks, accordingly, of those unmoved German citizens waiting for a train on a station platform, compelled to hold their noses in revulsion as the freight cars, after passing through miles of unpeopled countryside, disgorge their dehumanized prey—a "relief stop" conceived in malice and derision. In his final chapter, "Letters from Germans," Levi quotes a correspondent who pleads with him "to remember the innumerable Germans who suffered and died in their struggle against iniquity." This letter and others like it bring Levi to the boiling point. He scorns the apologists, the liars, the "falsely penitent." He recalls his feelings when he learned that *Survival in Auschwitz* would be published in Germany:

> yes, I had written the book in Italian for Italians, for my children, for those who did not know, those who did not want to know, those who were not yet born, those who, willing or not, had assented to the offense; but its true recipients, those against whom the book was aimed like a gun, were they, the Germans. Now the gun was loaded . . . I would corner them, tie them before a mirror . . . Not that handful of high-ranking culprits, but them, the people, those I had seen from close up, those from among whom the SS militia were recruited, and also those others, those who had believed, who not believing had kept silent, who did not have the frail courage to look into our eyes, throw us a piece of bread, whisper a human word.

He quotes from *Mein Kampf*; he reminds his "polite and civil interlocutors, members of a people who exterminated mine," of the free elections that put Hitler into office, and of *Kristallnacht*; he points out that "enrollment in the SS was voluntary," and that heads of German families were entitled, upon application, to receive clothing and shoes for both children and adults from the warehouses at Auschwitz. "Did no one ask himself where so many children's shoes were coming from?" And he concludes with a *j'accuse* directed toward "that great majority of Germans who accepted in the beginning, out of mental laziness, myopic calculation, stupidity, and national pride, the 'beautiful words' of Corporal Hitler."

The Drowned and the Saved is a book of catching-up after decades of abstaining. It is a book of blows returned by a pen on fire. The surrender to fury in these burning chapters does not swallow up their exactness—the scientist's truthful lens is not dissolved—but Levi in the violated voice of this last completed work lets fly a biblical ululation that its predecessors withheld: *thy brother's blood cries up from the ground*. I do not mean that Levi has literally set down those words; but he has, at long last, unleashed their clamor.

And what of the predecessor-volumes? What of their lucid calm, absence of hatred, magisterial equanimity, unaroused detachment? Readers have not misconstrued Levi's tone, at least not until now. *The Drowned and the Saved* makes it seem likely that the restraint of forty years was undertaken out of a consistent adherence to an elevated *idée fixe*, possibly to a self-deception: a picture of how a civilized man ought to conduct himself when he is documenting savagery. The result was the world's consensus: a man somehow set apart from retaliatory passion. A man who would not trade punches. A transparency; a pure spirit. A vessel of clear water.

I spoke earlier of creeping fuses, mutedness, the slow accretion of an insurmountable pressure. "The Furies . . . perpetuate the tormentor's work by denying peace to the tormented." But all that was subterranean. Then came the suicide. Consider now an image drawn from Primo Levi's calling. Into a vessel of clear water—tranquil, innocuous—drop an unaccustomed ingredient: a lump of potassium, say, an alkali metal that reacts with water so violently that the hydrogen gas given off by the process will erupt into instant combustion. One moment, a beaker of unperturbed transparency. The next moment, a convulsion: self-destruction.

The unaccustomed ingredient, for Levi, was rage. "Suicide," he reflects in *The Drowned and the Saved*—which may be seen, perhaps and after all, as the bitterest of suicide notes—"is an act of man and not of the animal. It is a meditated act, a noninstinctive, unnatural choice." In the Lager, where human beings were driven to become animals, there were almost no suicides at all. Améry, Borowski, Celan, and ultimately Levi did not destroy themselves until some time after they were released. Levi waited more than forty years; and he did not become a suicide until he let passion in, and returned the blows. If he is right about Améry—that Améry's willingness to trade punches is the key to his suicide—then he has deciphered for us his own suicide as well.

What we know now—we did not know it before *The Drowned and the Saved*—is that at bottom Levi could not believe in himself as a vessel of clear water standing serenely apart. It was not detachment. It was dormancy, it was latency, it was potentiality; it was inoperativeness. He was always conscious of how near to hand the potassium was. I grieve that he equated rage—the rage that speaks for mercifulness—with self-destruction. A flawed formula. It seems to me it would not have been a mistake—and could not have been misinterpreted—if all of Primo Levi's books touching on the German hell had been as vehement, and as pointed, as the last, the most remarkable.

The Phantasmagoria of Bruno Schulz

HALF A CENTURY AGO, Bruno Schulz, a fifty-year-old high-school art teacher in command of one of the most original literary imaginations of modern Europe, was gunned down by a Jew-hunting contingent of SS men in the streets of an insignificant provincial town in eastern Galicia. On the map of Poland the town hides itself from you; you have to search out the tiniest print to discover Drogobych. In this cramped crevice of a place Schulz too hid himself—though not from the Nazis. Urged on by a group of writers, the Polish underground devised a means of escape—false papers and a hiding place. Schulz chose to die unhidden in Drogobych. But even before the German storm, he had already chosen both to hide and to die there. He knew its streets, and their houses and shops, with a paralyzed intimacy. His environment and his family digested him. He was incapable of leaving home, of marrying, at first even of writing. On a drab salary, in a job he despised, he supported a small band of relatives, and though he visited Warsaw and Lvov, and once even went as far as Paris, he gave up larger places, minds, and lives for the sake of

Drogobych—or, rather, for the sake of the gargoylish and astonishing map his imagination had learned to draw of an invisible Drogobych contrived entirely out of language.

In English there is virtually no biographical information to be had concerning Schulz. It is known that his final manuscript, a novel called "The Messiah," was carried for safekeeping to a friend; both friend and manuscript were swallowed up by the sacrificial fires of the Europe of 1942. All of Schulz's letters, and two-thirds of the very small body of his finished work—two novels, one novella—remain untranslated and, so far, inaccessible to American readers. It is a powerful omission. Think what our notion of the literature of the Dark Continent of Europe would be like if we had read our way so late into the century without the most renowned of the stories in *Red Cavalry*, or without "Gimpel the Fool," or without *Metamorphosis*. A verbal landscape stripped of Babel or Singer or Kafka is unimaginable to us now, and it may turn out, in the wake of *The Street of Crocodiles**, that Schulz can stand naturally—or unnaturally—among those writers who break our eyes with torches, and end by demonstrating the remarkable uses of a purposeful dark.

In this dark the familiar looms freakish, and all of these —Babel as Cossack Jew, Singer purveying his imps and demiurges, Kafka with his measured and logical illogic— offer mutations, weird births, essences and occasions never before suspected. *The Street of Crocodiles*, at one with that mythic crew, is a transmogrified Drogobych: real town and real time and real tasks twisted and twisted until droplets of changed, even hateful, even hideous, beauty are squeezed out of bolts of cloth, ledgers, tailors' dummies, pet birds, a

* *The Street of Crocodiles* by Bruno Schulz, Penguin Books, 1977.

row of shops, a puppy, a servant girl. As in Kafka, the malevolent is deadpan; its loveliness of form is what we notice. At the heart of the malevolent—also the repugnant, the pitiless—crouches the father: Schulz's own father, since there is an inviolable autobiographical glaze that paints over every distortion. The father is a shopkeeper, the owner of a dry-goods store. He gets sick, gives up work, hangs around home, fiddles with his account books, grows morbid and sulky, has trouble with his bowels, bursts out into fits of rage. All this is novelist's material, and we are made to understand it in the usual way of novels.

But parallel with it, engorging it, is a running flame of amazing imagery—altogether exact and meticulous—that alters everything. The wallpaper becomes a "pullulating jungle . . . filled with whispers, lisping and hissing." Father "sitting clumsily on an enormous china chamberpot" turns into a prophet of "the terrible Demiurge," howling with "the divine anger of saintly men." Father shrinks, hides in closets, climbs the curtains and perches there like a baleful stuffed vulture, disappears "for many days into some distant corner of the house." Schulz's language is dense with disappearances, losses, metamorphoses. The dry-goods shop is flooded by a "cosmogony of cloth." Crowded streets become "an ultra-barrel of myth." The calendar takes on a thirteenth month. Rooms in houses are forgotten, misplaced. A bicycle ascends into the zodiac. Even death is somehow indefinite; a murk, a confusion. Father "could not merge with any reality and was therefore condemned to float eternally on the periphery of life, in half-real regions, on the margins of existence. He could not even earn an honest citizen's death." Father, alive, lectures on manikins: "There is no dead matter . . . lifelessness is only a disguise behind which hide unknown forms of life." A dog represents "the most essential secret of life, reduced to this simple, handy, toy-like form." Wallpapers become bored; furniture, "unstable, degenerate," breaks out into rashes. The maid rules the master with ominous and magisterial positions of her fingers—she points, waggles, tickles. She is a kind of proto-Nazi. Father takes up ornithology and hatches a condor like "an emaciated ascetic, a Buddhist lama," an idol, a mummy—it resembles father himself. (A fore-echo of Kosinski, another Pole obsessed by fearful birds.) Father loathes cockroaches, violently pursues them, and is transformed, undertaking at last their "ceremonial crawl."

> He lay on the floor naked, stained with black totem spots, the lines of his ribs heavily outlined, the fantastic structure of his anatomy visible through the skin; he lay on his face, in the grip of an obsession of loathing which dragged him into the abyss of its complex paths. He moved with the many-limbed, complicated movements of a strange ritual in which I recognized with horror an imitation of the ceremonial crawl of a cockroach.

In Kafka's myth, it is the powerless son who turns into a cockroach; here it is the father who has lost control. Everything is loosened; it is not that the center does not hold; there never *was* a center. "Reality is as thin as paper and betrays with all its cracks its imitative character." "Our language has no definitions which would weigh, so to speak, the grade of reality." Given these hints, it may be misleading to anticipate *The Street of Crocodiles* with so "normal" a signal as *novel*: it is a thick string of sights and sinuosities, a cascade of flashes, of extraordinary movements—a succession of what television has taught us to call "film clips," images in magnetic batches, registered storms, each one shooting memories of itself into the lightnings of all the others. What is being invented in the very drone of our passive literary expectations is Religion—not the taming religion of theology and morality, but the brute splendors of rite, gesture, phantasmagoric transfiguration, sacrifice, elevation, degradation, mortification, repugnance, terror, cult. The religion of animism, in fact, where everything comes alive with an unpredictable and spiteful spirit-force, where even living tissue contains ghosts, where there is no pity.

Such metaphysical specters have their historical undersides. Home shifts, its forms are unreliable, demons rule. Why should these literary Jews of twentieth-century Slavic Europe—Babel, whose language was Russian, two years younger than Schulz; Kafka, who wrote in German, seven years older; Singer, a Yiddish writer, a dozen years younger; and finally (one is tempted to enter the next generation) the American Kosinski—why should these cultivated Slavic Jews run into the black crevices of nihilism, animalism, hollow riddle? Why, indeed, should these writers be the very ones almost to *invent* the literary signposts of such crevices? Gogol came first, it is true; but it is the Slavic Jews who have leaped into the fermenting vat. The homelessness and ultimate pariahship felt by Schulz—an assimilated, Polish-speaking Jew, not so much a Jew as a conscious Pole—in the years before the fiery consummation of the Final Solution may explain why the real Drogobych took on the symbolic name Crocodile Street, and became the place where "nothing ever succeeds . . . nothing can ever reach a definite conclusion." But it did, in gunshot, on the streets of Drogobych in 1942. "Over the whole area," Schulz writes of his visionary town, "there floats the lazy licentious smell of sin."

The shock of Schulz's images brings us the authentic bedevilment of the Europe we are heir to. Schulz's life was cut short. His work, a small packet, reminds us of father: "the small shroud of his body and the handful of nonsensical oddities." Some of the packet was lost in the human ash heap. As for the little that remains: let us set it beside Kafka and the others and see how it measures up for truth-telling.

Italo Calvino: Bringing Stories to Their Senses

NOT LONG BEFORE his death in 1985, Italo Calvino undertook to write five stories on the five senses. He completed three—on the powers of tongue, ear, nostrils—gathered now in a nervous, narrow, dazing volume; a cerebral accident swept him away before he could arrive at the fingertips and the eye.

The trio of tales in *Under the Jaguar Sun** are not "experimental." Calvino, an authentic postmodernist (despite the clamor, there are not so many of these), does not experiment: the self-conscious postmodernist is also a devil-may-care post-experimenter. No one has understood the gleeful and raucous fix—or tragedy—of the latter-day artist more penetratingly than Italo Calvino. The writer's quest has traditionally been to figure out the right human questions to ask, and if we still love the novels of, say, George Eliot, it is because we are nostalgic for the sobriety of a time when the right questions could be divined. In the disorderly aftermath of Joyce, Kafka, Agnon, Borges, all

* Published by Jonathan Cape, 1991.

the questions appear to be used up, repetitive, irrelevant; and their answers—which only recently *did* take on experimental form—have been marred by struggle, stoicism, and a studied "playfulness" more plucky than antic. After Kafka, after Borges, what is there to do but mope?

Calvino sets aside both questions and answers for the sake of brilliant clues and riddling intuitions. He gives up narrative destination for destiny, clarification for clairvoyance. He invents a new laughter suitable to the contemporary disbelief in story. In short, Calvino re-addresses—and magisterially re-enters—the idea of myth, of "the tale." In earlier works, he imagined Marco Polo as Scheherazade, mesmerizing Kublai Khan with jewellike accounts of walls, images, weather, names, humors, fates; or he noted that "the objects of reading and writing are placed among rocks, grass, lizards, having become products of the mineral-vegetable-animal continuum." He even invoked—in the exhilarating pages of *If On A Winter's Night A Traveler*—a Father of Stories, "the universal source of narrative material, the primordial magma." A learned, daring, ingeniously gifted magus, Calvino has in our own time turned himself into the Italian Grimm: his *Italian Folktales*, a masterwork of culling and retelling, is devoted precisely to the lure of the primordial magma—myth spawned by the body of the organic and inorganic world.

The three tales of *Under the Jaguar Sun* are, accordingly, engendered by the human nervous system—the body as a cornucopia of sensation, or as an echoing palace with manifold windows, each a shifting kaleidoscope. The modernists have already hinted at how the fundamental story-clay, the myth-magma, can spring out of taste—remember Proust's madeleine; or smell—Mann's diseased Venice; or sound—Forster's *ou-boum* in the Marabar Caves.

Yet these merely metaphorical resonances will not content Calvino. He slides back behind them to the primary ground of perception: ganglia and synapse. He fuses fable with neuron. By driving story right down to its biological root, to cell and stimulus, he nearly annihilates metaphor. Calvino's postmodernism is a literalism so absolute that it transports myth to its organic source, confining story to the limits of the mouth, the ear, the nose.

But what seems to be confinement and limitation—the mouth, after all, is only a little chamber—widens to rite and mystery. The title story opens with a scrupulous recounting of Mexican cuisine (the reader is likely to salivate), and winds up in a dazzlement of wit and horror. The narrator and Olivia, a tourist couple who are vaguely estranged, are in Mexico on a holiday. They are diligent about seeing the sights and obsessive about trying every exotic dish. The husband is somewhat apathetic ("insipid," Olivia calls him, as if he needed seasoning) while Olivia is intense, inquisitive, perilously inspired. Her passion for food is sacerdotal, almost creedal. Studying her "voluptuous mastication," the narrator is overcome by a revelation of his own: "I realized my gaze was resting not on her eyes but on her teeth . . . which I happened to be seeing for the first time not as the radiant glow of a smile but as the instruments most suited to their purpose: to be dug into flesh, to sever it, tear it."

Husband and wife investigate the "gastronomical lexicon" of various localities, including *chiles en nogada*, "wrinkled little peppers, swimming in a walnut sauce whose harshness and bitter aftertaste were drowned in a creamy, sweetish surrender," and *gorditas pellizcadas con manteca*, "plump girls pinched with butter." The very name of the latter returns them to their hotel room in a rare state of sexual arousal. And meanwhile their days are given over to exploring the ruins of ancient Aztec and Olmec civilizations—temples where human sacrifice was practiced, with the complicity of willing victims, by priests who afterward consumed a certain "ritual meal." Olivia presses their guide to speculate on the possible flavors of that unspecified dish—following which, during a supper of shrimp soup and goat kid, the husband fantasizes that "I could feel her tongue lift me against the roof of her mouth, enfold me in saliva, then thrust me under the tips of the canines . . . The situation was not entirely passive," he reflects, "since while I was being chewed by her I felt also that I was acting on her, transmitting sensations that spread from the taste buds through her whole body." Without such reciprocity, "human sacrifice would be unthinkable."

Of course this is also a comic immersion in the psychology of that "universal cannibalism," as the well-chewed narrator terms it, that "erases the lines between our bodies and . . . *enchiladas*." And incidentally makes marriages work.

If the mouth can both smile and devour, the ear is all petrified anxiety. To listen acutely is to be powerless, even if you sit on a throne. In "The King Listens"—the crown of this extraordinary collection—the suspected eavesdropping of spies, unidentifiable movements and whispers, signals of usurpation, mysterious knockings, the very noise of the universe, imply terror and imprisonment. The ear turns out to be the most imagining organ, because it is the most accomplished at deciphering; still, on its own, it cannot be confident of any one interpretation, and wheels frenetically from conjecture to conjecture. In the end, the monarch around whom the life of the palace stirs does not know whether he is a king or a caged prisoner in the palace's secret dungeon.

Transposition of ruler and ruled—the theme, to be sure, of Chekhov's "Ward No. Six," and even (more frivolously) of J. M. Barrie's *The Admirable Crichton*. But Calvino's mythopoetics has no theme; the primordial magma is beyond, and below, what story is "about." And the palace itself, we soon recognize, is a maze leading to a tunnel: the configuration of the human ear.

The last and shortest tale—"The Name, the Nose"—is not, I think, a success, though here as in the others the brilliance of language never falters. Calvino's aim is to juxtapose the primitive and the rococo, the coarse and the highly mannered, in order to reveal their congenital olfactory unity. To emphasize the bond of nose with nose, he constructs a somewhat blurry triptych. A decadent French gentleman visits Madame Odile's *parfumerie* in search of the scent of the vanished lady he waltzed with at a masked ball. A neanderthal man-beast runs with the herd in pursuit of females, lured by the explicit odor of a single escaped female. After a bleary night of beer, marijuana, and sex, the drummer of a London rock band wakes up in a cold and filthy rooming house fixed on the smell of the girl he slept with, though she has long since cleared out. In brief, the nose, no matter who is wearing it, is an aboriginal hunter. It is all too artful, too archetypal, too anthropological—and especially too programmed and thematic. No use sniffing here after the primeval mythos. The sophisticated aroma is of Calvino, writing.

James Whistler—acclaimed a master painter in his own time, if not in ours—once declared that "the master stands in no relation to the moment at which he occurs." Possibly. But it is also a sign of the masterly imagination that it will respond lavishly to the moment's appetite—and appetite is elemental, the opposite of fashion. Calvino occurring in any span of decades other than those vouchsafed him is inconceivable. He was meant to flourish on the heels of Kafka. That he flourishes in an English prose equal in brio and originality to Nabokov's is owed to his noteworthy translator, William Weaver, who brings to Calvino's voice the ear, the savor, and the quizzical nostrils of a fellow poet.

The Sister Melons of J. M. Coetzee

THE LITERATURE OF conscience is ultimately about the bewilderment of the naive. Why do men carry guns and build prison camps, when the nurturing earth is made for freedom? To the outcast, the stray, the simpleton, the unsuspecting—to the innocent—the ideologies that order society are inane, incomprehensible. Comprehension comes unaccoutered, stripped, uninstructed—like Huck Finn on the loose, who merely knows what he knows. And what the pariah Huck knows, against the weight and law and common logic of his slaveholding "sivilization," is that the black man is whole, the rightful owner of his life and times.

In *Life & Times of Michael K,* J. M. Coetzee, a South African born in 1940, has rewritten the travail of Huck's insight, but from the black man's point of view, and set in a country more terrible—because it is a living bitter hard-hearted contemporary place, the parable-world of an unregenerate soon-after-now, with little pity and no comedy. Conscience, insight, innocence: Michael K cannot aspire to such high recognitions—he is "dull," his mind is "not quick." He was born fatherless and with a disfigurement: a harelip that prevented him from being nourished at his mother's breast. When he needs some tools to make a cart to transport his dying mother, he breaks into a locked shed and takes them. The smallest transgression, undetected and unpunished, the single offense of his life; yet nearly every moment of his life is judged as if he were guilty of some huge and undisclosed crime—not for nothing is his surname resonant with the Kafkan "K." His crime is his birth. When as a schoolchild he is perplexed by long division, he is "committed to the protection" of a state-run orphanage for the "variously afflicted." From then on he is consistently protected—subject to curfews, police permits, patrols, convoys, sentries, guns, a work camp with wire fences, a semi-benevolent prison hospital: tyranny, like his school, "at the expense of the state."

Though a mote in the dustheap of society, he is no derelict. From the age of fifteen he has worked as a gardener in a public park in Cape Town. His worn and profoundly scrupulous mother also lives honorably; she is a domestic servant for a decent enough elderly couple in a posh seaside apartment house. They have gone to the trouble of keeping a room for her—an unused basement storage closet without electricity or ventilation. Her duties end at eight o'clock at night six days a week. When she falls ill, she is dependent on the charity of her employers. The building is attacked, vandalized, the residents driven out. Michael K is laid off. The country is at war.

The purpose of the war, from one standpoint—that of a reasonable-minded prisonmaster—is "so that minorities will have a say in their destinies." This is indisputably the language of democratic idealism. In a South African context such a creed unexpectedly turns Orwellian: it means repression of the black majority by the white minority. Yet in Coetzee's tale we are not told who is black and who is white, who is in power and who is not. Except for the reference to Cape Town and to place names that are recognizably Afrikaans, we are not even told that this is the physical and moral landscape of South Africa. We remain largely uninstructed because we are privy solely to Michael K's heart, an organ that does not deal in color or power, a territory foreign to abstractions and doctrines; it knows only what is obvious and elemental. Another way of putting this is to say that—though there is little mention anywhere of piety or faith, and though it is the prison-masters alone who speak sympathetically and conscientiously of rights and of freedom—Michael K responds only to what appears to be divinely ordered, despite every implacable decree and man-made restraint. He names no tyranny and no ideal. He cares for his mother; he cares for the earth; he will learn how they come to the same in the end.

With laborious tenderness, with intelligent laboriousness—how intelligent he is!—Michael K builds a crude hand-drawn vehicle to restore his mother to a lost place that has become the frail ephemeral text of her illness, no more substantial than a vision: a bit of soil with a chicken run, where she remembers having once been happy in childhood. The town nearest this patch is only five hours away, but without a permit they may not go by train. No permit arrives. They set out clandestinely, the young man heaving the weight of his old mother in the cart, dodging military convoys, hiding, the two of them repeatedly assaulted by cold and bad weather and thugs with knives. To Michael K at the start of the journey, brutality and danger and stiffness of limb and rain seem all the same; tyranny feels as natural an ordeal as the harshness of the road.

On the road his mother deteriorates so piteously that Michael K must surrender her to a hospital. There he is shunted aside and she dies. Without consultation her body is cremated and given back to him, a small bundle of ashes in a plastic bag. He holds his mother's dust and imagines the burning halo of her hair. Then, still without permission, he returns her to the place of her illumination and buries her ashes. It is a grassy nowhere, a guess, the cloud-rack of a dream of peace, the long-abandoned farm of a departed Afrikaaner family, a forgotten and unrecorded spot fallen through the brute mesh of totalitarian surveillance.

And here begins the parable of Michael K's freedom and resourcefulness; here begins Michael K's brief bliss. He is Robinson Crusoe, he is the lord of his life. It is his mother's own earth; it is his motherland; he lives in a womblike burrow; he tills the fruitful soil. Miracles sprout from a handful of discovered seeds: "Now two pale green melons were growing on the far side of the field. It seemed to him that he loved these two, which he thought of as two sisters, even more than the pumpkins, which he thought of as a band of brothers. Under the melons he placed pads of grass so that their skins should not bruise." He eats with deep relish, in the fulfillment of what is ordained: the work of his hands, a newfound sovereignty over his own hands and the blessing of fertility in his own scrap of ground. "I am becoming a different kind of man," he reflects. For the first time he is unprotected. When he has grown almost unafraid, civilization intrudes.

A whining boy who is a runaway soldier takes over the farmhouse and declares himself in need of a servant. A group of guerrillas and their donkeys pass through by night and trample the seedlings. Michael K flees; he is picked up as a "parasite" and confined to a work camp. But because he has lived in the field as a free man—in the field "he was not a prisoner or a castaway . . . he was himself"—he has learned how to think and judge. "What if the hosts were far outnumbered by the parasites, the parasites of idleness and the other secret parasites in the army and the police force and the schools and the factories and offices, the parasites of the heart? Could the parasites then be called parasites? Parasites too had flesh and substance; parasites too could be preyed upon."

From the seed of freedom Michael K has raised up a metaphysics. It is not the coarse dogma of a killer-rebel or a terrorist; he does not join the guerrillas. He sees vulnerable children on all sides—the runaway who wants to be taken care of, the careless insurgents who are like "young men come off the field after a hard game," even the young camp guard with diabetes, callous and threatening, yet willing to share his food, who will end up as a prisoner himself. "How many people are there left who are neither locked up nor standing guard at the gate?"

But behind the gate Michael K cannot eat, cannot swallow, cannot get nourishment, and now Coetzee turns his parable to one of starvation. Repression wastes. Tyranny makes skeletons. Injustice will be vomited up. "Maybe he only eats the bread of freedom," says a doctor in the camp for "rehabilitation," where Michael K is next incarcerated. His body is "crying to be fed its own food, and only that." Behind the wire fences of a politics organized by curfew and restriction, where essence is smothered by law, and law is lie, Michael K is set aside as a rough mindless lost unfit creature, a simpleton or an idiot, a savage. It is a wonder, the doctor observes, that he has been able to keep himself alive. He is "the runt of the cat's litter," "the obscurest of the obscure." Thus the judgment of benevolent arrogance—or compassion indistinguishable from arrogance—on the ingenious farmer and visionary free man of his mother's field.

Coetzee is a writer of clarifying inventiveness and translucent conviction. Both are given voice gradually, seepingly, as if time itself were a character in the narrative. "There is time enough for everything." As in his previous novel, *Waiting for the Barbarians,* Coetzee's landscapes of suffering are defined by the little-by-little art of moral disclosure—his stories might be about anyone and anyplace. At the same time they defy the vice of abstraction; they are engrossed in the minute and the concrete. It would be possible, following Coetzee's dazzlingly precise illuminations, to learn how to sow, or use a pump, or make a house of earth. The grain of his sentences is flat and austere, and so purifying to the senses that one comes away feeling that one's eye has been sharpened, one's hearing vivified, not only for the bright proliferations of nature, but for human unexpectedness.

If *Life & Times of Michael K* has a flaw, it is in the density of its own interior interpretations. In the final quarter we are removed, temporarily, from the plain seeing of Michael K to the self-indulgent diary of the prison doctor who struggles with the entanglements of an increasingly abusive regime. But the doctor's commentary is superfluous; he thickens the clear tongue of the novel by naming its "mes- sage" and thumping out ironies. For one thing, he spe out what we have long ago taken in with the immediac intuition and possession. He construes, he trans Michael K is "an original soul . . . untouched by do untouched by history . . . evading the peace and . . . drifting through time, observing the seasons, trying to change the course of history than a grain of sand does." All this is redundant. The sister-melons and the brother-pumpkins have already had their eloquent say. And the lip of the child kept from its mother's milk has had its say. And the man who grows strong and intelligent when he is at peace in his motherland has had his say.

Coetzee's subdued yet urgent lament is for the sadness of a South Africa that has made dependents and parasites and prisoners of its own children, black and white. (Not to mention more ambiguously imprisoned groups: Indians, "coloreds," the troubled and precarious Jewish community.) Moreover, Coetzee makes plain that the noble endurances and passionate revelations of Michael K do not mask a covert defense of terror; although he evades no horrors, existing or to come, Coetzee has not written a symbolic novel about the inevitability of guerrilla war and revolution in a country where oppression and dependency are breathed with the air. Instead, he discloses, in the language of imagination, the lumbering hoaxes and self-deceptions of stupidity. His theme is the wild and merciless power of inanity. Michael K suffers from the obdurate callowness of both sides, rulers and rebels—one tramples the ... the other blows up the pump. At the end of the story, ...ns of drinking the living water drawn out of his ...rth, if only drop by drop, if only from a tea-

...f the innocent, time is Coetzee's hope.